The Canine Aggression Workbook

James O'Heare

www.GentleSolutions.net
www.acbt.ca

The Canine Aggression Workbook

Published by Gentle Solutions (www.GentleSolutions.net),
Ottawa Ontario Canada

National Library of Canada Cataloguing in Publication Data

O'Heare, 1971 -
The Canine aggression workbook

Includes bibliographical references.
ISBN 0-9689668-0-2

1.Dogs--Training. 2.Dogs-Behavior. 3.Aggressive behavior in animals. I.Title.

SF431.043 2001 636.7"08877 C2001-903041-X

Other Books by James O'Heare

The Canine Separation Anxiety Workbook

Canine Neuropsychology

Table of Contents

Acknowledgments

I would like to express thanks to those who helped me with this project.

Brenda Rushman for advice, support, proof reading and editing. Any remaining errors are mine though.

Angelica Steinker for advice and support.

Brandy Oliver of doggiedoor.com for being my devil's advocate.

Beth Duman of Wolf Park for confirming for me that dogs are not wolves.

Laura MacDonald for the illustrations inside the book.

Susan Dillon for the cover illustration and some typo checking.

My wife Pascale who let me spend thousands of dollars and thousands of hours getting this book ready.

W. Thomas Leroux for computer related book production; again, a weak point of mine.

Thanks to all the students and faculty of the ***Academy of Canine Behavioral Theory*** from whom I have learned a lot.

Others I would like to thank for inspiration: Jean Donaldson, Pamela Reid, Pat Miller, Karen Pryor, Deb Jones, Sue Sternberg, Chris Bach, Ian Dunbar.

Dedication

I dedicate this book to all of the shelter dogs I have known and worked with over the years. They have taught me more than any book or any person has.

Preface
Important; Read Me First

This is a work in progress. I have learned a fair amount about aggression in domestic dogs, through my studies and behavior counseling practice. This is a time of growth for the field of diagnosing and treating unwanted aggression in dogs. Debates rage regarding proper handling of aggressive dogs. To quote Brian Kilcommons, trainer, author of Good Owners, Great Dogs "*The only thing two trainers can agree on is that the third is wrong.*". I urge the reader, who is either studying for a career with dogs, or who is dealing with their own dog's aggression, to read multiple sources on the topic and to formulate what you believe is valuable and not-so-valuable. Refer to the suggested reading section at the back of the book, and really THINK about what you're reading.

Science does not provide us with all the answers we need in order to deal with aggressive dogs. Where possible, I rely on science. I will use references throughout the book, when I feel that the source supports my views. What is not referenced, are my own assumptions and opinions, based on my experience or inferences from the science. So, rather than qualify every statement in this book with "In my experience..." I will say here that the theories contained here are mine. I believe they are correct, based on what I know at this time, but they are debatable, and perhaps even incorrect. For the field of dog behavior counseling to evolve into a science-based and respected profession, we must be clear on what we can back up with science, what is peer-reviewed and generally considered true, and what is theory, not yet backed by science or peer review. My theories, as presented here, are offered for public and peer review. I do not claim that what I say is the final word on the matter. Science is a process.

I make use of proper and precise terminology. I will define the terminology in use. You do not have to be familiar with the jargon of dog behavior and training before reading this book, but you will be when you have finished it. This will make further study far easier, when faced with documents which do not define terminology. If you are a dog owner and do not want to work through the jargon and details, at the end of each chapter will be a section called "The Take Home Message". In that section I will review the chapter's contents, without jargon and in the simplest terms. So, if you have a hard time getting through a chapter, "The Take Home Message" should help to make things more clear.

Here is why I wrote a book on aggression; a topic many trainers and behaviorists say should not be handled by an owner with a book, or even with phone consultation with a dog behavior counselor: first, there is not a whole lot of information out there in book form, regarding aggression in dogs. There are only a handful of books, many of which are not easy to find, many are quite dated. Of the books that are out there, I disagree with much of what is written which makes it difficult for me to recommend one. The next reason is that the recommendation to "contact a trainer or behaviorist near you" simply does not happen. People do not tend to do this, for a variety of reasons; and even if they did, I am uneasy suggesting to owners that they contact a trainer or behaviorist near them, knowing that many traditional trainers are out there still using methods that we now know do more harm than good. It is a roll the dice, and I am wary of suggesting it to people. The next reason is that, while professionals are really useful, in the end it is YOU, the owner, that must understand the dog and do the work. The owner with an aggressive dog must become the expert, and this does not always happen when spending a hour with a professional, even if it is every week for 6 weeks. I do think that professionals have way more experience than they used to, and than the average dog owner, and they can see things owners cannot. I wish people would and could get in touch with a dog behavior counselor or behaviorist who is up on the latest information and knows what they are doing. That would be ideal, but in my experience, this does not happen. So, I hope that you will read this book, consider your options as defined in the book, consult with a qualified counselor or behaviorist, and develop a plan of action, rather than continuing to simply live with the problem as it grows out of control. That is why I have written a book on a topic that, ideally, should be seen in person by a qualified professional.

This is a big book on aggression, and there is a lot of information here. There is a tight rope that is walked by behaviorists: on the one side, you need to avoid overloading the client with information and work, so that he does not tune out and quit; and on other side the client must get enough information and hands-on skills that they can effect a change. As the owner, this is YOUR dog, and as long as he will remain your dog YOU will have to become an expert on aggression and retraining. YOU will have to deal with this problem, not a professional somewhere, because it is YOUR relationship with YOUR dog that needs salvaging. YOU need to fully understand the PRINCIPLES on which general guidelines are built, because life is variable. Every dog has 2 trainers in his life: you, and the environment. The environment works to change his behavior 24 hours per day. In order to be efficient, YOU, the owner, MUST understand how this affects you and your dog, and you must understand how to counteract this. If you are simply given a few steps to follow, you will invariably come across situations that do not quite fit the rules. These situations are the ones that will mess up a plan, unless YOU understand how to design the plan yourself. The knowledgeable, effective owner and trainer understands WHY we do things, and how behavior is affected by environmental factors, and so is able to build the plan from the ground up. YOU will have to become an expert, fast, and "dumbing this book down" to a set of quick tips or presumptuous guidelines will not be nearly as helpful. So, as you will see, I fall on the side of giving you too much to do. If you tune me out and quit, then you tune me out and quit. But if you hang in there, you will get the information you need to deal with the problems you are having. When I have a client with an aggressive dog, we develop an understanding of what the problem is, and then set a carefully designed plan into motion. But, then I do not just walk away and leave it like that. If I did, my success rate would plummet. I do follow-up consults to trouble-shoot the inevitable issues that pop up along the way. Plans sometimes need to be adjusted, and sometimes abandoned in favor of a new ones. So please, read carefully and absorb the information here. Then, reread and study it, because YOU will have to deal with this, not the book, and not a trainer; YOU. Have you gotten the impression yet that it is all about YOU (and your dog)? You love your dog, or you would not be here; but you have a problem. Let's deal with it.

If you are a dog owner dealing with an actual case you will be called upon to do some homework. You will need a file folder to keep it in, and you will need to make notes. When you see the word HOMEWORK, that is your indication that you will have to prepare something for your file. The file will turn out to a be a complete and comprehensive description of the problem, and what you plan to do about it. Please do not skip these exercises. I know it's tempting, but the information you will develop from it is invaluable, and you cannot hope to simply hold it all in your head. And, if you decide to contact a knowledgeable counselor for help, they will need this information. No one likes homework, but then no one likes an aggressive dog, either, so lets get to work, shall we?

Chapter 1

Understanding Aggression

Understanding Aggression

The Human Dog Bond

Dogs and humans have a unique relationship. No other symbiotic relationship in history has been like that of dog and mankind. Dogs allow us to experience a companionship that is supremely honest and extremely forgiving. Dogs do not plot behind our backs or act out of spite. Dogs feel what they feel and express those feelings honestly. We can count on the integrity and truth of their actions. Being domesticated means that dogs have evolved to form close bonds with humans. Dogs offer us the kind of bond that can be very difficult to find in the human world.

Sometimes bonds and relationships are strained. Aggressive behavior can lead to the deterioration of the bond and relationship which often spells the end of the relationship. The goal of treating aggression will ultimately be to return the relationship to a safe and mutually beneficial one.

The bond that exists between you and your dog or the possibility of regaining a bond will realistically be the only thing that will get you through this crisis. In many cases guilt may also influence the process but in the long run it must be the bond that unites you and provides incentive to manage and treat the problem. Try to think from your dog's perspective and know that if he felt he had a choice he would rather behave prosocially rather than antisocially. He either does not believe it would be safe to do so or is acting instinctively. It will be our job to convince him to act in a different way. It will also be our responsibility as ethical beings to not use aversive methods in the process. Much of aggression is based in aversion and using aversion to battle aversion cannot lead to a close bonded relationship; the basis of solving aggression problems in pet dogs.

Denial and the Stages of Grief

Grief may seem like an odd word to describe the emotional turmoil that a dog owner will go through in response to their dog displaying aggressive tendencies, but this is a very common process that owners of aggressive dogs do and must go through. Many owners get stuck at a particular stage and this holds up not only the healing process but also the recognition of the problem, and treatment for the dog.

1. Denial

No other problem in pet dogs provokes such denial as aggressive behavior. This must stop. People experience denial because it is horrible to face the realization that one's companion is dangerous. Nobody wants to face that kind of reality. The problem is that this does not solve the problem; it just puts it off. It is also not a conscious choice altogether. People's minds will only allow them to face what they are prepared to face, and until you are ready to face something your mind will rationalize and deny. Denial is a complicated demon; one you must fight. Many people convince themselves that a growling adolescent dog is cute or that predatory or defensive behavior will go away by itself as the dog matures. Some people latch onto the notion that an obedience class will solve aggressive behavior problems: obedience class is no place for an aggressive dog. While learning obedience will likely improve your relationship with your dog (by providing a common language and predictability), the average obedience class simply isn't suited to providing the necessary guidance for an owner of a dog with aggression problems. Some people cling to the idea that the dogs are just sorting out who is the boss when their dog jumps all over other dogs on a regular basis. Aggression cases almost never get better without intervention. There are no excuses to be made. Yes aggressive behavior is normal but we can and must still prevent or modify it. Urinating on your rug is also normal for a dog but we prevent and modify that too. Yes the dog may have been abused in his previous home but the problem must be addressed. Please do not ignore signs that your dog is developing or has a problem with excessive aggressive behavior. It will not just go away. It IS serious. Have you heard your dog growl at someone? if yes, then you have a problem. Has your dog ever snapped at anyone? If yes then you have a problem. No ifs or buts. This indicates a problem. Be open to that.

2. Anger

This stage usually involves the person becoming angry with the person trying to point out that their dog has a predatory or defensive behavior problem. It can also be directed at the "other dog" or person who the predatory or defensive behavior is directed at for some real or imagined offense. It may also be directed at the predatory or defensive dog, for being predatory or defensive. This is a coping mechanism and another form of denial. Guard against this. If someone points out that your dog is aggressive pay close attention to the feelings you have at that moment. Reflect upon those feelings later. Take control of yourself and responsibility for your actions. If you feel angry, accept that feeling, don't deny it. But, then take ownership of the feeling and identify the function for the anger. Ask yourself how you used anger as a defense mechanism to avoid dealing with the problem at hand. Even if someone did act inappropriately by charging up to your dog and petting him on the head without permission you can still educate this person without becoming angry. Nor does that change the fact that you dog growled or lunged in response to it. And if you do experience anger, do not deny it but also do not let it prevent you from seeing the reality of the situation. If your dog bites someone who walks right up to pet your dog that indicates a real problem. Even if your dog leaves the room every time a child visits that could be a red flag. Pay attention. You are ultimately and legally liable for your dog's actions, and your dog's actions reflect on every other pet-owner and dog in the world, like ripples in a pond. Take responsibility, and work to effect a change in your dog's behavior.

3. Bargaining

This is the stage most often dealt with by behavior counselors. Bargaining may be another avoidance technique; a defence mechanism. These stages help you come to a resolution. They are there for a reason. If you are scared or confused these mechanisms help you ease the blow. But, you must work to get through each stage as honestly as possible. By bargaining with your trainer or behaviorist (or even your dog) you attempt to diminish the required intervention and hence the seriousness of the problem. A full treatment intervention requires that you admit that there is a future to this problem unless it is dealt with. There cannot be any bargaining regarding treatment. Action must be taken and so you must work your way through this stage toward acceptance. Guard against bargaining by being conscious of your feelings and assessing the function for them honestly.

4. Depression (and Guilt)

Once you have exhausted other defence mechanisms you may find that you internally direct feelings that allow you to suspend action. Guilt and depression are real but, as a defense mechanism, the function for this behavior is to allow you to avoid responsibility and suspend the taking of action. Work through this stage by reminding yourself that aggressive behavior is normal and largely genetic; aggressive behavior serves a purpose, in all life forms. However, dogs are unable to use reason in the same way that humans do, and therein lies the rub: the dog doesn't seem to understand that his aggressing may cause you to lose your home, or him to lose his life. Accept that your feelings exist but that does not mean you should ignore the function as a defence mechanism. Feel and assess your feelings and thoughts. Do not deny them but also do not deny the need to move on when possible.

5. Acceptance

Be careful of this one. Acceptance is easy to rationalize. It is easy to say you accept the problem and you may even believe it. It can be difficult to know when your acceptance is itself a rationalization or genuine. My advice is not to worry too much about it. Just accept your feels when they happen. Be conscious of your thoughts and feelings and explore them. You may get to acceptance a few times and notice new levels of acceptance each time as you deal with previous stages. There is no set time frame for these levels and they can jump around quite a bit.

In summary. Guard against denial. Accept your feelings. Be conscious of them and explore their function as a defense mechanism. They have value. You must go through these stages. Try not to rush them by pretending to jump to another level. Be conscious and take responsibility for them. Own your feelings.

What You Are Up Against

There is no cure for aggression. A dog who is aggressive will always tend toward aggressive responses, because aggressive responses are habit-forming. When an animal is stressed they respond habitually because the reasoning portion of the brain is inhibited. They must rely on behavior that is almost automatic; that they do not have to think about. Experiencing fear, frustration and anger puts a dog in the position to rely on that default (habitual) behavior. Your goal will be to heighten the thresholds related to those emotions and to train replacement habits. This is an uphill battle. Old, bad habits die hard and under stress those old habits are always a potential result. With a high level of commitment and a lot of work you may very well get to the point where you do not get aggressive behavior but you will not be able to rely upon that. Just as an alcoholic remains a recovering alcoholic for life so too does an aggressive dog remain a recovering aggressive dog for life.

There are no easy answers. Aggression is not a simple problem. It is very complicated and resistant to modification because of how deep-seated the behavior is. Dogs are biologically prepared for using violence just as people are. Many popular books that deal with aggressive behavior in pet dogs oversimplify the problem. Their goal presumably is to make it readily understandable by their audience but in the process they give the impression that treatment should be successful given a little bit of work (or a lot of work). I am here to tell you that in some cases even a lot of work will not solve the problem.

Think about an aggressive or violent person you may have known. Even if they recognize they have a problem they usually have a very difficult time changing their personality (temperament) or behavior. Even with medication and psychotherapy they may learn to control their behaviors to a certain extent but their basic personality (temperament) and aggressive behavioral strategies remains unchanged in most cases. When things go wrong and push comes to shove, the habits return. It's almost a cliche, the violent husband apologizing for a violent outburst explaining it will never happen again, for the tenth time. Ya right. The same is probably true of dogs except that they probably do not even feel that same sense of guilt the husband does. The dog probably feels he did the right thing.

I do not want to inappropriately discourage you. It is true that there are the occasional dogs whom I don't think are treatable but the vast majority are treatable. In most cases if an owner is willing to manage their dog's behavior and commit to a treatment plan they can live a fulfilling, safe life. But, if that is what you want you cannot be under the impression that a few weeks or even months will cure the problem. It will be an ongoing issue. If you really commit to the program you are far more likely to regain a healthy relationship with your dog. Be realistic and you will be more likely to succeed.

Legal Issues

Generally in most places dogs are considered property and any damage done by that property will be the responsibility of the owner. On top of that owners are held to the same duty of care as anyone else. Criminal offenses may be able to be demonstrated against those who are negligent in the handling of their dog. If you know that your dog poses a risk and do not take all reasonable precautions then you may be guilty of an offense. This is a general precaution. I am not a lawyer and will not attempt to precisely interpret the law regarding this issue. It is my advice that if you have a dog who poses a risk to society then consult a lawyer regarding your obligations and safeguards. I'll suggest you check out http://www.dogbitelaw.com/ for more information. It can be a very useful web site.

Your Options

One of the first things you will have to do if your dog has a problem with aggression is to decide what you will do about it. Take into consideration the following factors when deciding how to approach the problem.

1. Risk. Are there children in the house? How serious is the problem at this time? Does the dog bite to break skin? Can you predict when he will bite or does it seem unpredictable? Can you prevent the circumstances that provoke an predatory or defensive behavior or not?

2. Willing and able. Do you have the inclination to put a LOT of time and effort into this problem? Do you have the time to spend on this?

3. On board. Is everyone in the household on board for the retraining? Those who are not can ruin a program.

4. Money. Can you afford veterinary checkups, medication, behavior counselling, equipment etc.?

5. Able to accept criticism and change. Are you willing to consider while reading a book or hear while consulting a professional that your behavior is a big

part of what causes or maintains the behavior? Are you willing to accept this and modify your own behavior?

Here are some of your options.

Option #1. Take a management approach. If this is a safe option and you are able to prevent provoking the dog then this is one option you have. Management refers to avoiding contexts in which the dog becomes predatory or defensive and using equipment to control any problems. It can be a risky option to try to avoid triggers so this should only be considered in level one biters or less. This will be discussed further on.

Option #2. Rehome the dog. If there is someone that will take this problem on who is in a better position to deal with it then this is an option. If you or a particular part of the environment the dog presently lives in is triggering defensive behavior then this is a viable option. You must be very clear with the new owner what the problems are. I almost never suggest this option. It is unrealistic in most cases.

Option #3. Euthanasia. In some cases this is the only safe or humane option available.

Option #4. Treatment. Treatment refers to teaching the dog adaptive behavioral strategies or coping skills. This option inevitably involves management options as well. If you are realistic about your commitment and the risks, this is an option. Treatment in some cases is unsuccessful. When and if this happens euthanasia may be the next step.

Understanding Canine Aggression

Unified Theory of Aggression

Aggression is complex. What follows is an exploration of the defining characteristics of aggression and it's motivation.

What is Dog Aggression

Aggression is a species-specific threat or attack response to a stimulus. The term aggression is used here, not as a precise diagnostic definition, but rather a general term referring to threat or attack behavior. Defining exactly what constitutes aggression is problematic. Many people consider any behavior that is likely to harm to be aggression while others insist that the dog must intend to harm. Deciding at which point excitement or arousal becomes aggression is arbitrary. The arbitrary nature of defining aggression makes it unlikely to be defined to everyone's satisfaction. Aggression here will be a general term applied to problem behavior involving threat and attack behavior.

Why Dogs Aggress

Evolution selects for survival of the most adaptable. Survival itself is the ultimate goal of adaptive behavior. In order to achieve survival an animal must adapt and control events that impact upon it's needs. Aggression is one behavioral response toward that goal. Aggression is adaptive. Animals are genetically prepared to use behavior that will ensure control of the environment and hence maximize reinforcers and minimize punishers. That is, aggression is all about control. Control is a function of adaptation which is a function of survival. Action patterns such as biting, growling and snarling are available to the dog toward these ends.

There is more than one way to answer the question of 'why do dogs aggress'. One way is to simply say that dogs aggress because they either want to kill prey, they have learned to play inappropriately or because they get scared or angry just like people do. Scared dogs, like scared humans defend themselves if necessary. Different dogs, like different people see that necessity differently. Angry dogs like angry humans, may use violence to express their rage. Hunters, whether human of dog use violence to get their prey. We use guns; they use teeth.

Aggression is a strategic behavior also. *Animals use aggression to maximize reinforcers and minimize punishers.* This is a very important concept in understanding aggressive behavior, because in "maximizing reinforcers", the dog's goal may be (for example) to put distance between himself and something scary. That distance is a reinforcer. By the same token, the *lack* of distance would be considered to be a punisher that the dog would seek to minimize that, by increasing distance.One cannot consider behavior without considering the role of learning. Aggression is not merely an automatic and reflexive response to a stimulus, although it may seem that way sometimes. The brain evaluates incoming stimuli and devises a response based partially on what has previously worked and failed to work in the past to achieve what they want. Aggression is complex and multi-factorial.

To sum up the above, aggression is naturally adaptive behavior for dogs which is meant to help them get things they want and avoid / escape things they do not want. The dog is biologically prepared to use aggression if need be and with every single experience of it's use adaptive learning modulates it's expression toward that same ubiquitous goal of survival: rehearsal of the aggressive behavior creates habitual behavior as the dog learns that aggression works. Aggression has innate qualities and is further modulated by learning and emotional evaluational processes.

Aggression can be conceptually divided into two functionally divergent forms. Threat and attack behavior can be either:

- Affective
- Nonaffective

Affective aggression is highly emotional and stimulates sympathetic autonomic arousal. This class of aggression includes all forms of aggression except predatory behavior and involves significant emotional content. Nonaffective aggression is nonemotional and does not stimulate sympathetic autonomic arousal. Nonaffective aggression involves attack behaviors related to predatory action patterns.

Nonaffective Aggression

Noneffective aggression involves the use of segments of the predatory sequence in ways that are deemed inappropriate, dangerous or inconvenient to humans. A general model of carnivorous canine predatory sequence is offered by Coppinger:

Orient>eye>stalk>chase>grab-bite>kill-bite>dissect>consume.

[Coppinger,206]

Part of the domestication and evolution of dogs has involved enhancing certain parts of this sequence and deleting, or making latent, others. Some dogs such as the border collie for example have evolved an orient>eye-stalk>chase sequence which they use to herd sheep. They also possess the disect>consume sequence because they must eat after all, but it is separated from other parts of the sequence so that it does not interfere with their job. Grab-bite occurs occasionally and is considered a fault which is not bred for (toward deletion) but for the most part it is latent. Grab>kill is even less likely and more latent than grab>bite. [Coppinger,209] A good livestock guarding breed will only have the sequence consume. Other segments have been made latent. [Coppinger,209] Each breed and individual has a variation on the basic predatory sequence that is genetically coded in them which is the basis for selective breeding and the adjustment of such behaviors within a breeding program. As mentioned, nonaffective aggression does not provoke sympathetic (emotional) arousal; the dog is not scared or angry - he is hunting. In many cases normal predatory behavior is found to be dangerous and highly inappropriate to humans. People buy a hunting or herding breed to live in their house and are surprised when it applies these hard wired behaviors. In some cases variation within the sequence can be unusual for the breed standard. For example a border collie may possess the grab-bite segment and use it in ways that the humans find inappropriate or dangerous.

Affective Aggression

Affective aggression, provokes sympathetic arousal. This form of aggression, involves significant emotional content. The basis of this form of aggression as with human aggression is emotional provocation. The question is: what emotional states provoke aggressive outcomes.

The field of emotions and cognition is highly controversial and debatable. There is no agreeance yet on the exact relative role of one to the other. It is commonly suggested that emotion is influenced by thought processes and that thought processes are influenced by emotions. It used to be thought that emotionality is detrimental to and at odds with rational thought but it is now believed that without emotional evaluation and content, behavior would be inadequate. Studies of human patients with lesions that eliminate emotional processing show behavior that is not completely rational as one might expect but completely inappropriate and out of context. Emotion is ever-present and highly influential over behavior. Emotion allows for evaluation of stimuli which in turn allows for adaptive behaviors and survival. One can also effect emotional states, thought processes and even physical changes. If you breath deeply and smile you can reduce the physiological consequences of anxiety or anger. If you think counter to your emotional state you can shift your mood. Certainly there is a very complicated interaction between emotion and cognition.

One model of emotion suggests that the stimuli an animal perceives is directly inputted into two systems: one system identifies and discriminates, and the other system effectively evaluates its significance. This means that the animal simultaneously identifies the stimulus in terms of it's features and also evaluates it's significance. The evaluation process seems to be distinctly divided into two processes; positivity and negativity. Within this evaluation system the stimuli are perceived emotionally as positive or negative, good or bad, safe or dangerous. Whether a particular stimuli will be perceived and evaluated as positive or negative is relative, that is, it depends on a very complex system of evaluation. A cold water stimulus may be evaluated as good or bad depending on how hot the environment is, for example, or how thirsty the animal is. Whether food is evaluated as good or bad will depend on how hungry the dog is, and their past experience with the food item. The evaluation will also depend on the dog's innate drives and sensitivities as well as any emotional learning that has taken place and relates to the stimulus. The relative evaluation of how good or bad a thing is can be a very complex process. If a stimulus is determined to be negative, avoidance / withdrawal behaviors will be activated, whereas if the stimulus is determined to be positive, approach / investigative behaviors will be activated. The avoidance of bad and the approach of good is a basic survival principle and seems to be hard wired right into the dog's innate species-specific system and emotional responses. A single stimulus can even provoke conflicting evaluational determinations. A dog, for example, could be imprinted with humans and still feel fear of them for some other reason. In such a case there would be a conflict in the approach / avoidance responses.

Another important set of emotional principles that should be understood is positive offset and negativity bias. Positive offset suggests that at low levels of evaluation activation a weak positive motivational output is prepotent over a negative output. [Cacioppo] This means that with normal or low levels of stimulation a dog tends toward a mild optimism.Without this emotional drive animals would not approach potential sources of novel food, shelter, social contact or other needs. Negative bias on the other hand suggests that moderate or intensely negative stimuli are responded to more strongly than moderate or intensely positive stimuli. [Cacioppo] The evolutionary and adaptive value of this tendency is evident when one considers that a dangerous or noxious stimulus ignored may prevent death, while a pleasant stimulus ignored simply means a lost opportunity for pleasure at intense levels, but in day to day life animals must possess a mild optimism in order to function optimally.

So what emotional states are involved in the expression of canine defensiveness (affective aggression)? The two most likely candidates are anger and fear as they are both considered by many theorists to be basic emotional states related to avoidance.

"Anger is usually caused by the frustration of attempts to attain a goal, or by hostile or disturbing actions such as insults, injuries, or threats that do not come from a feared source." [Gale Encyclopedia of Psychology] "Like fear, anger is a basic emotion that provides a primitive mechanism for physical survival. The physiological changes that accompany anger and fear are very similar and include increased heart rate and blood pressure, rapid breathing, and muscle tension. However, anger produces more muscle tension, higher blood pressure, and a lower heart rate, while fear induces rapid breathing. Unlike the adrenalin-producing "fight or flight" response that characterizes fear, anger is attributed to the secretion of both adrenalin and another hormone, noradrenalin." [Gale Encyclopedia of Psychology] Both anger and fear originate from the evaluation of a stimulus and determination at an emotional level as negative. This next quote from the Gale Encyclopedia of Psychology is written to describe anger in humans but it keenly describes common dog behaviors. "In the classroom, a passive aggressive student will display behavior that is subtly uncooperative or disrespectful but which provides no concrete basis for disciplinary action. Passive aggressive acts may even appear in the guise of a service or favor, when in fact the sentiments expressed are those of hostility rather than altruism. Some of the more extreme defenses against anger are paranoia..." [Gale Encyclopedia of Psychology]

Anger and fear are both threshold responses. The stimulus must reach a certain intensity before the emotional response of anger or fear is triggered. As mentioned also there are many dimensions of relativity in the emotional evaluation of stimuli. Another complicating factor is attempting to determine from the observable behavior whether anger or fear is the driving emotional state for the aggressive behavior. In the simpler cases the fear motivated dog will show avoidance / withdrawal behaviors and move to more active defensive strategies only once escape is made impossible. The anger motivated dog will respond actively aggressive in response to an apparent frustrative event. In less than simple cases fearful dogs can learn to act more offensively and less defensively thus confusing the presumed motivational state. This is called avoidance motivated aggression and will be discussed in detail below. This is why it is not that easy to simply label an aggressive display as anger motivated vs. fear motivated. It may also be suggested that there is a fine line between anger and fear since they both derive from the same drive to control and survive and from the same evaluation of negativity. Anger could be described as a result of a fear of not being able to adapt and control (frustration). Drawing a line between anger and fear in many cases will not be easy. Again, aggression is complex.

Signs of Aggression

- Biting
- Growling
- Snapping
- Lunging
- Snarling
- Barking menacingly
- Staring
- Stiffening gate
- Raised hackles
- High, flagging tail
- Dilated pupils
- Mouth always closed prior to active attack

Biting is the most clear expression of aggression. When a dog bites it is either accidental, inappropriate play behavior or it is predatory, fear or anger motivated aggression. A dog who snaps is warning or threatening. Growling is complex and involves various levels of threat from the mere vocalized expression of discomfort or frustration to the expression of a clear warning that if the provocation continues he will move onto the next level. In considering the growl as an expression of aggressive intent, one must also consider breed differences and propensities. However, this is too broad a discussion for this forum. Suffice it to say for the intent of this book that the growling described here is a peripheral vocalization; it is expressed as part of a defensive repertoire that also includes other physical expressions as outlined above. This is also true of snapping, as many herding breeds are seen to snap in play. It's important to distinguish between these behaviors, and those included in a defensive repertoire. One form of growl involves the dog growling in a higher pitched tone that resembles a howl. The dog will not usually direct the growl at anything in particular. This is the whining or complaining kind of growl that indicated initial levels of discomfort and perhaps frustration. When a dog growls deeply and stares at the provocative stimuli this indicates a more serious threat and seems more anger motivated in most cases than fear motivated. If it is accompanied by tensing of the muscles, dilation of the pupils, hackles going up, tail going up and possibly tail wagging in a wide flagging motion, snarling etc. then the risk and threatening intent is higher. The fearful dog just wants the aversive stimuli to go away while the angry dog is more dangerous because he wants to unload on something. Each dog has various thresholds on what it will take to get them to go to the next level. Many dogs can easily be stimulated to growl but never proceed to snapping or biting no matter how intensely they are exposed to the provocative stimulus. Some dogs have thresholds so close together that the step from growling to biting is virtually invisible. Dogs can also learn to bypass lower levels. This is called avoidance motivated aggression and will be discussed below.

When attempting to read a dog's intent look for the combinations of behaviors rather than just one indication. For example you can gauge fairly well the intentions of a dog by the behavior of the tail but you will have much better predictive results by looking at the synergy of behaviors. If the dog makes himself look smaller by hunching with tail between legs and ears down while he snarls or backs away you know that this dog is scared and could be dangerous if he is cornered. These dogs will occasionally strike as the feared stimulus retreats. If on the other hand the dog makes himself look bigger while he stands leaning forward with ears and tail up while he stares and growls or barks you will know that this dog is more actively defensive and is more likely to bite without having to be cornered first. As mentioned this dog is angry and wants to express that. These dogs will be more likely than the fear motivated dog to go out of their way to pursue their target. Remember, anger does not mean the dog has no reason to fear the stimulus. Perhaps in many of these cases fear turns to anger. When assessing the aggressive intensions of a dog look at the ears, tail, eyes, hackles, stance, retreat vs. advance motions. Listen to the pitch of barking or growling. Generally the lower the pitch the more serious and actively defensive will be the dog. Look and listen to the whole event.

Note: as the dog's owner, you understand which events and circumstances are likely to trigger the situations outlined above. It's important that you *not* purposely set out to cause or allow these to occur. It's simply not necessary for the re-training process, and can be quite detrimental. As aggressive behavior is highly predisposed to becoming habitual, each time the dog is allowed or caused to rehearse the behavior it will make the pattern stronger and more resistant to change. Please utilize all the management tools at your disposal to ensure that the dog is not put into a position of having an opportunity to express these behaviors. Set the dog up to succeed.

Active and Passive Defensiveness

Defensiveness can be expressed via:

- Active defensive behaviors (fight) (aggression)
- Passive defensive behaviors (flight, freeze, appease)

It is tempting to identify active defensiveness as anger motivated defensiveness and passive defensiveness as fear motivated defensiveness. Active and passive describe observable behavior while fear and anger describe motivational emotional states. Because of the overlap in expression it is safer to use observable indicators and not rely heavily on the identification of motivational substrates. Part of the reason for this is because learning effects the behavioral strategy chosen. A fearful dog can learn that acting passively does not work nearly as well at increasing social distance as does more active strategies. The resulting active defensiveness hence results from fear, not anger. This is why active vs. passive is a better model for classifying defensiveness in dogs. When it comes to active aggression assuming motivational emotional state is too highly speculative. Refer to avoidance motivated aggression below.

Which strategy the dog will use will depend on various factors:

- Learning history
- Drives and sensitivities
- Temperament
- Availability of escape option
- Affect of initial strategy attempted

Learning history refers to what strategy has been most effective in the past. Dogs will do more of what works best. If fleeing works best then a dog is more likely to flee. If fighting has worked best in the past then the dog is more likely to choose that strategy.

Drives are that which the dog likes and seeks to gain. Sensitivities are that which the dog does not like. Some propensity of drives and sensitivities is inherited but they can be inhibited and cultivated through learning especially in the sensitive periods of youth. How driven a dog is regarding some stimuli involved or how sensitive the dog is toward a stimuli will contribute to the expression of defensiveness. It will contribute motivational factors.

Temperament refers to the dog's basic genetic behavioral makeup. Temperament is a complex amalgam of inherited potential and development of the brain when the dog is as a very young puppy. During this time nurture changes nature into the final product. Temperament is not nature or nurture but a product of the interplay between the two as pointed out by Coppinger.

Research indicates that flight is generally prepotent over fight. If leashes, fences, verbal commands to stay etc. cause the dog to feel flight is not an available option fight will become more likely.

If a dog attempts freeze or appease and the threat continues and flight does not work fight can become more likely. If one strategy does not work another will be attempted.

Lindsay frames aggression this way:

"...aggression can be adequately understood and controlled only by recognizing that it is motivated and emitted under the influence of both emotional (reflexive) and purposive (instrumental [operant]) components. Functional aggressive behavior depends on the presence of significant setting events (broad contextual and motivational variables), transient emotional establishing operations (e.g., frustration, irritability, and anxiety), and an evocative target or situation toward which the threat or attack is directed. The goal of aggression is control." [Lindsay,175] A beautifully concise framing of the concepts discussed above.

From a physiological perspective affective aggression is an aroused response to aversive stress response (negativity) to regain control and or avoid loss of control. By stress I mean any force applied to a dog that requires or demands change or adaptation. This is a rather wide definition including almost all stimuli. Aversive means that it was perceived as unpleasant or fear / anger provoking for the dog in question. Arousal is the dog's response to that stress - activation of the nervous system toward assessment and evaluation of the stimulus and response to it. A dog becomes aroused beyond his triggering threshold and experiences an aversive (negativity) stress response. Stress also acts to lower many thresholds. During this aversive stress response the dog's brain is flooded with physiologically addictive chemicals (producing both euphoria and analgesia) that all together form what is commonly referred to as the dog's fight or flight mechanism (active or passive defensiveness) or display of anger. This chemical bath accounts for the intrinsic reinforcement for the aggressive behavior. The consequences or outcome of the behavior (if effective) accounts for the extrinsic reinforcement for the behavior. Reinforcement is that which influences an increase in said behavior.

Each dog possesses varying thresholds before they trigger into aggression and the stressful stimuli must be of an aversive nature, as perceived by the dog, as that is what effects the appropriate neurological substrate in the brain for the stress response activation to occur. Various stimuli possess various aversive or fear / anger provoking qualities which can vary from context to context. Refer to Jean Donaldson's description of bite thresholds in her book The Culture Clash.

It is important to note that the dog does not choose to experience a stimulus as aversive any more than we choose to experience something as aversive. They may perceive a stressor as aversive because of inappropriate socialization, because it has proved dangerous, because the dog is genetically predisposed to frustrative arousal, fearfulness or possibly for various other reasons. In any case the dog starts by experiencing an aversive stressor. Arousal levels begin to rise. Arousal is complex and may be integrally caused by involuntary response factors as well as voluntary ones. Some dogs have higher thresholds before they reach the next level than others. Some dogs have learned through training to cope better than others. At some point the aversive stress threshold is surpassed and the dog's limbic system is activated. The limbic system is the part of the brain involved in emotional responses. As this happens the cerebral cortex is inhibited. This is the part of the brain responsible for higher cognitive function and learning. The chemical bath continues and forms what we call an aversive stress response; fight or flight.

It is important to note that many dogs who have never been trained have a low threshold for stress. This is relatively easy to rectify through the use of clicker training. As the training progresses, the natural succession requires the use of small amounts of stress (withholding the click) to cause the dog to try new behaviors. A by-product of this technique is that the dog learns to stay operant through the stressful events. It is a wondrous change to behold!

Evolution has allowed for a fast response to danger (negativity bias). Dogs cannot take the time to reason through all hazardous situations, especially the quick one. If they did they would die. Hence a mechanism that will inhibit or shut down rational thought and create an emotional response that puts hazard avoidance behaviors into action far faster than a rational approach could. At this point the dog is not thinking, hearing or able to respond to cues. He is RE-ACTING.

What determines how the dog will act is a combination of species specific defensive behaviors and what has been learned. They have lost conscious control. We can heighten this threshold through teaching impulse control / coping strategies and attempt to teach the dog at that base level how to respond less harshly but once the aversive stress response is activated the dog is not thinking; he is acting. Once arousal has diminished he will learn from the event but it will invariably be a combination of intrinsic and extrinsic factors that contribute to that learning. The fact that this is a neurological and physiological response and that the intrinsic reinforcement is salient means that the lessons learned are unlikely to be positive from your perspective. How can you compete with the physiologically addictive mind bath and the success of the behavior? You cannot.

Initially the feelings that provoke affective aggressive behavior are not pleasant. A dog does not perform aggressive behavior because he feels elation but because he feels aroused, frustrated, fearful, angry. The experience itself can often become highly reinforcing and even physiologically addictive. The result may in many cases produce a strange physiological elation. As both intrinsic and extrinsic reinforcement is experienced the aggressive behavior can become a conflicted amalgam of frustrative arousal (anger) or fear arousal, physiologically addictive and analgesic experiences, relief and of course deterioration of the social bond. Dogs are short sighted and in the very short term these behaviors are reinforcing and necessary. In the long term the dog really only has constant stress and euthanasia to look forward to.

The Role of Learning in Aggression

Dogs are obedient to the laws of operant conditioning (so long as operant conditioning does not collide with what is termed instinctive drift). There are four available outcomes for a behavior:

- Present subjectively pleasant stimuli (Positive Reinforcement) [Increase Behavior]
- Remove subjectively pleasant stimuli (Negative Punishment) [Decrease Behavior]
- Present subjectively unpleasant stimuli (Positive Punishment) [Decrease Behavior]
- Remove subjectively unpleasant stimuli (Negative Reinforcement) [Increase Behavior]

Note: Access to reinforcement is what drives behavior, and so we will only use the first 2 consequences in our training: offering rewards (positive reinforcement), and removing rewards (negative punishment). Reward-based training is highly effective, and there is virtually no fallout associated with it. Reward-based training will not make an aggressive dog more aggressive.

Sources of operant consequences:

- People / dogs (Animate)
- Environment (Inanimate)
- Physiology (sensation / emotion; physiological change within the dog himself)

Dogs may be born with predispositions and tendencies but with every experience from then on they will adapt through the process of learning. They will learn to predict consequences and they will learn which behaviors cause which consequences. If the outcome or consequence is subjectively pleasant then the behavior will be strengthened. If the outcome or consequence is subjectively unpleasant the behavior is weakened. These pleasant or unpleasant consequences can come from within the dog himself or from without, from both animate and inanimate objects. When a dog aggresses his brain is flooded with a brain bath of physiologically addictive chemicals such as adrenalin, cortisol and endorphins which provide a huge intrinsic reinforcement for the behavior. If the behavior works to achieve the goal then the behavior is both intrinsically and extrinsically reinforced. Relief reinforces also. If a fear or anger eliciting stimulus can be driven away then whatever behavior achieved that will become positively reinforced. Learning takes on a major role in aggressive behavior in dogs especially over extended time frames with repeated trials.

The paragraph above is incredibly important: this is why we cannot allow rehearsal of the behavior patterns. Dogs are very prone to "single-event learning": Circumstances that are either very scary or very reinforcing are likely to form habits in only one or 2 rehearsals. You can see why it's so critical to manage the situation, so that the dog doesn't have the opportunity to rehearse the repertoire.

Generalization

Aggression generalizes. It seems ironic that when it comes to training new desirable behaviors we are always talking about how badly dogs generalize but when it comes to aggression they seem to generalize fairly well. Fear is initially elicited by a specific stimulus. As time goes on and the response is repeatedly elicited or emitted the dog will search desperately for common denominators (discriminative stimuli) in the events in an attempt to be able to predict it and hence avoid it - adaptation (normal animal behavior). With each event the dog collects more data which become integrally associated with the fear or anger. If the original stimulus was say a stranger with a hat the dog may initially fear that person but soon he will fear all strangers with hats. From there it is a short trip to fearing hats or all strangers or perhaps males. Soon it becomes impossible to identify the original stimulus through all of the generalizations. This argues for catching defensiveness early before it generalizes and becomes very much more difficult to modify.

Nature vs. Nurture

Every behavior possesses environmental (nurture) and genetic (nature) components. It is impossible to say how much of each is important. They are both very important. Dr. Ian Dunbar likes to respond to the question of nature or nurture with the question "is it a prospect or product?". If you are a breeder, or one who wants to legislate breeding in order to control aggression, then the dog is a prospect and the answer is "do not breed aggressive dogs because nature is very very important". If you just adopted a puppy then you have a product and the answer is "nature means very little at this point so socialize the little puppy's brains out because nurture is very very important". The genetics of aggression is a very complex problem since it is what they call polygenetic. That means aggression is a big part of almost every gene in the dog's body. Suffice it to say here that nature and nurture are intertwined and each contributes significantly to the final product of an aggressive dog. Lindsay, referring to the nature vs. nurture problem puts it this way: "However, to compare the relative importance of the two factors separately is analogous to asking whether hydrogen or oxygen is more important in the makeup of water." [Lindsay,pg.167] Genes do not directly create behavior just as behavior does not directly create genes. [Lindsay,pg.168] Genes impact upon the biochemical substrate which then impacts upon behavior in a more direct way. "Behavioral and biological development take place within a context of inherited constraints, sufficiently variable to allow for change according to the necessity dictated by an animal's unique experience and interaction with the environment. This adjustment to the demands of the physical and social environment depends on learning, but learning is possible only to the extent that an animal is genetically prepared to learn." [Lindsay,pg.168] When a dog is born his brain continues to grow. It changes both in size and shape. The shape refers to the kinds on neural connections it makes. The experiences the dog has when he is a young puppy change the shape and size of his brain which means that what he is born with in terms of temperament is not what will exist in the adult. The development of the fetus and being born are just the first stages of the development of the dog's temperament. The final product will be a combination of nature and nurture. [Coppinger]

Personality Profiling and Aggression

Understanding a bit about the dog's personality can help in understanding why a dog uses aggression.

Personality is:

- Temperament
- Learning and socialization history so far

One way of describing a dog's personality is to describe his:

- Drives
- Sensitivities

Drives are what motivate a dog to act toward performing a behavior. They are what drives behavior. The word "drives" defines, on a general level, what this particular dog views as reinforcement. It's incredibly important that the dog be viewed as an individual on all counts, but it's particularly important, here: each dog is driven by different things. These drives can both define the dog's targets, and give us the ammunition necessary to successfully re-train.

Sensitivities are common aversive associations with specific environmental stimuli. They are what dogs do not like and are motivated to avoid or escape.

A dog may have varying levels of many qualities that make up their set of drives and sensitivities. A dog can have a very strong or high social drive or a very strong or high predatory drive. These drives motivate many behaviors within the dog's life and contribute to the gestalt of his personality which in turn helps to explain why he behaves the way he does and helps us predict how he might respond toward various stimuli. A dog can have a sensitivity to social pressure or to handling specifically. These sensitivities, like drives, help us explain why a dog behaves the way he does and also helps us predict his future responses. Strong sensitivities over ride drives. For example a dog may be very food-driven, but may not eat or play when scared. The sensitivity over-rides the drive.

Drives and sensitivities are both inherited and learned. Many dogs are born with a predisposition toward high drives or sensitivities but they can be created or cultivated to some extent also. Dogs tend toward the growth of sensitivities which would help explain why aggressive dog's do not tend become more prosocial without intervention.

A particularly strong drive or sensitivity can help explain why a dog aggresses.

HOMEWORK Each aggressive dog should have a list made of his primary or most influential drives and sensitivities. These lists will help define this dog's personality. Personality profiling will help you understand what motivates that particular dog and it helps you predict how relationships may go or how that particular dog may respond to various environmental stimuli. Know your dog. Know his general drives and sensitivities. A knowledge of a dog's drives and sensitivities can help explain the function for the dog's aggression and help you prevent, manage and treat the problem.

Classifying Aggression (Inventory)

There are two schools of thought on classifying aggression cases. One school suggests that classifying aggression is either a waste of time or misleading. The argument goes that we cannot read a dog's mind and hence we cannot effectively know what is motivating the dog to aggress. The argument continues that what should be addressed is the trigger stimuli and not a convoluted conceptual label. This school of thought seems to suggest that the behavior should be addressed the same way regardless of the motivation since no attempt to define the motivation is made.

Another school of thought suggests that we should classify aggression cases. The argument goes that by attempting to understand the motivational substrate of the aggression we can better design a treatment plan that addresses those actual motivations. This school of thought recognizes that different motivational functions of aggression require different approaches in treatment to address the actual motivation for the behavior.

The often suggested scenario for argument is that if a dog bites a child is it worth while to differentiate the behavior as a result of a fear response or a predatory response? The first school would suggest that the behavior is either wanted or not wanted and that is the only distinction. This behavior is not wanted and so the dog is then managed and treated for the behavior. The other school would suggest that it is unwanted *and* that it is significant to treatment to know what motivates the behavior. The first school would then typically ask whether knowing this effects the plan (suggesting that it would not affect theirs) and the second school would answer yes (suggesting that it would affect their choice of treatment). From this common account of this debate it can be assumed that the wanted vs. unwanted group design a treatment plan heavy on teaching of adaptive replacement behaviors in a very general way whereas the classifier group teach replacement behaviors addressed to the presumed motivation. The classifier group may suggest predatory outlet activities for the predator and counter conditioning and systematic desensitization for the fearful dog. The nonclassifier group may simply focus on training a solid heal or sit and make eye contact and proof it in high distraction situations.

Both schools of thought make very valid points. We cannot read a dog's mind. We will not know for sure what motivates him to aggress and trying to pigeon hole it may distract us from the real problem. But, understanding why a dog aggresses is the foundation for more specific and accurate decisions on what to do about it. I have had many aggression cases that I could not be certain of the motivation, in which case I simply classified it as unwanted and we got right to work on it. So whether you are a classifier or a nonclassifier be prepared to settle for "not wanted" sometimes and then just address the actual triggers.

This book will reconcile this debate in the following way. The framework for a unified theory of aggression has already been presented. This theory allows for abstraction and generalization. It is basic. What will follow will be more in-depth discussion in an inventory format of various readily identifiable and characteristic "forms" of expression. As a primary theory of aggression an inventory format classification system is problematic. It does not allow very well for abstraction or generalization and there is significant over lap. It describes many expressions of aggressive behavior but fails to offer a unified theory that can be used. This inventory will act only for illustration purposes. It will be an exploration of easily identifiable "types" of defensive expression and a more in depth appreciation for the motivational substrates involved. It is hoped that this more in-depth exploration will aid in designing a treatment plan. Diagnosis will not make use of inventory type classification. Aggression is either wanted or unwanted and diagnosis will attempt to identify the "function" for the behavior but not pigeon hole it into a classification. The difference between identifying a function and a motivation is presumptuousness. When we define the function we identify the consequences that reinforce a behavior and the cues that make those consequences available. This is made evident by behavior emitted or elicited. Motivation requires us to presume more than mere function. The basic theory outlined will act to explain why at a basic level and function will identify why at a more specific level. Treatment will include a foundational program and will then include more specific behavior modification techniques that address the actual trigger stimuli. A discussion of common tricks and tips will be offered based on the inventory but these are offered for illustration purposes only to aid in the design of a treatment plan. The counselor or owner must be flexible in the use of any approaches outlined.

The next important issue involves the problem with classification systems. There have been about as many classification systems designed as there are theorists out there giving thought to the matter.

One system defines aggression in terms of either offensive aggression or defensive aggression. It is unclear whether the system in meant to describe the expression of the behavior (active or passive defensiveness) or the intension of the animal (fear or anger) or both.

Another system has defined aggression in terms of either fear aggression or dominance aggression. This system lacks functionality and rests on some very problematic assumptions regarding the underlying motivation for certain behaviors.

Most if not all systems recognize the significant difference between predatory behavior and other behaviors that lead to attack outcomes. Some sources exclude predatory behavior from their definition of aggression because of this significant difference in motivational state. Many systems include predatory behavior as a form of aggression, probably due to the fact that it does result in the same destructive outcome of attack and so that it can be differentiated from other forms.

There have been many variations on the system of functional inventory for aggressive behavior. This system has been criticized (Lindsay,vol.2) as being overlapping and not allowing for abstraction or generalization. As noted, here a motivational inventory system will be used but more basic distinctions are made to allow for theoretical exploration. Although it will be different than many other inventories it will be very similar to most in many ways. Actual dog behavior does not always (or even usually) fit neatly into any category system that I have yet seen. This is another fine argument for defining aggression cases as either wanted or unwanted. This system is not meant to have owners attempt to jam square pegs into round holes. The classification system is more for illustration purposes and allows the owner or behavior counselor to design more motivationally directed treatments based on as objective a system of classification as possible.

Dog - Dog vs. Dog - Human Aggression

There are often differences in the common motivational substrates of aggression targeted toward other dogs or toward humans. Typically, aggression targeted toward humans is fear motivated. We do not share many of the same drives and because we are a different species: more subtle communication is less effective. Also, there are often socialization deficits and sensitization problems that contribute to this fear.

Typically, aggression targeted toward other dogs on the other hand seems to be based in competition or frustration. Dogs share the same drives in many cases; certainly they are more closely aligned than those of human to dog. This leads to competitive problems especially among dogs who reside together. Regarding dogs who do not reside together: fear or escalation of aggression through clashing personalities or through socialization deficits is a common cause of aggression. One of the most typical scenarios though involves one dog learning that he can be more of a bully simply because it works so well on a day to day basis. These dogs become impatient and frustrated easily. The above are typical motivations; no doubt many dogs are motivated atypically and fear another dog they reside with or feel competitive with human family members, but these are less common.

Fear Related Aggression

Signalment

Any dog may experience fear related aggression. Female dogs tend to be more fearful than male dogs. [Beaver,166] The margin between socialized dogs and unsocialized dogs displaying aggression is not as big as many think which lends to a more genetic theory of etiology. [Overall]

Characteristics

Typically, fear related aggression presents active defensive behavior only after passive defensiveness fails or is impossible. The exception to this rule would be the experienced dog performing avoidance motivated aggression discussed below.

Triggering Stimuli

Triggering stimuli are usually well defined at least until they generalize and work toward avoidance motivated aggression.

Fear and Aggression

Passive defensiveness (flight, freeze, appease) is a prepotent response in normal dogs over active defensiveness (fight). Fear inhibits aggression because it activates the flight response. A dog will gravitate quickly or gradually toward active defensiveness under the following conditions:

- Flight fails to achieve an increase in distance
- Flight is made impossible to even attempt
- Flight has a history of failure for a particular dog
- The dog has a predisposition to fight

Fear related aggression is used to avoid or take control of a fear inducing stimuli (threat).

Fear may develop out of the following situations:

- Undersocialized to the triggering stimuli
- The triggering stimuli may have proven dangerous through some event or series of events
- Genetic predisposition

Neophobia and Investigative Drive

Dogs have an innate mechanism for avoiding danger; a fear or apprehension of the unfamiliar and potentially dangerous. The way it works is the very young puppy is afraid of little or nothing. He has a very high investigative drive. He is so curious that he wants to check everything out. This drive is there so that he will have the chance to be introduced to all the things he will need to know how to interact with *for his life time*. Out in the wilderness this is not impossible. This period of high curiosity correlates to when mother is supervising so that he remains safe but is socialized to things he needs to be socialized to. As the puppy gets older and he is a few months old the investigative drive is gradually taken over by neophobia. He will become less curious and more and more leery of things he has not yet experienced in a positive way. Now he has learned what can be trusted and what cannot. What cannot be trusted is anything he was not exposed to in puppyhood. He becomes more independent and needs his mother less as a supervisor. The cycle of socialization works as such very well in the wild. In our society a dog is exposed to so many novel stimuli that it is close to impossible to work within these boundaries. That is why socialization is so important. If you miss the critical period you are playing catch up for the rest of the dog's life. So if you missed the boat regarding socialization the dog is at a higher risk of developing a fear based aggression.

Single Event & Learning Fear Aggression

Dr. Ian Dunbar tells a story about a man who having never hit his dog before comes home to some intolerable event performed by the dog, puts his keys down and hits the dog. The next day the man is getting ready for work, feels bad about hitting the dog he gets all his stuff together to leave, including his keys, and the dog bites him. Dr. Dunbar was illustrating how a single experience can provoke an intense emotional response in a dog and produce an aggressive event. The story is told in a way that makes it seem as though it will be easy to figure out what the trigger is. Most cases involving a single event learned aggression involve complex and obscure triggers that are not identified. They can also evolve into a set of obscure triggers that are very unlikely to be identified. These can be perplexing cases. This is really a fear based aggression but is described as a sub-set of fear aggression due to it's unique evolution. The best way to determine these triggers is to identify every single contextual stimulus prior to each event that is common and then to perform a functional analysis on them. Functional analysis is a way of manipulating events to get at the key factors. A story is told by Pamela Reid about her dog having liked children all along and then one day a child barks at the dog and from that moment on the dog was terrified of children and would lunge at them if given a chance. This illustrates how apparently (to us) benign experiences can lead to this form of aggression. These stories also help us appreciate how complex aggression problems can be. The origin of this aggression problem may never have been identified if it was not observed first hand by a professional. This could have easily been a bizarre and mysterious seeming case even after extensive questioning of the owner. Even an owner that saw this might not bring it up under questioning. Single-event learned aggression can be the bane of attempts to determine the motivation of an aggression case.

Avoidance Motivated Aggression

If fear related passive defensiveness fails to provide relief and then so does active defensiveness the result may be learned helplessness or neurosis. This can result if nothing appears to provide relief. Another potential result may be frustrative rage. In most cases humans fail to recognize passive defensive strategies. The dog who walks out of the room when children arrive is displaying passive defensiveness. He leaves. This is often not recognized by humans as a sign of fear (or at least at that point discomfort). If this strategy fails to bring relief through increased distance or if it simply becomes too frustrating the dog will respond with more active defensiveness strategies. If these are reinforced then those strategies will increase in frequency. The dog does what works. Chances are that they will not be reinforced every single time. Each time relief is not forthcoming the aggressive strategies will become more and more active. Fleeing and appeasing fail to reinforce the behavior and it goes into an extinction burst. Extinction is what happens when a behavior fails to get reinforced. The behavior becomes variable until some variant is reinforced and that becomes the behavior of choice. That little burst of variability is called an extinction burst. The dog growls and the parents remove the child from the situation or remove the dog. Either way relief and hence reinforcement occurs. As time goes on the parents are absent through a few more events and the children fail to respond and hence they fail to immediately reinforce the growling. The next step is a snap. The dog no longer even attempts to flee. That has been extinguished because it did not work. What did work? Well, for a while growling did. Now snapping is the reinforced behavior. The behavior is being shaped through encouraging the dog to vary his behavior, then a more intense version is installed. As time goes on the dog not only learns operantly what behaviors work and which do not work, but he also learns how to predict the aversive situation. The presence of children becomes the trigger for the active defensive response. As this situation progresses the dog becomes more active in his own defense and the triggering stimuli has become highly predictable. The next stage is the preemptive strike. The fear is elicited with the mere presentation of the child and the snapping is emitted. By this point there are few if any passive strategies being employed and the dog is not waiting for the children to make contact. The dog is now motivated to avoid the situation as quickly as possible. The final result is an immediate and very offensive looking and active attack on the mere suggestion of the presentation of the stimulus (child in this hypothetical). This is what is meant by an experienced fearfully aggressive dog. At this point with no obvious signs of passive defensiveness it becomes difficult if possible at all to distinguish this fear motivated aggression from an anger motivated aggression.

There is another way of looking at this behavior pattern. It could very well be that repeated elicitation of fear provokes frustration and eventually anger. It could be that fear provokes passive defensiveness and that anger provokes active defensiveness. If this model is true then one would be able to classify all flight behavior as fear motivated and all fight behavior as anger motivated. This model may very well be the correct one. It would be difficult to test this hypothesis and until it is tested it remains an untested model - theory that may be plausible but is not yet a valid inductive conclusion. One way to add validity to this model might be to measure heart rate, respiration rate and neurotransmitter release. We could match the results up with flight vs. fight responses and against what we know about the physiologic difference between fear and anger.

Control Complex Aggression

Control complex aggression describes an abnormal and maladaptive emotional state. These dogs are control freaks with low thresholds for frustration and anger. They are socially incompetent.

Signalment

65% to 90% of dogs displaying behaviors associated with control related aggression are male. [Beaver,157] 90% of those dogs are intact at the time they are presented to a professional for help. [Beaver,157] Of the females presenting with this complex most are spayed. [Overall] Signs are usually present at sexual maturity (6-12 months) to those who observe carefully but it escalates and becomes obvious even to poor observers by social maturity (18-24 months). [Beaver,157] The typical age of presentation to a professional is 1 to 3 years of age [Beaver,157] Pure breeds are more at risk of developing this form of aggression (82-87%). [Beaver,157] Certain breeds are more at risk for developing this form of aggression. Certain lines of dogs in breeding programs have been found to be overrepresented in aggression statistics related to behavior associated with this complex.

Characteristics

Control complex aggression seems to be characterized by the following:

- Very low frustration threshold (easily angered)
- Frustrated arousal response to perceived social control or competition
- Socially controlling (aggressive and manipulative) responses to frustrative arousal
- Relatively uninhibited aggressive response (characteristic of anger or rage)

Control complex aggression dogs tend to perform subtle manipulative control seeking behaviors. The behaviors are associated with affection and nonaggressive attention seeking in most dogs.

Subtle controlling behaviors reported by Overall (1997):

- Pushing on people or other dogs
- Placing paws or head on the person's or dog's shoulders, head or back.
- Standing over people.
- Blocking access through narrow spaces such as doorways.
- Staring the person down, often with dilated pupils.
- "Talking back". This means barking at the person in response to being given a directive or reprimand.
- Guarding beds, couches, toys, air molecules and any other place or thing.

"...most dominance [read control complex] aggression appears to be the result of social confusion, frustration, irritability, contact aversion, and learning. Rather than being socially dominant, many dominance aggressors simply appear to be socially incompetent and unable adaptively to navigate the social and interactive demands placed upon them without biting." [Lindsay,vol2,241]

Dogs with this exceptionally low threshold for frustrative arousal are abnormal in the sense that they are not average in their responses. They apparently experience a lack of social confidence. They experience various stimuli as survival imperatives when in fact they are not. These dogs are defensive and guided by survival and control but they lack the ability to judge what is truly a threat and what is not. These are NOT social ladder climbers; they are control freaks. The theory of dominance aggression suggests that these dogs are supremely confident. This seems ridiculous to me as a truly confident animal would not feel such a need to control. If you have known an aggressively controlling human you know that they are not supremely confident; they are insecure and overcompensating. Same thing with dogs. They are not confident at all. They are socially incompetent and frustrated.

Control complex is not synonymous with dominance because I do not believe the premises that these dogs are highly confident and that they are status seeking; dominance theory is tenuous if not flawed completely. It is impossible to confirm that dogs are status seeking and that presumption rests on some flimsy premises of cognitive ethology. Is a dog capable of using aggression to attain a symbolic title of alpha because it will allow them access to future privilege? It seems more likely that these dogs are not confident or socially competent. Reference to status seeking has historically lead to a resentment based confrontational and combative relationship between owners and their dogs. Given the unlikely premises of 'confidence' and 'status seeking' and the highly problematic and relationship degrading qualities of pack theory I reject it. Control complex is a syndrome. It helps us account for the various behavioral phenomena observed that has in the past resulted in a diagnosis of dominance aggression. There may be various reasons or motivational substrates involved in producing this temperament and control complex is a theoretical model designed to account for it.

Trigger Stimuli

Trigger stimuli may include any of the following:

- Attempt by human (or other dog) to remove or reach for valued resource (resource guarding)
- Disturbance of the dog from resting place (startle reflex or location guarding)
- Attempts to handle the dog especially the head, muzzle, rump, paws, neck or back (dog hasn't been taught to accept this handling)
- Reprimands or punishment (compromised trust)
- Disturbing dog while in company of particular family member (often while on their lap) (resource guarding)
- Being put in crate (has no safety or reward history with the crate)
- Staring at the dog (or in some cases making any eye contact) (punitive history associated with eye contact)
- Leash correction (compromised trust)

Note: in parentheses above, you'll find the most likely reasons why these behaviors occur. Many of them have to do with compromised trust, safety history, and reward history. Punitive methodology compromises all of these aspects of your relationship with your dog; it is critical that you entirely give up all punitive and correction-based methodology, in order to re-build your relationship with your dog.

Dog - Dog Control Complex Aggression

As noted, dog - dog control related aggression seems to be motivated primarily around competitive factors with in many cases a learned 'bully' component. Access to resources is the most common proximal cause for control related aggression toward other dogs. These dogs are very easily frustrated. This is distinguished from plain possessive aggression in that the control of the possession seems obsessive and excessive or relentless. It is also usually accompanied by other sings of excessively controlling behaviors. This is a maladaptive and abnormal response in most dogs. Many dogs are competitive but control complex aggression dogs are triggered by extremely low level stimulation by objectively innocuous triggering stimuli (social control / even mild competition).

Dog - Human Control Complex Aggression

As noted, dog - human control complex aggression is guided by the same extremely low threshold for frustrative arousal by socially controlling triggering stimuli. Given that humans are not typically very good at reading the intentions of dogs humans are at risk of seemingly "out of nowhere" aggressive incidents. The warnings are not always recognized prior to the dog triggering. Most incidents relate more to a build up of irritability due to contact aversion rather than direct competition. These dogs typically become more irritable when touched or controlled.

The Competitive Component

The competitive component to control complex aggression usually relates to interactions among dogs. Competitive conflict between dogs and humans happens but is less typical. Lindsay [vol2,203] suggests that sexual imperatives may be the reason for this, accounting for much of the competitive tension among dogs. Sexual competition or gender role competition may help explain why aggression among dogs is primarily intergender. The social behavior of dogs seems to revolve around the balance of competitive / defensive distance increasing activity, and, affiliative bonding distance decreasing activities. Most dogs are socially driven. Dogs will compete for access to valued resources including sexual activity, comfortable and familiar places and familiar social objects. Competition is often a source of conflict among dogs. For dogs with a control complex aggression mentality even minor competitive events drive the dog to perform active distance decreasing defensive behaviors. Frustration is the result of perceived ineffectual or unsuccessful competition. Dogs with such high drives to compete and low thresholds to experience frustration are dangerous because they appear to view various, usually objectively innocuous, events as competitive and hence frustrative. This frustration appears to provoke anger and out of context and inappropriate aggressive responses. The more irritable and angry the dog becomes the more of a survival issue it becomes and less inhibited the response will be. Control complex aggression mentality dogs are abnormal in their admixture of competitive drives and frustrative arousal thresholds.

There is a learned component to this process also in many cases. If a dog learns that he will be competitively successful all the time (spoiled rotten dog or just the biggest and most driven dog) then he will expect to be competitively successful every time. After repeated lessons to this effect, a dog will become frustrated easily when he does not get things his way. He is not used to it and does not fully know how to cope with that particular stress. The frustration leads to anger. This dog is impatient and easily frustrated. They appear pushy or bossy. Dogs do not spoil each other, that is a human issue that creates a lot of dogs that are then labeled dominant aggressive. Then, the owner is instructed by their traditional trainer to dominate the dog which causes more frustration on the part of the dog and bang you have a huge problem on your hands. Do not spoil your dog rotten or he may come to be a spoiled rotten dog.

Many control complex dogs could be described as sociopathic. Often it is observed that these dogs will perform playful behaviors or affection seeking behaviors only to trigger once the invitation is accepted. These dogs are observed to offer a toy to a human or other dog only to attack once the toy is accepted. These dogs may show deferential behaviors or play solicitous metasignals (signals like a play bow that indicate that what they are about to do might look aggressive but it is really just play) to other dogs or humans and then trigger when the other dog or human respond affectionately or playfully. These dogs often do not offer affection but demand it. They do not seem to experience social joy at all in many cases and when they do it seems to be a perverse kind of challenge.

Distinguishing Between Control Complex Aggression and Pathophysiologic Aggression

Various pathophysiologic and neurologic disorders produce low threshold, unpredictable and uninhibited forms of aggression. It is vital that a full medical evaluation be completed by a veterinarian experienced with ruling out medical causes for aggressive behavior.

Contact Aversion

Many control complex aggression dogs are independent and aloof. They lack a "social buffer" as Sue Sternberg would say that inhibits most dogs from becoming frustrated or irritable in the face of restrictive social control. The relation between the owner and dog can erode or fail to develop to the point that mere contact between the dog and owner can be frustrative to the dog. Continued or repeated contact may produce a cumulative contact aversion and irritability that can lead to contact becoming a potent triggering stimulus. This irritability may lower frustrative thresholds.

Lindsay proposes the contact aversion theory to account for the following facts:

"1. Aggression is often selectively directed.

2. Aggression often takes place in areas associated with affectionate activity (e.g., on sofas and beds).

3. Aggression often occurs under the influence of minimal stimulation, such as when the dog is being reached for in a non provocative way.

4. Aggression is often explosive and inappropriate, suggesting an accumulated tension building up over time.

5. Dominance [read control complex] may become progressively resentful of affectionate contact and resist efforts to elicit play." [Lindsay,vol2,248]

Summary of Control Complex Aggression Etiology

Control complex aggressive dogs tend to have a very low threshold for frustration. Frustration leads to an uninhibited and actively defensive manner. These dogs are often lacking a social buffer and are independent-minded. They become irritable and anger easily. Requiring the dog to do something he does not want to do or preventing him from doing something he wants to do is often the triggering stimulus. These dogs are abnormal in their threshold levels for frustrative arousal or in many cases competitive drive. These dogs maladaptively and actively defend themselves against irrational perceptions of threats to their ability to survive.

Territorial Aggression

Signalment

Primarily adult males. Dogs on a high protein diet are more prominently shown in statistics. [Beaver,180] Intact males may act slightly more intensely once they have triggered but neutering does not typically affect this form of aggression significantly. [Beaver,180]

Characteristics

- Territorial aggression involves the defense of an area.
- The area defended is almost always a highly familiar area, usually the dog's home or yard.
- Territory is defended against "outsiders"; those who are unfamiliar
- Territorial aggression characterized by alarm barking
- Expression at least when the stranger is at a distance is very active and demonstrative

Triggering Stimuli

The approach or presence of an unfamiliar or feared person or dog into ones territory.

Fear or Anger Related

Defense of territory is usually active in expression, including alarm barking, growling, snarling, lunging and in some cases biting or snapping. Anger stemming from frustration or fear could be the impetus of this behavior.

Fear Related Territoriality

Fear-related active defensive strategies are experimented with and are reinforced frequently. Over time defensiveness becomes more and more active and more and more intense. In many of these cases the defensiveness generalizes to any unfamiliar intruder. The mail man is an excellent example of how this form of territoriality develops. The mail man arrives which provokes discomfort in the dog. The dog probes the situation with a light "woof woof" and then silence while he attempts to determine the effect of the behavior. The mail man leaves after depositing the mail. The dog feels relief which is highly reinforcing. After a few trials of this the dog gains more confidence in performing more active defensive strategies. Now he barks menacingly at the door. Each time the behavior is reinforced. It becomes habitual and almost reflexive. Not only is the behavior now being reinforced by the retreat of the intruder but the chemical mind bath and adrenaline rush experienced in the fight intrinsically reinforces the behavior. A big part of this may be the development of avoidance motivated aggression as defined under fear related aggression.

Frustration or Territoriality

Many situations involving what looks like territorial aggression seem to be related more to frustration than fear. Many cases of fence fighting between dogs, usually intact males, seem attributable to frustration. Labelling these dogs as territorial is problematic. Here is the etiology. Dogs become aroused by the presence of the other dog either because they want to interact or because they resent the intrusion. Irritability and tension build with each frustrative encounter. These dogs will often run back and forth barking, lunging and charging at the other dog. Each incident makes the trigger more firm and the behavior more habitual. The act of aggressing reinforces the behavior and a highly frustrated form of aggression results. The meetings of these dogs are typically unpredictable. If the motivation was defense of an area then you would expect active defensiveness if the fence is removed. In many cases this does not happen. Many times the meeting does result in an explosion of apparent anger (release of frustration), but in many cases with the trigger stimuli (the fence or denied access, not the area itself) gone the dogs display affiliative (prosocial) behaviors. These meetings are unpredictable. When fence fighters are introduced away from the "territory" they typically get along better. This may be accountable to removing them from the territory or to removing more trigger stimuli for the conditioned aggression. In many cases territorial aggression may have initiated the process but it becomes difficult to defend this phenomenon as territorial aggression.

Tied-Out Dogs and Aggression

Another situation often difficult to label is the aggressive behavior exhibited by dogs who are tied up in the yard. We know that tied-up dogs are at a significantly increased risk of developing aggressiveness but it is often motivated by frustration. Tie outs prevent the escape option which in and of itself promotes more fear and high frustration levels. Confinement makes the dog feel vulnerable to attack. Teasing by cats, children or others increases frustrative arousal and or fear. These dogs will often take the first chance they get to preemptively strike or explode in a rage. If a child walks within the reach of such a dog the dog may attack with little or no inhibition. This indicates frustration. In many cases these dogs initially were fearful of the lack of passive options. In many cases this situation may be described in avoidance motivated aggression paradigms. Aggression resulting from this situation is often described in the light of territorial aggression but if this were true then this effect would happen only on the dog's territory. It is often suggested that territory can be floating and follow the dog but this seems to render the notion of territoriality less useful. It may also be that the dog was more confident in familiar surroundings and hence fear did not inhibit expression of anger. Territoriality may be related solely to the lack of inhibition in a familiar place. An unfamiliar place may simply produce more anxiety and fear which inhibits active defensive behavior. This may be an argument for rejecting the notion of territory.

Possessive Aggression

Signalment

Any dog can be possessive. The more valued the object the more possessive a dog will be of it and deprivation often increases the object's value. Dogs who are not used to sharing are also at increased risk because they have not learned that removal of an object can be reinforcing or is likely to be reinforcing.

Characteristics

Dogs displaying possessive aggression use active aggressive strategies to get or keep valued objects. Dogs do not understand the concept of property rights or permanent possession. Dogs tend to live in 'the here and now' as they say and possessions of value to the dog in the moment may be guarded. A possession or resource can be just about anything including toys, food, bed, couch, crate, person, other dog etc.

Triggering Stimuli

- Approaching a dog who is in possession of a highly valued resource
- Attempting to remove or reaching for a highly valued resource that a dog is in possession of
- Attempting to remove a dog from a highly valued place

Dogs assign varying levels of value to various items. Attempts by either another dog or a person to take control of that resource or to remove the dog from that resource may trigger defensive behaviors. This is an adaptive behavior and may be built right into the dog's genetic construction. Left to their own devises most dogs would develop some form of resource guarding (possessiveness). Possessiveness can be thought of as a form of hoarding behavior, another form of aggression commonly referred to as protective aggression. This is likely a form of resource guarding or hoarding and is adequately described in that light rather than as a classification of its own.

Maternal Aggression

Signalment

Intact female dog behavior. Occasionally remains in spayed females, especially if the spay was done too soon after heat but this is more accurately termed learned aggression or possessiveness.

Characteristics

Active aggression resembling possessive aggression but experienced by intact female dogs in the following states:

- Pregnancy
- Pseudopregnancy
- Whelping
- Postpartum

This behavior is highly influenced by genetics and hormonal activity.

The dog will choose a place as a nesting area to guard or a possession, often a soft object like a slipper or stuffed toy, to guard as if it were a puppy. For dogs that are truly pregnant or whelping the puppies or nesting area are guarded.

Trigger Stimuli

Approaching or attempting to remove or in some way control:

- Puppies
- Object in place of actual puppy
- Nesting area

Pathophysiological Aggression

Jean Dodds, DVM, is widely considered to be a leading researcher in the field of medical causes of aberrant behavior and much of this section relies on her experience and professionalism.

There are a number of medical problems in dogs that may cause the dog to respond aggressively. The aggression is medical in nature if an illness known to produce aggressive behavior is identified and treated whereupon the aggressive behavior significantly reduces in frequency and intensity. Aggression can always have a learned component also, so if the aggression has been present for quite a while, curing or managing an illness will not necessarily stop aggression. The learned component must still be dealt with. It has become a habit. It has become behavioral strategy plan A.

All cases of aggression should involve ruling out common potential medical causes first, but there are certain circumstances in which medical causes should be suspected and more elaborate medical diagnostics should be explored. If the onset of aggression is sudden, medical causes should be suspected. If the aggression seems explosive or excessively inappropriate to the trigger, medical causes should be suspected. If the aggressive behavior has no apparent trigger or is related to general reclusiveness or grumpiness, medical causes should be suspected. If the dog is acting at all such that you would characterize it as weird or bizarre then medical causes should be suspected. If the onset of aggression correlates to the use of a medication or the beginning of some injury or illness then the two should be suspected as having a relationship. If any of the above characterize your dog's situation you should request that your veterinarian perform more invasive testing to evaluate and rule out medical causes. You may often hear of ruling out medical causes. *It is important for you to know that you never really rule out medical causes.* What you do is rule out some, depending on the extent of testing, of the more common causes of aggressive behavior. This does not mean that the problem is not medical. It just means that it is unlikely to be caused by the medical causes that were suspected and then tested for.

"Abnormal behavior in dogs can have a variety of medical causes; it also can reflect underlying problems of a psychological nature. Your veterinarian follows a systematic diagnostic approach in searching for medical causes when a per exhibits unusual or unacceptable behavior. As summarized by Landsberg (Canadian Veterinary Journal, 31:225-227, 1990), this includes:

1.) a complete patient history;

2.) clinical examination and a neurological work-up;

3.) routine laboratory testing of complete blood count, blood biochemistry and thyroid profiles, urinalysis, fecal exam and X-ray;

4.) additional specific laboratory tests as indicated (e.g., other hormonal tests, bile acids, blood ammonia, glucose tolerance immunologist assays and tests for toxins, fungi and other infections;

5.) examination of cerebral spinal fluid; and

6.) more specialized neurological examinations such as an electroencephalography and computerized axial tomography scan.

Diagnostic steps 1 through 3 are usually completed first; additional tests such as steps 4 through 6 are performed if indicated." [W. Jean Dodds, DVM, As published in Dog World Vol. 77 No. 10, October 1992]

Pain can cause an otherwise well tempered, well socialized and trained dog to have various antisocial thresholds lowered. Hip dysplasia, ear infections, stomach cramps, allergies and any other number of pain causing conditions can cause an aggressive response. Partial blindness or deafness can cause aggression if the dog is startled by the approach of people because he cannot sense them coming. Even the memory of pain can provoke a response. If a dog stepped on a nail he may never be comfortable with having that foot touched. Some breeds and some individuals are more pain sensitive than others. A pit bull is less likely to respond aggressively to pain than most other breeds for example because he is very pain insensitive by design.

Canine Epilepsy and Aggression

One common form of health related aggression involves seizure activity.

Canine epilepsy is a catch-all term referring to a diverse category of disorders. Canine epilepsy is a disorder of the brain in which abnormal electrical activity triggers further uncoordinated nerve transmission which scrambles messages to the muscles. This inhibits coordinated function of the muscles. Canine epilepsy is broadly divided into idiopathic disorders and symptomatic disorders.

Seizures produced by canine epilepsy can be generalized or partial. Partial seizures, also called focal seizures involve an electrical storm in a localized part of the brain as opposed to generalized seizures which involve an electrical storm that encompasses the whole brain at once. Partial seizures can be divided into simple focal seizures when consciousness is preserved or complex focal seizures when consciousness is altered. "A complex partial seizure will originate in the area of the brain that controls behavior and is sometimes called a psychomotor seizure. During this type of seizure, a dog's consciousness is altered and he may exhibit bizarre behavior such as unprovoked aggression or extreme irrational fear." [http://www.canine-epilepsy-guardian-angels.com/CanineEpil.htm] "The seizures are often spaced several weeks to months apart, and occasionally they appear in a brief cluster. In some cases the animals become aggressive and attack those around them shortly before or after having one of these seizure episodes." [W. Jean Dodds, DVM and Linda P. Aronson, DVM]

If your vet can find no other cause for what may be seizure activity she may want to do a complete history, a neurological exam, a complete blood cell count, serum chemistry profile and a thyroid test. Nutritional counseling is also an important aspect of seizure history, as some breeds exhibit a propensity for allergic or hyper-sensitivity reactions to ingredients that may manifest as seizure activity. You will be asked to describe in detail the event, before, during and after. You should note the time of day, any common denominators that may act as triggers including exactly what activity the dog was performing at the time the seizure started. Depending on what is found or not found other tests may include cerebrospinal fluid analysis (spinal tap), magnetic resonance imaging (MRI), and electroencephalogram (EEG).

Medication may be an option which you will discuss with the veterinarian. Phenobarbital or Potassium Bromide are the initial treatments of choice for dogs that require drug therapy. It may be unrealistic to expect all seizure activity to go away once treatment has started.

Difficulties may arise in having the appropriate tests done, let alone achieving a diagnosis, because many seizures do not present the typical convulsion type result. It may be difficult to convince some veterinarians that the behavior you are witnessing may be a seizure or seizure related.

Hypothyroidism and Aggression

It remains unclear how diminished thyroid function affects behavior. There is some indication that hypothyroid dogs have reduced cortisol clearance. "Hypothyroid patients have reduced cortisol clearance, and the constantly elevated levels or circulating cortisol mimic the condition of an animal in a constant state of stress, as well as suppressed TSH output and production of thyroid hormones." [W. Jean Dodds, DVM and Linda P. Aronson, DVM] There has been a clear connection demonstrated between dopamine and serotonin reception in aggressive pathways in the central nervous system. "In dogs with aberrant aggression, a large collaborative study at Tufts University has shown a favorable response to thyroid replacement therapy within the first week of treatment". [W. Jean Dodds, DVM and Linda P. Aronson, DVM] "Dramatic reversal of behavior with resumption of previous problems has occurred in some cases if only a single dose is missed." [W. Jean Dodds, DVM and Linda P. Aronson, DVM]

"The major categories of aberrant behavior were: aggression (40% of cases), seizures (30%), fearfulness (9%), and hyperactivity (7%); some dogs exhibited more than 1 of these behaviors. Thyroid dysfunction was found in 62% of the aggressive dogs, 77% of seizuring dogs, 47% of fearful dogs, and 31% of hyperactive dogs." [W. Jean Dodds, DVM and Linda P. Aronson, DVM]

"Typical clinical signs include unprovoked aggression towards other animals and/or people, sudden onset of a seizure disorder in adulthood, disorientation, moodiness, erratic temperament, periods of hyperactivity, hypoattentiveness, depression, fearfulness and phobias, anxiety, submissiveness, passivity, compulsiveness, and irritability. After the episodes, a majority of the animals were noted to behave as if they were coming out of a trance- like state and were unaware of their previous behavior." [W. Jean Dodds, DVM and Linda P. Aronson, DVM]

Ensure your veterinarian performs the following test:

- Thyroid Antibody DST Profile, which tests for T3, T4, Free T3 & T4, T3 & T4 Autoantibodies.

For more information on the internet:

- http://www.canine-epilepsy.com/testinst.html
- http://www.oxfordlabs.com/vetlabs.htm

Idiopathic Aggression (a.k.a. Rage Syndrome)

Idiopathic aggression is a very controversial classification. Many behavioral theorists believe that this form of aggression is purely medical or that if it occurs in normally healthy dogs then it merely relates to low thresholds or severe avoidance motivated aggression. The term idiopathic aggression is also often used in cases in which a classification cannot be identified. This is not the way the term will be used here.

Idiopathic aggression is a term given to a form of aggression characterized by particularly violent and unpredictable attacks on people, other animals or inanimate objects. The dog may look confused immediately before and after the attack. The dog may take on a blank, glazed over stare prior to attack. "This look could be the result of a sympathetic nervous system reaction that enhances tapetal reflection". [Overall,125] Occasionally twitching may be noted in these dogs while in an attack. These dogs are usually not generally aggressive but simply experience episodes of extreme rage. It is known to exist with greater occurrences in certain breeds and within specific breeding lines which has lead to speculation that there is a strong genetic basis. Cocker Spaniels and Springer Spaniels are most commonly afflicted which has lead to alternative names such as cocker rage syndrome or springer rage syndrome. St. Bernards are often included in lists of likely breeds for idiopathic aggression. This is a controversial form of aggression as many are possibly medical (seizure) in nature. The label idiopathic aggression or rage syndrome may be inappropriately used resulting in medical avenues which are not explored. This diagnosis should only be made when seizure disorder has been ruled out either through testing or through a trial course of anti-seizure medication (e.g. phenobarbital). "Idiopathic aggression seems to appear most often in dogs 1 to 3 years of age,... This is also, unfortunately, the age at which most idiopathic epilepsy develops." [Overall, 1997, pg126] "One of three dogs in the study by Dodman and co-workers responded to phenobarbital" [Overall, 1997, pg126] The cause of non-seizure-related idiopathic aggression is not known. This classification is NOT to be used as a catch all for cases in which aggression cannot be diagnosed. It is not a label for undiagnosed aggressive dogs.

Predatory Aggression

Signalment

Predatory aggression involves the inconvenient, inappropriate or harmful application, by the dog, of some part of the predatory sequence. Terriers and herding dogs are most prevalent but any dog may perform predatory behavior.

Characteristics

Refer to description of nonaffective aggression above. Predatory behavior is characterized by a lack of emotional response and absence of sympathetic arousal as is the case with all other forms of aggression. The attacks often follow stalking behavior and are usually quiet. Many times the initial bites are to the back of the legs. Then as the prey goes down biting may proceed to the neck and then to the trunk and head. [Lauridson,1993] Predatory aggression will not usually involve growling or snarling as a preliminary display. [Unruh,1996] Occasionally a dog will stop short of the prey and bark. [O'Farrel,1986] It is thought that this is because the prey differs significantly enough from the dog's mental expectation of what prey constitutes. It could also be a probe behavior in situations determined to be more dangerous to the dog. For example if a rabbit ran from a dog and the dog's prey drive was stimulated he would probably respond typically. But if he chased a squirrel and the squirrel turned to fight back the dog may test the danger level with a few barks or snaps and lunges. Or if a child triggers the prey drive it is possible that the barks may be a displacement behavior brought on by the fact that he was stimulated but the prey does not resemble exactly normal prey. This may be a confused response. You may have a dog who under all other circumstances would not bite hard at all even when provoked but then if his prey drive is triggered he may act completely instinctively. This can be a very difficult type of aggressing to modify and very dangerous also.

Predatory Drift

When aggression is between a small dog and a big dog with the big dog being the aggressor predatory aggression should be considered. This is called predatory drift. The dogs may be playing and seem fine together but some action or sound made by the small dog may trigger a response in the bigger dog. This can result in very serious injuries.

Trigger Stimuli

Quick moving objects (often small and often producing high pitched sounds and moving in a jerky fashion)

Play Aggression

Signalment

- Most often associated with high energy dogs such as those of the sporting group but may include any breed or individual.
- Most often associated with dogs with a history of rough play allowed by owners and perhaps in which bite inhibition exercises were not carried out.

Characteristics

This kind of aggression does not involve increasing social distance at all; no fear or anger. The only reason this will be considered here as aggression is because it is dangerous and should not be confused with other forms of aggression. "The two favorite ways dogs love to play are chasing and mock-fighting. Developing hunting skills is the primary goal of the former, and the later serves to develop social skills and to strengthen social ties between individuals. Through play, appropriate as well as inappropriate social behaviors are learned. It really depends on how the dogs play partners may or may not guide the interactions." [www.petpsych.com/reflib.htm] The cause of this behavior is primarily a matter of encouraging inappropriate play or failing to train limits to play. If the dog thinks that lunging and biting is fun and allowed he will do so. If he believes that humans can handle hard bites because bite inhibition was never installed then he will bite hard. This is not to say that some dog's are not genetically predisposed to bite hard. It would seem that many are. If the owner responds to play with wrestling either meant playfully by the owner or meant to punish the inappropriate play, the dog is likely to take that as reinforcement and continue to play in an inappropriate manner. These dogs invariably feel they are allowed to initiate these play sessions also. In some cases the dog will respond to subtle cues from the owner that mean to him that play is to begin. Often the owner who uses force to punish this behavior will stare down the dog in an attempt to "tell" him not to but the dog takes it as the challenge for mock-combat sort of like a play bow. They may think it's the human version of the play bow; an invitation to play. When situations get tense some dogs will use a play bow to indicate no threat. This play bow could become full contact play. The initiation of play could be working quite well for some dogs to turn off punishment. This is again another strategy behavior.

Sometimes play can become arousal-related aggression. In this case the dog is playing initially but becomes highly aroused and switches from play to aggression. This is not so much about anger or fear as much as it is a carnivorous predator (domesticated or not) who becomes over stimulated and gets carried away.

Redirected / Displaced Aggression

This type of aggression can occur when a dog is highly aroused and responding aggressively to one stimuli and you present another at that moment. The dog may respond toward that stimuli in place of the original one. That means that if your dog is fighting with another dog and you pull him away he may turn and snap at you or bite. You were not the original target but were in the wrong place at the wrong time. Another example is a dog who is highly stimulated by a dog walking past the house and then if you present yourself at that moment you may become the target. This form of aggression does not tend to relate to any specific age. If you participate in a dog sport which creates a very high arousal level and you get problems with aggression at these times then you should consider this form of aggression in your differential diagnosis list.

Dog - Dog Same Gender vs. Opposite Gender Aggression

Aggression between dogs is more likely to occur between same gender opponents. Within the household interfemale aggression is most common. Between dogs who do not reside together intermale aggression is most common. Lindsay describes one etiology for the occurrences of males in conflict with females. He terms it Virago Syndrome. This occurs when a female initiates aggressive or competitive conflict with a male and the male responds primarily with confusion due to his inability to view the female as a competitor and source of aggression. In that case the male only half heartedly defends himself whereupon the female develops the expectation of getting what she wants which reinforces the behavior and promotes continued fight-picking with males. It is as though the female realizes that she can compete with males because they do not see her as a competitor and don't defend themselves. This is the edge she needs to get a "big head" so to speak: this female becomes a bully. This sets her up for a rude awakening when she faces a testosterone-driven male dog that responds actively and without inhibition. It is thought that these aggressive females were affected by vagrant testosterone prior to birth.

Resident Directed Aggression

Aggression between dogs that live together often involves spayed females. It is thought that spaying removes progestrone, a calming hormone, which accounts for higher incidents of aggression among spayed as opposed to intact females. For whatever reason, in a household it is most likely to be familiar females who experience conflict. The conflict is also usually more intense than male conflict and more damage is usually done.

One etiology for aggression among dogs living in the same household is the learning of impatience. Dogs who live together learn to expect what consequences come from their social behavior. They learn who they can successfully push around to get what they want and who they cannot and all in what contexts. If one dog is regularly competitively successful or allowed to bully another dog, they will expect to continue to be competitively successful and be a bully (if that is their bent) until such time as their expectation is disconfirmed. The dog who is regularly competitively unsuccessful similarly learns to expect to be unsuccessful in competitive events. Sometimes both parties take comfort in the consistency of their relationship. Even the usually competitively unsuccessful dog can simply learn to work around the other dog in most cases if the expectations are consistent. In some cases with repeated rehearsal of the behavior the bully simply becomes less and less tolerant and impatient while the other dog becomes more and more traumatized or anxious and fearful. This is made worse if the events are not predictable for the unsuccessful dog. If he cannot adequately take action to adapt and work around the other dog within a consistent system he will be at greater risk for experiencing ill psychological effects. Either way, in this system of continued rehearsal of conflict, impatience is rewarded and frustration thresholds lowers. At the heart of understanding the etiology of this problem you must appreciate that dogs are competitive and can experience impatience and frustration. If a dog is repeatedly rewarded for impatience and pushy behavior then he will simply become more pushy and impatient and act more like a bully. The dog needs to learn that bullying will not work and that patience and impulse control does work: this occurs through active training and management protocols.

It would probably be wise to dismiss the old theory of 'supporting the hierarchy' in which owners are instructed to identify the "alpha" dog and support their rein. Yes this would promote consistency but it would be consistent rehearsal of pushy behavior and rewarding of impatience and lack of impulse control. Often over time the supported "alpha" dog will develop an unrealistic and problematic sense of self-importance. These supported dogs can develop a control complex. It is often these dogs that are labeled dominant but perhaps a part of the reason they have a control complex is because their behavior has been reinforced for so long or just so effectively that they have become hair trigger, control freaks with low thresholds for frustration. This is much like the spoiled child who has not only learned that that behavior works but who has internalized it and genuinely expects everything to be served up on a silver platter. Life doesn't always work that way and so conflict arises. Perhaps these so called "dominant" dogs are out of control spoiled rotten children.

Another common cause for excessive conflict among household dogs is breed type. Different breeds have different sociabilities. Some breeds possess genetically lower thresholds for reactivity. Some breeds are not nearly as social with other dogs. A house full of hair trigger Jack Russel Terriers is a recipe for conflict. Terriers in general are reactive. Some guarding and fighting breeds have been bred specifically to have very high thresholds for feeling pain. This lack of consequence in terms of pain when fighting can lead to particularly damaging fights. Many of these dogs are known to bite hard and not let go readily.

Yet another cause of conflict can be miscommunication. Ritualization is not present in dogs nearly to the extent that it is found in canids such as wolves. Not only do they not communicate ritualistically as much as wolves, but we have also selectively bred them to look threatening to other dogs and to not be able to communicate true intentions. We breed dogs to be forward and up, a threat communication among dogs. We breed some dogs without tails or we surgically remove them, eliminating one of the dog's key means of communications. The same kind of thing is done with eyes and ears. It is no wonder that dogs are aggressive when they simply use ritualization less and the ritualization they do use is convoluted with miscommunications.

Non Resident Directed Aggression

Aggression directed toward unfamiliar dogs who do not live in the same household is usually a male phenomenon and within that context an intact male issue. Testosterone modulates other difficulties these dogs may have making the conflict more quick to develop and more intense when it does occur. Much non-resident-directed defensiveness relates to fear or self protection.

Competitive conflict among dogs that do not reside together occurs also. Again many dogs are allowed to rehearse being a pushy dog. They come to expect that everything should go their way all the time. They have learned very little patience or impulse control. When two dogs like this meet there is usually conflict as they become frustrated and their expectations are met with resistance. These dogs can be like spoiled children throwing a temper tantrum, simply because they never learned how to be patient. They never learned that things do not in fact always go their way right away.

Another cause is undersocialization. If a dog does not learn how and when to appropriately use affiliative behaviors or even ritualized defensive behaviors when he is a pup and adolescent then he may use sloppy communication skills as an adult. Even being socialized can lead to problems. If as a puppy or dog develops an expectation of being a competitively successful dog, he may be at risk of becoming a bully. If he developed an expectation of always being unsuccessful he might develop a sensitivity to canine social pressure and become defensive.

Yet another cause of conflict can be miscommunication as described above.

Trauma can cause lifelong sensitivities. One attack by a strange dog is often enough to create a sensitivity toward a specific breed, gender, color of dog or even to dog's in general. They will often generalize the triggering stimuli. One bad experience is often all it takes and the dog may never be as confident as he was or could have been.

As mentioned above breed type is also very important. Some breeds seem to have no personal space. The lab for example tends to bounce right into other dogs. This is generally their style, and for many other breeds who do have personal space and are perhaps more reserved or aloof (akita, for example) this imposition can be perceived as very rude and frustrating. Some breeds (pit bulls, rotties) are very physical in play and perform heavy hip checks and other rough behaviors that more delicate or sensitive breeds cannot handle. These are all sources of conflict among unfamiliar dogs.

A special area of concern is the location of the bites. If a dog (whether he lives with the target or not) bites another dog's feet or legs then this dog is very serious. Among many wild canids biting and breaking the front paws or legs, causing injury, is a precursor to a fatal attack. This is why normal dogs are so leery about having their paws touched. It is very taboo for a dog to fight this way and represents a very serious and dangerous problem. Biting the abdomen is also very serious, and is sometimes considered to be prey-driven.

Dog - Dog Aggression or Play

When dogs interact they may play, argue or fight. Understanding the difference will help you know whether you are dealing with a problem or not. There are no really solid hard and fast guidelines to differentiating rough play from and argument or fight because mock combat is the method of choice for play. There are some generalizations that you can look for, though, in helping you decide.

In appropriate play all of the dogs involved are consenting participants. Look for the dog that tried to run and get away. Often a dog will not feel like he can get away, though, and chasing is a normal play behavior so try separating the dogs when things get going. Try to remove the dog who seems to be the primary bully first but either way simply separate them. If they choose to go back for more then chances are they were just playing. If one tries to get away or hiding behind or under a chair or something like that then it was getting out of hand.

Vocalizations can help you make a determination. If one dog yelps pay particular attention. It might have been an accident or it might be that one dog is getting carried away or becoming frustrated. The proper response by the dog who caused the yelp is a doggie apology. They should back off a bit or show cut off behaviors (discussed below). If this is the case and the dog who yelped seems to accept the apology then things are probably okay for now but you will want to monitor this situation. If the dog who caused the yelp does not apologize in this way and the other dog does not accept the apology then you have a conflict. In some cases the yelp will stimulate the bully to strike even more intensely. These dogs must be separated. This bully must not learn that he can pick on other dogs without it ending all of his fun. Picking fights is not okay. Growling is normal play behavior but often if it is turning more into a fight the growling will get deeper in tone. Pay close attention to the escalation of intensity. If the vocalizations get louder, more frequent and yelp or lower pitched for growling and less barking occurs then it is escalating. It may just be arousal but conflict and arousal are integrally linked.

Behaviors to look out for include mounting or putting of paws or chin on the other dog's shoulders. These can be okay behaviors but if they seem relentless then this dog may be trying to intimidate the other dog. This does not mean the other dog will feel intimidated. More sensitive dogs will be intimidated while the less sensitive ones may not be at all. Either way the arousal level is escalating. It may not be a conflict yet but it may soon be. This would be a time to test whether one of them feels like not interacting. Separate them and see if they both still choose to interact. The break will help reduce the arousal level also.

Ideally you want dogs to learn how to play and even how to argue effectively. If they break the rules you want them to learn how to apologize and how to accept apologies. Play is good and even appropriate conflict if it is handled properly by the dogs but fighting teaches the dogs nothing positive. When you note that the intensity is escalating or an argument is not being resolved quickly and appropriately it is your job to step in. The indications above will give you an idea of whether you are dealing with playful dogs or conflicted dogs.

Neuropsychology of Aggression

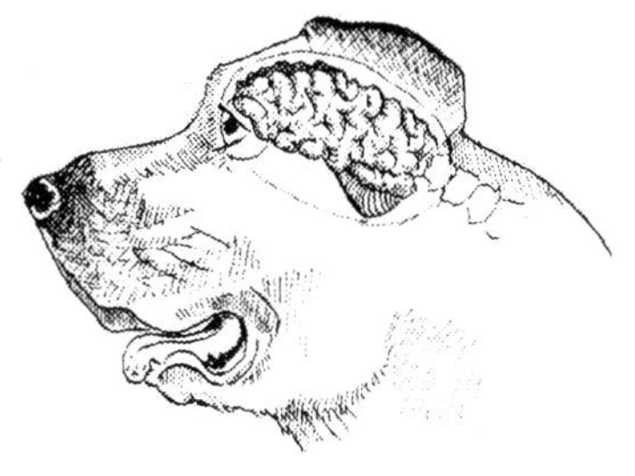

The Nervous System - The Brain

The brain is made up of the forebrain, the midbrain and the hindbrain. The midbrain and hindbrain make up the brain stem and control basic life functions such as cardiovascular and respiratory activity. The forebrain comprises the limbic system and the cerebral cortex among other parts. The limbic system comprises the amygdala, cingulate gyrus, fornix, hippocampus, hypothalamus, olfactory cortex and the thalamus. The cerebral cortex is the outer portion of the forebrain and made up of frontal lobe, occipital lobe, parietal lobe and the temporal lobe.

Limbic System

The limbic system comprises a complex circuit of neural structures involved primarily in the expression and experience of emotions. Some learning and emotional memory are coordinated here also. [Lindsay,vol1,82]

The thalamus takes sensory input and emotional responses and mediates their processing through the body, limbic system (emotional center) and cerebral cortex (cognitive center). [Lindsay,vol1,78] The thalamus enables the dog to selectively focus or concentrate on one thing at a time. [Lindsay,vol1,79] The thalamus is a relay or middle man so to speak.

The hypothalamus generally performs regulatory functions of basic biological activities such as appetite, thirst and various homeostatic functions such as blood pressure, temperature regulation and blood sugar regulation. [Lindsay,vol1,79] The hypothalamus regulates eating, drinking, body temperature, the reproductive system and ANS. [Lindsay,vol1,79] It controls the endocrine system and is also integral in regulating sleep and awake cycles. The hypothalamus orchestrates both parasympathetic and sympathetic nervous activity. [Lindsay,vol1,185] The hypothalamus is part of the hypothalamic-pituitary-adrenal (HPA) system which is profoundly involved in the homeostatic control of the body's response to both stress and threat. [Lindsay,vol1,185] Another function of the hypothalamus is as part of a negative feedback loop for circulating testosterone levels. As testosterone levels decline the hypothalamus secretes gonadotropin-releasing factor which causes the pituitary gland to release luteinizing hormone which in turn stimulates the testes to produce more testosterone. The hypothalamus ceases production of the releasing factor when testosterone levels rise to the appropriate level. [Lindsay,vol1,185]

The amygdala, part of the limbic system, mediates the expression of fear and modulates aggression. [Lindsay,vol1,83] Many of the neurons in the amygdala possess a low threshold of excitability and are prone to seizure activity which can lead to explosive aggression. [Lindsay,vol1,84] "With the use of electroencephalograms (EEGs), abnormal electrical activity has been identified in the amygdala of aggressive persons. It does seem reasonable that some seizure activity in the amygdaloid complex could result in heightened aggressiveness, vigilance, intolerance, disorientation, and the periodic exhibition of inappropriate explosive rage." [Lindsay,vol1,84] It has been associated with predatory behavior as well as inhibition or excitation of the expression of other forms of aggression and social behavior. [Lindsay,vol1,84] It plays a central role in emotional learning. [Lindsay,vol1,85] It is a part of the limbic system which initiates survival responses. It also controls some hormonal secretions.

In humans the cingulate gyrus coordinates sensory input with emotions, emotional responses to pain and regulates aggressive behavior. In dogs the cingulate gyrus probably serves a similar purpose.

In humans the hippocampus functions to consolidate new memories, emotions, navigation and spatial orientation. In dogs the hippocampus probably serves a similar purpose. In dogs, the hippocampus seems to be important as a neural substrate for mediating low fearfulness thresholds and prolonged states of generalized anxious arousal. [Lindsay,vol1,192]

In humans the fornix functions to connect the hypothalamus to the cerebrum. In the dog the fornix probably serves a similar function.

In humans the olfactory cortex functions to cause conscious awareness of odors, identifies odors and receives sensory information from the olfactory bulb. In dogs this area of the brain is probably significantly more important.

Aggression and the Limbic System

"Certain brain areas have been associated with aggression in dogs. Removal of the septal areas or ventromedial hypothalamus results in an increase in aggression or irritability. Stimulation of the amygdala, diencephalon, periaqueductal gray, tectum, or reticular regions can result in aggression. Fear and defensive responses occur when the dorsal area of the amygdaloid nucleus is stimulated, so bilateral destruction of the amygdaloid nuclei may or may not be used to treat aggression, primarily fear-induced aggression. Stimulation of parts of the hypothalamus, the so called aggressive center, results in an attack or ingestion of food. This region is normally controlled by the aggressive inhibition center in the anterolateral hypothalamus, so lesions here can also result in increased aggression. Other areas that inhibit aggression have been isolated in the amygdala (corpus amygdaloideum) and frontal lobes in the cortex." [Beaver,156]

Cerebral Cortex

The cerebral cortex is the outer part of the brain and last to develop. The cerebral cortex is thought to be the primary site of consciousness and intelligence. It performs the most complex associative functions. [Lindsay,vol1,90] The cerebral cortex is intimately involved in the elaboration of various cognitive functions such as learning and problem solving. [Lindsay,vol1,91] Once input makes it's way to the prefrontal cortex the input is assessed and a course of action is decided upon. The expression of that action plan will fall within species-typical action patters. The prefrontal cortex performs such assessments based on learning history. [Lindsay,vol1,91] The prefrontal and orbitofrontal cortex is probably involved in controlling impulsive behavior such as panic and aggression. [Lindsay,vol1,92] The connection from the amygdala (the part of the brain associated with emotional impulse control) to the cortex is stronger than the connection from the cortex to the amygdala and this is thought to explain why some dogs cannot seem to fully control fearful and aggressive impulses. [Lindsay,vol1,92] The cortex is divided into four lobes. The frontal lobe is involved in planning, execution and control of movement. The parietal lobe is involved in translating sensory information. The occipital lobe is involved in translating visual information. The temperal lobe is involved in translating auditory information and is closely related to the limbic system and hence some emotional information is processed here.

Limbic System vs. Cerebral Cortex (Emotion vs. Cognition)

Information perceived by the senses as well as emotional information proceeds from the peripheral nervous system to the thalamus. From the thalamus the information goes to the posterior lobes of the brain for decoding. Information is decoded and the brain analyzes the significance of the information based on previous learning and experience and then it goes to the frontal lobe where it is used to formulate a plan of action. [Strong, The Dog's Brain,11] The limbic system and the cerebral cortex work together to produce the gestalt of emotional content and higher cognitive content. Information is inputted, organized, assessed, processed and then outputted in the form of behavioral responses be they involuntary reflexes or voluntary behaviors. The limbic system and the cerebral cortex have an intimate relationship as it relates to dog behavior and implications for training.

"In the complicated circuitry of the brain, scientists have discovered an inverse relationship between activation of the cortex and activation of the limbic system. When one is activated, the other is inhibited. A dog or person who is in the grips of a strong emotion (i.e., the fight or flight response is activated) literally cannot think straight. This is not necessarily a conscious choice, but a neurochemical reality." [Clothier,Body Posture & Emotions,25] "Under the adverse conditions of stress, however, subcortical activities are amplified while, at the same time, corresponding cortical regulatory functions may be temporarily disrupted. In particular, acute stress has a robust excitatory effect on the amygdala, which, in turn, coordinates the expression of numerous preparatory systems that mobilize an organism for impending emergency action. During such stressful activation, increased levels of NE and dopamine are released in the prefrontal cortex. Although increased catecholamine activity appears to have a facilitatory effect on subcortical processes, the release of these neurotransmitters in the prefrontal area has an opposite effect, causing it temporarily to suspend its efficient functioning." [Lindsay,vol1,112] The information contained in these quotes indicates a very important principle in dog training and behavior modification which is central to this book. They indicate that if a dog is allowed to become enthralled in emotional responses then he is unlikely to learn properly. This has implications with the treatment of separation anxiety and aggression among other problems. Sensitized responses in these problems must be avoided while treatment proceeds. They indicate that concentration on a cognitive task can help maintain focus while fending off sensitized stress responses. The basis of a systematic desensitization program may be habituation without sensitization.

Neurotransmitters

The nervous system conveys information from one place to another place by way of nerve cells (neurons). Neurons have two processes; dendrites are projections that accept chemical messages from the body and bring them to the brain and is referred to as the afferent system, and, axons which are projections that direct messages from the brain and bring them to the body, referred to as the efferent system. Axons and dendrites do not actually touch. There is a small gap between them called the a synapse where the nervous impulses jump from one neuron to the next.

Electrical chemical secretions called neurotransmitters travel from one cell to another on their way to their destination. Neurotransmitters contain and convey information. They excite, inhibit or modulate the activity of other neurons. Neurotransmitters are synthesized from precursor substances some of which the body produces itself and some must be attained in the animal's diet. Once a neurotransmitter in finished it's function it will either be taken back into cell (called re-uptake) or it is destroyed and thereby deactivated.

Some of the more important neurotransitters include dopamine, norepinephrine, serotonin, glutimate and GABA (gamma-aminobutric acid).

Dopamine

Dopamine is involved in motor coordination, attention, reinforcement and reaction time. A deficiency in dopamine can cause an inability to learn, irritability, anxiety and a decline in endorphins, the dog's natural pain killers. Dopamine influences the brain's pleasure center and so a decline in dopamine can cause a lack of the capacity to enjoy life. Depleted levels of dopamine in the brain will result in diminished positive feeling. [Lindsay,vol1,78] Excess dopamine will promote agitation impulsive behavior and over reactivity. A dog who is governed by a strong dopaminergic activity system tends to get in perpetual trouble. [Lindsay,vol1,90]

Adrenaline and Norepinephrine

Adrenalin, a hormone, is released into the blood stream when the dog is frightened (acute stress). The heart beats faster and the blood flow is guided away from skin and intestines toward the muscles in preparation for fight or flight.

Norepinephrine NE, is related to adrenalin. NE is responsible for, among other things, a dog's energy level. If NE is depleted the body shuts down it's energy expenditure. In a dog, lethargy and depression can represent inhibition or depletion of NE. The body can only operate for so long under depleted NE (chronic stress) before it shuts down completely. Depletion of NE is associated with learned helplessness. [Lindsay,vol1,78] High levels of NE will cause aggression, over arousal, impulsive behavior and high levels of excitability. Trauma and prolonged stress result in depleted NE. [Lindsay,vol1,78]

Serotonin

Serotonin regulates mood, pain and arousal levels. Low levels of serotonin can result in impulsive, aggressive behavior, impaired learning, anxiety and obsessive behavior. Serotonin is produced in the hindbrain [Lindsay,vol1,77] from it's precursor dietary tryptophan. "Serotonin plays an important role in the regulation and inhibition of aggressive behavior - decreased serotonergic activity in these systems is associated with an increased likelihood of aggressive impulsivity under conditions of threat or frustration." [Lindsay,vol1,90] Excess serotonin in the brain is recaptured by neurons and broken down by monoamine oxidase (MAO). [Lindsay,vol1,96] "Monoamine oxidase A (MAOA) deficiencies have been associated with aggression in humans and mice. This enzyme normally degrades serotonin and norepinephrine. Acetylcholine and androgenic hormones activate the aggressiveness center of the hypothalamus, whereas serotonin tends to inhibit it." [Beaver,156] "Besides controlling sleep-wake cycles, serotonin projections terminating in the limbic system play an important role in inhibiting anger and aggression. Further, serotonin directly attenuates the subjective experience of pain occurring during highly emotional displays involving anger or aggression, thereby mitigating against the effectiveness of physical punishment in the control of emotionally charged (affective) aggression." [Lindsay,vol1,96] Reisner and colleagues (1996) have determined that dogs demonstrating control complex aggression possess lower levels of serotonergic and dopaminergic metabolites in their cerebral spinal fluid. Investigators suggest that those dogs who fail to warn before biting as well as dogs who bite hard when they do bite are different from dogs who do deliver warnings prior to biting and do not bite as hard are different from one another in a neurochemical way. The warners/soft biters tend to have a supply of serotonin while the other group has low levels or depleted serotonin. [Lindsay,vol1,98] This would suggest that learned bite inhibition may not be the only important determinant in the development of soft biting and that brain chemistry has a role to play. "Studies of animals and humans (Mench and Shea-Moore, 1995 Appl Anim Behav Sci 44(2/4):99-118) suggest that an increase in central nervous system (CNS) serotonin (5-HT) activity inhibits aggression, while decreased 5-HT activity increases aggression." [http://www.aes.ucdavis.edu/AnStress/Partic/WELD.htm] "Like its catecholamine cousins, adrenaline, noradrenaline, and dopamine, serotonin acts all over the body" [http://www.life-enhancement.com/displayart.asp?ID=208] "In the blood vessels, 5-HT constricts large arteries, thus helping to balance excessive dilation required for proper normal blood pressure control. In the intestines, 5-HT controls GI motility (movements of the stomach and intestinal musculature). In the periphery, 5-HT is a major factor in platelet homeostasis which could be of benefit in the treatment of diabetes. As Stevenson portrayed so well in Jekyll and Hyde, altering serotonergic activity may even be capable of inducing profound changes in personality." [http://www.life-enhancement.com/displayart.asp?ID=208] "Serotonin's influence over aggressive tendencies goes way back in the evolution of life. Studies over a wide range of species, from crustaceans to fish to lizards to hamsters to mice to dogs to nonhuman primates to human beings, have all demonstrated essentially the same results: reducing serotonergic activity leads to increases in aggressive behavior, and enhancing serotonergic function decreases aggressive behavior." [http://www.life-enhancement.com/displayart.asp?ID=208]

Glutimate & GABA

Glutimate transmits excitory messages [Lindsay,vol1,94] while GABA is the principle inhibitory neurotransmitter preventing other neurons from firing uncontrollably. Low levels can cause mental instability. "Glutimate and GABA balance and check each other through a complex excitory-inhibitory process of neural homeostasis." [Lindsay,vol1,94] These neurotransmitters regulate the homeostasis of neural activity. With an imbalance of one, neural activity would either fire out of control or cease to fire effectively. Obviously this is a very important relationship. Glutimate and GABA are formed from the amino acid glutamine, a non-essential amino acid.

The Endocrine System

As mentioned the nervous system works closely with the endocrine system which is responsible for chemical coordination in the body. The endocrine system is made up of several glands that secrete hormones under the direction of the Hypothalamus. The endocrine system is chiefly concerned with the homeostatic control of chemical secretions in the body and does this by secreting these hormones when they are called for and then ceasing production when not called for. The glands of the endocrine system are ductless which means that the secretions are excreted directly into the blood stream. The blood stream carries these hormones to all tissues in the body. Hormones are not sent only to the organs they are meant to influence. Rather each hormone has a target organ and affects only that organ. So a particular hormone goes everywhere but only affects a particular organ.

The hypothalamus is located at the base of the brain. It signals the pituitary gland which is located nearby. The pituitary gland upon receiving releasing factors from the hypothalamus secretes various hormones that stimulate the other endocrine glands to secrete their hormones. One of the important hormones secreted by the pituitary gland includes adreno-corticotropic hormone (ACTH). ACTH stimulates the adrenal cortex to produce cortisone which is a very important hormone involved in the stress response. Another important hormone secreted by the pituitary gland is luteinizing hormone (LH) which stimulates the male testicles to produce testosterone which affects male sexually dimorphic behavior and can modulate aggression. LH stimulates the female ovary to release it's ovum (eggs). The endocrine portion of the pancreas releases the hormone insulin which is involved in the digestion and absorption of glucose which is sugar in the blood stream. Insulin production affects neurotransmitter access to the brain by removing some competitor neurotransmitters and releasing stored tryptophan. The adrenal gland is made up of the adrenal cortex (the outer portion) and the adrenal medulla (the inner portion). The adrenal cortex produces several hormones called steroids which regulate glucose metabolism, produce sex hormones and maintain proper levels of minerals. One of the more important hormones produced by the adrenal medulla is adrenaline (also known as epinephrine). Adrenaline is one of the more important hormones that works with the sympathetic nervous system helping the body prepare for emergency situations.

Cortisol & the Hypothalamic-Pituitary-Adrenocortical (HPA) System

Cortisol is a hormone secreted during times of stress. This hormone is secreted as part of the stress response for the purpose of readying the body for response. "Under conditions of stress, the hypothalamus secretes corticotropin-releasing factor (CRF), which signals the pituitary gland to secrete a tropic hormone - adrenocorticotropic hormone (ACTH) - into the bloodstream. ACTH stimulates the adrenal cortex to release various steroidal hormones, including cortisol (corticosterone). Cortisol serves many biological functions (regulation of blood pressure, control of glucose levels in the blood, and acceleration of the breakdown of protein into amino acids) to help an animal cope effectively with stress, injury, or defense. The release of cortisol into the bloodstream completes the circuit when it reaches the hypothalamus, where it inhibits CRF production and thereby inhibits ACTH production by the pituitary. The reduction of circulating ACTH causes the adrenal cortex to decrease production and secretion of cortisol. This slower stress-activated system is known as the hypothalamic-pituitary-adrenocortical (HPA) system." [Lindsay,vol1,79]

Stress, Fear, Anger, Anxiety and Aggression

We have already established that a significant emotional response will tend to inhibit clear thinking and lead to the activation of the dog's emergency response system - the flight or fight mechanisms. An examination of the effects of stress, fear and anxiety - significant emotional responses - on the dog follows. Stress is so important because it tends to lower thresholds of tolerance.

Stress Defined

"Stress occurs when any demand is placed upon a dog to change or adjust." [Lindsay,vol1,109] Any biological or psychological demand will result is stress. The demand does not necessarily have to involve an aversive for stress to occur.

If a demand is placed upon the animal the animal will respond to it. This response requires effort and the animal prepares for the energy expenditure. This preparation and activation of resources is what the experience of stress involves. Stress can come from within as occurs when an animal thinks about a demand or from outside as when any part of the environment places demands on the animal. Minute by minute new demands are placed upon all animals. Normal levels of stress that are managed well by the animal are referred to as stimulation. Stress can become pathological if the stress threshold is surpassed. Stress that is perceived as aversive may also trigger fight or flight mechanisms or aversive stress responses.

Stress Threshold

The stress threshold is the upper limit point at which stress surpasses the dog's stress tolerance. Many dogs can handle high levels of stress without reaching their stress threshold while others cannot handle even small amounts of stress without the dog's becoming anxious. This stress tolerance is an inherited trait, suggest some researchers (Burns). "To a large extent, differences in emotional thresholds are affected by a limbic/autonomic inheritance present at birth. Some individuals are genetically disposed to being more calm and emotionally balanced under the influence of limbic modulation and parasympathetic tone (parasympathetic dominant), where as others (sympathetic dominant) are much more sensitive and reactive to fright-freeze-fight stimulation, hyperemotional, tend to persevereate in negative emotional states, are subject to neurotic elaborations and disequilibrium, and are prone to develop psychosomatic disease." [Lindsay,vol1,185] Dogs with low stress thresholds may be sympathetically dominant. Stress, in general, affects the dog but when stress surpasses the stress threshold a cascade of electrochemical reactions takes place called a stress response. We call this level of stress beyond the threshold "over-stress". Over-stress affects the weakest link in the organism first but eventually affects the whole dog. Over-stress creates chemical and functional disturbance. As an aside, dogs, like some people, can become physiologically addicted to the chemical reaction of acute stress. The more aversive or unpleasant the stress is the more likely the dog is to trigger.

Acute Stress Response

When experiencing a sudden or acute onset of stress or fear the amygdala is bombarded with excitory signals which in turn stimulates the rest of the mind and body to activate emergency processes. Adrenalin is released into the blood stream when the dog is frightened. The heart beats faster and the blood flow is guided away from skin and intestines toward the muscles in preparation for fight or flight. NE and dopamine are released in the prefrontal cortex. The increased activity of these neurotransmitters in the prefrontal cortex causes a temporary suspension of proper function of the prefrontal cortex which is responsible for learning and higher thought processes. This is also the part of the brain responsible for previous learning, impulse control and social inhibition. Inhibition, impulse control and previously learned coping mechanisms may become inaccessible by the dog, thereby provoking species-typical aggressive flight or fight tendencies. The threshold for aggressive behavior is lowered in dogs under stress. Furthermore, the limbic system may enhance these responses. Acute stress stimulates the body and mind to prepare to fight or flight and it suspends rationality.

Chronic Stress Response

Many dogs maintain a chronic level of stress. During this stress response the body maintains an emergency state for an extended period and depletes itself of valuable resources including those that affect immune system health. Serotonin is stored in the brain and is converted to melatonin and back again to serotonin. This conversion is what makes up the rhythmic clock that guides sleep and awake times. Deeply involved in this process are the temperature coordinating mechanisms, cortisol which is the body's chief stress fighting hormone and the process of sleep cycles. Of particular interest to us here is cortisol. When cortisol secretion is high the body is prepared to face stress. As the stress continues, serotonin, NE and dopamine become depleted. As NE becomes depleted, so does endorphin function. Endorphins are the bodies pain relieving chemicals. NE is responsible for, among other things, the dog's energy level. If NE is inhibited, the body shuts down it's energy expenditure. In a dog, lethargy and depression may represent inhibition of NE. The body can only operate for so long under inhibited NE before it shuts down completely. As stress continues the resulting depletion results in disrupted sleep patterns, difficulty in thinking clearly, disruption of the rational activity of the mind, oversensitivity to pain and a lack of ability to experience reward or pleasure.

Signs of Stress

When experiencing over-stress the dog will express the consequences in various ways. Some may be difficult to detect while others are unmistakable. You may notice that some signs relate to an increase in activity and reactiveness while others relate to a decrease in activity or shutting down. If acute stress occurs adrenaline takes on the major role and the dog activates. He will go into full red alert mentally and physically. If chronic stress occurs NE, serotonin and dopamine depletion take on the major role and the dog will deactivate. In either case the dog is suffering an over stress-response. What follows are simply a few of the many signs of stress.

Rapid shallow or deep forceful panting. Panting is normal for dogs who have been exercising or who are hot, but these should be deeper respirations with a relaxed tongue. When stressed, the lips will be pulled back in a wide grin which will also cause furrows in the skin under the eyes and on the forehead. Take it in context along with the situation and other signs of stress.

Lack of focus or attention. If your dog fails to respond to cues, he may be very distracted by a squirrel or some other stimulus. He may also be stressed out. Watch for the context. While in this state the dog is not ignoring you. He cannot even hear you let alone pay attention to what you want. His mind has forced a tunnel vision and tunnel attention that makes it impossible for him to respond to you. Can you remember any time when you were so stressed out that you could barely function and simple tasks seemed impossible? Not a fun place to be.

Sweaty paws. Just like when people get nervous they get sweaty palms, dogs also get sweaty paws. You may see them when the dog walks on a hardwood floor or in his crate or when he steps off of the veterinarians exam table. This is a product of the body forcing fluid from out.

Yawning. This is a very common sign of stress and fairly reliable. Unless the dog is under no stress and about to settle into a nap it will represent stress. The yawns tend to be more intense than normal. The dog will usually tuck his chin into his chest and yawn intensely.

Hyperactivity. A dog who is severely stressed may activate as a defense mechanism. They may look frantic or panicked or you may interpret their behavior as fooling around or simple hyperactivity. This is the quintessential activation stress. Dogs cannot maintain this for long before the system is drained, a deactivated stress sets in and the dog shuts down.

Increased frequency of urination and defecation. If your dog urinates and defecates more frequently than normal he may be suffering an illness or he may be suffering stress. If he voids inside it may be a house training issue or a sign of severe stress. When the body is stressed it will force fluid from itself. The dog will have an undeniable urge to urinate and defecate and do so inside the house if he has to. This is one reason why we should never punish a dog for voiding under any circumstances.

Vomiting & diarrhea. Stress reeks havoc on the mind and body, and the digestive system is usually the first system to react poorly. There may be many reasons why a dog vomits or has diarrhea and these can become, or be caused by medical problems but they, many times, represent a high stress situation.

Stretching. If your dog wakes up from a nap and stretches, he is just limbering up but if he is in a situation that he finds stressful then he may be showing his stress. Often when faced with a crowd of people or other dogs they will stretch to relieve stress. Stress tends to make muscles tense up. Stretching may be a way to relax tense muscles.

Shaking as if he just came out of water. Dogs who are stressed will attempt to "shake off the stress". You see this a lot in dog classes and at dog parks. When dogs finish with a tense confrontation they will often give a shake.

Confusion. A dog who is over stressed may act strangely and in a confused manner. Remember the tunnel attention? This could also be a medical problem such as a seizure or diabetic emergency so you must exercise caution when interpreting this behavior.

Self mutilation. The behaviors in this category may include tail biting, or chewing a paw or his flank. This is a tricky one. There may be many reasons a dog self mutilates, including a genetic predisposition or medical problems (e.g.allergies). It may have been unknowingly taught or reinforced or may be part of a true compulsive disorder. The dog may also have an injury or illness that causes pain in that area. Arthritis in the front hocks area is a common reason why geriatric dogs may lick or bite their fronts legs, for example. Regardless of these causes you can be sure that stress is taking place when a dog self mutilates.

Excessive grooming. A dog who excessively grooms will usually lick at an area excessively. Some common areas include, paws, the flank or genitals. Damage can be done. Again, there may be an injury or illness or an underlying obsessive compulsive disorder that causes this. The most likely culprit is allergies but stress is a possible cause also.

Sleeping excessively. Some dogs are lazy. For example if you have a Greyhound or and English Bulldog then you may have a normal level of laziness if he lays on the couch 18 hours out of a day. Every dog has a different energy level and so this may be a difficult sign to recognize until after a stress reduction program. Many people notice in hindsight that their dog seemed to be shut down with no energy before they started managing their dog's stress level. This is the quintessential sign of chronic stress; shutting down; serotonin depletion. It is important to note that these dogs usually will not experience a satisfying sleep. This is why they are always trying to sleep.

Skin disorders. Many people (Turid Rugaas among them) believe that many skin disorders such as hot spots and allergies are physical expressions of severe chronic stress. It is difficult to assess this for sure. Certainly stress can reduce immune function and allow for infection and sensitivity. Skin problems should be brought to a veterinarian.

Immune system disorder. Many people believe that autoimmune disorder is heavily correlated with chronic stress. It would be wise to consider treatment for stress as a part of the total treatment plan for immune system disorder.

Excessive thirst. A dog who is drinking more than normal may be suffering an illness but may also be performing a behavior in an attempt to ease stress. It may be a redirected frustration or an obsessive behavior but in any case correlates to stressful states. I have seen a dog who, when placed in a stressful situation, would drink water until the situation was over, no matter how long it took. Was he all of a sudden thirsty? I doubt it. Perhaps he avoided dealing with the situation by doing something else. Perhaps it is a calming signal which we will discuss shortly.

Obsessive compulsive behaviors. If a dog spends a significant amount of time barking, digging or tail chasing then he may be suffering high levels of stress. These may be strategies employed by the dog to keep stress at bay. If it goes on and on and on without apparent cause, stress could be cause. Serotonin and other neurotransmitters have been implicated in obsessive compulsive disorders which may make it intimately related to stress responses. When stressed, certain behaviors can become obsessive compulsive after a while.

Overly reactive. If your dog cannot relax when you get up off the couch then he may be overly reactive. If he jumps to attention when faced with the slightest environmental contrast he may be too wound up or high strung. This may relate to ineffective sleep patterns.

Stiffness. When stressed out the dog's muscles will become stiff, producing a very stiff gate and tail movement. If you feel the dog, his muscles will be extremely hard.

Shivering. Many dogs suffering excess stress will shiver. Context will tell you if he is cold or stressed.

Displacement behaviors. When you ask a severely stressed dog to do something he may perform other behaviors. That is, if you can keep his attention long enough to have him hear you. This is one expression of confusion.

Cut off behaviors. Dogs will display certain behaviors as a normal part of interactions with other animals and fellow dogs in order to calm them down. They may perform these pro-actively in order to prevent poor relations with others or they may perform them to calm an already tense situation. Dogs may use cut off behaviors when stressed in order to calm a stressful situation. Some of the common cut off behaviors include:

- Turning the head away or averting the eyes.
- Turning completely away.
- Sniffing at the ground (very common).
- Quick (often lizard like) licking of the lips.
- Freezing in place.
- Moving excruciatingly slowly.
- Sitting or laying down.
- Play bow position.
- Yawning (which we already mentioned).

Fear Stimulation

Fearful responses are much the same as highly stressful responses in dogs. The emergency response mechanisms of the mind and body are activated and high stress levels cause chemical imbalance in the brain.

"During fearful stimulation, sensory information relayed by the thalamus prompts the amygdala to instruct the periventricular hypothalamus to secrete CRF [corticotropin-releasing factor]. Subsequently, CRF stimulates the anterior pituitary gland to release ACTH [adrenocorticotropic hormone] into the bloodstream. ACTH is a hormone that acts specifically on the cortex of the adrenal glands, triggering the release of a variety of adrenal steroids. Once in the bloodstream, these hormones excite the emergency activation of a dog's bodily defenses. Among the steroidal hormones secreted by the adrenal glands is a group known as the corticoids, which include both inflammatory (aldostrones) and anti-inflammatory hormones (cortisol). In addition to it's anti-inflammatory effects, cortisol also serves to calm fearful dogs while preparing them for action" [Lindsay,vol1,109]

Anger

Anger is similar to a fear response except that "Unlike the adrenalin-producing "fight or flight" response that characterizes fear, anger is attributed to the secretion of both adrenalin and another hormone, noradrenalin [NE]." [Gale Encyclopedia of Psychology]

Put Simply (Neuropsychology of Aggression)

The brain coordinates neurochemical function in the body. The chemical responses of the brain affect the behavior of dogs. Certain chemicals increase or decrease to differing amounts in response to different stresses. These chemicals can be thought of as happy messengers and angry messengers. When a dog is over-stressed or fearful or angry, happy messengers are depleted and angry messengers take over prominence in their effect on the behavior of the dog. These chemicals can cause a dog to become aggressive and at the same time reduce his ability to think straight. This all leads to the conclusion that fear, anger and stress are not conducive to training or rationality.

Aggression Statistics

Much of what follows comes from www.dogbitelaw.com which is an excellent, valuable web site worth visiting.

"The number of dogs. Approximately 35 percent of American households owned a dog in 1994, and the US dog population exceeded 52 million. (Wise JK, Yang JJ. Dog and cat ownership, 1991-1998. J Am Vet Med Assoc 1994;204:1166-7.)

The percentage of bites from dogs. Dog bites account for 80% of animal bite injuries.

The number of victims. A survey by the national Centers for Disease Control and Prevention in Atlanta ("CDC") concludes that dogs bite nearly 2% of the U.S. population -- more than 4.7 million people annually. (Sacks JJ, Kresnow M, Houston B. Dog bites: how big a problem? Injury Prev 1996;2:52-4.) Almost 800,000 bites per year are serious enough to require medical attention. Bites to children represent more than 50 percent of the total number cases. Twenty-six percent of dog bites in children compared with 12 percent in adults require medical care. (Ibid.) Every year 2,851 letter carriers are bitten. (US Postal Service.) An American has a one in 50 chance of being bitten by a dog each year. (Centers for Disease Control [CDC].)

The number of fatalities. In the U.S. from 1979 to 1996, 304 people in the U.S died from dog attacks, including 30 in California.The average number of deaths per year was 17. Most deaths occurred in children. (Centers for Disease Control,

"Dog-Bite-Related Fatalities -- United States, 1995-1996," MMWR 46(21):463-467, 1997.) The chances that victim of a fatal dog attack will be a burglar are one in 177; the odds that it will be a child are 7 out of 10. However, fatalities are highly unusual. For every fatal dog bite in the United States, there are an estimated 670 nonfatal cases requiring hospitalization, 16,000 involving a trip to the emergency room, 21,000 other medical visits and 187,000 bites that are not treated by a physician.

The number of victims: Los Angeles. Each year about 20,000 people are bitten by dogs in Los Angeles County, compared with about 4.7 million nationally.

The number of dangerous dogs: Los Angeles. In Los Angeles, more than 25,000 stray dangerous dogs roam the streets at any one time!

The financial impact of dog bites. Dog attack victims can suffer serious personal injuries, also called bodily injuries. These serious occurrences are addressed by tort law and sometimes criminal law. In monetary terms, these bites cause over $1billion in damages and losses in the U.S. every year. (Insurance Information Institute, Inc.) The average insurance pay out is $12,000. (State Farm Insurance.) One in three home owner insurance claims pertain to dog bites. (State Farm Insurance.) One in 5 dog bites require medical attention. (CDC.)

Dog bites are on the rise: The reported number of dog bites requiring medical care rose 36 percent between 1986 and 1996, from 585,000 to 800,000, according to a report by the National Center for Injury Prevention and Control. During that time, the number of dogs kept as pets rose only 2 percent. Experts attribute the rise in bites to the increasing popularity of dogs such as Rottweilers and pit bulls.

The scene of attack is home or a familiar place. The majority of dog attacks (61%) happen at home or in a familiar place.

Dogs bite family and friends. The vast majority of biting dogs (77%) belong to the victim's family or a friend." [http://www.dogbitelaw.com/PAGES/statistics.html]

"United States

Based on data from the National Center for Health Statistics National Hospital Ambulatory Medical Care Survey for 1992-1994 and the Centers for Disease Control and Prevention, it is estimated that dog bites in the United States are annually responsible for:

"4.7 million injuries

800,000 injuries requiring medical care

17 deaths

nearly 334,000 visits to hospital emergency departments (914 per day)

more than 21,000 visits to medical offices and clinics

more than 670 hospitalizations (severely injured patients stay an average of 4.2 days in the hospital)" [http://www.dogbitelaw.com/PAGES/statistics.html]

"Studies of dog bite injuries have reported that:

The median age of patients bitten was 15 years, with children, especially boys aged 5 to 9 years, having the highest incidence rate

The odds that a bite victim will be a child are 3.2 to 1. (CDC.)

Children seen in emergency departments were more likely than older persons to be bitten on the face, neck, and head. 77% of injuries to children under 10 years old are facial.

Severe injuries occur almost exclusively in children less than 10 years of age.

The majority of dog attacks (61%) happen at home or in a familiar place.

The vast majority of biting dogs (77%) belong to the victim's family or a friend.

When a child less than 4 years old is the victim, the family dog was the attacker half the time (47%), and the attack almost always happened in the family home (90%)." [http://www.dogbitelaw.com/PAGES/statistics.html]

"Studies also have shown that:

Dog bites result in approximately 44,000 facial injuries in US hospitals each year. This represents between 0.5% and 1.5% of all emergency room visits

The face is the most frequent target (77% of all injures). Mail carriers are an exception where 97% involve the lower extremities.

The central target area for the face includes the lips, nose, and cheeks." [http://www.dogbitelaw.com/PAGES/statistics.html]

"Injuries associated with dog bites and dog attacks were sustained most frequently by 5-9 year olds (28.5%). Of all injuries related to dog attacks, 57.9%

were male. Injuries occurred most often in the summer, 37.7%, and most frequently between the hours of 4 and 8p.m., (32.7%). Most injuries occurred at the victim's home, 34.2% or other home, 30.3%. The majority of injuries occurred when the patient had no direct interaction with the dog, 28.9%. Injuries that required advice only or minor treatment accounted for 57.9% of patients, while 36.8% of patients needed medical follow-up after leaving the emergency department and 4.5% were admitted to hospital. Overall, the most frequent types of injury were bites, 73.1%, and the body part most often affected was the face, 40.5%." [CHIRPP database, summary data for 1996, all ages]

"In 1996, dog bites and dog attacks represented 1.0% of all injuries in the CHIRPP database." [CHIRPP database, summary data for 1996, all ages]

Statistics Canada mortality data show that an average of one Canadian a year died from dog bites between 1991 and 1994. In the United States, an average of 17 people die every year from dog bites. [Sacks, Sattin, et al. 1989]

Take Home Message

The goal of this chapter was to introduce you to the most important concepts in understanding why dogs use aggression. Bellow are the most important take home messages that you, as a dog owner who may not be interested in the jargon or the intricate details need to know.

Dogs who are aggressive will always tend toward aggression. It's become a habit and old habits die hard.

Dogs aggress because they are hunting, they fear whatever it is they are aggressing upon, they are playing inappropriately or they have some organic problem. When a dog fears something he has the following options:

- Run away
- Fight back
- Try to make friends or calm the thing down

Whether they run or stay and fight depends on a lot of things but what is important to know is that just because they stay and fight does not mean that they are not afraid. Their goal is still to increase distance between themselves and the 'thing'.

When a dog is not hunting the aggression is a very emotional event. Fear and anger are the most likely emotions related to aggression. Anger is likely the result of frustration. Each dog is an individual and some get fearful or angry easily while others do not.

When a dog aggresses a number of chemicals flood the dog's brain. These chemicals are meant to ready the dog for action. Many of them can feel very good to the dog. The dog can even become addicted to the feeling. This means that each and every time the dog acts aggressively he is rewarded for it without you even having to do or say anything. This suggests that it is very important to prevent the dog from acting aggressively.

Stress can lower the threshold of fear or anger. If a dog is under a lot of stress he may be more irritable and aggressive than if he is not under as much stress.

It is very important to have a good understanding of how dogs learn since much of what drives their behavior is the result of learning. If a dog behaves in a certain way and it works or feels good in some way then they will probably behave that way more frequently. If it felt bad or did not work out for them then they are not so likely to behave that way again. It gets a little complicated because emotions are also at play here. If a dog is scared he will react whether reacting works for him or not. He is scared, much of what he does is habitual. But he will learn a bit; he will learn to some degree what works better than other things. The problem is that it is usually more aggressive behavior rather than alternative pro-social behavior that works. This is why aggression often gets worse or more intense. Continually keep in mind what a dog is learning or experiencing in his mind when he behaves. Is he being rewarded for the behavior? Remember also that merely behaving that way causes the chemicals to start flowing which rewards him so you really must prevent the aggressive response. Behavior can become habitual also. When a strategy works repeatedly it becomes almost automatic like a golf swing or even driving skills. This suggests what you will learn later and that is that you must first prevent the dog from reacting poorly and then through training give the dog some alternative behavior that will work for him and make him feel good. That means you will replace an old bad habit with a new productive (and safe) one.

To understand your dog better you should identify what drives his behavior. One way to help you do this is to identify his drives and sensitivities. This can give you insight into his behavior. Drives are anything that makes your dog want to do or get something. So for example some dogs are food driven or socially driven. That means they really want food and will act to get it or that they really enjoy being with people and will act to get it. Sensitivities are what a dog does not like and will act to avoid. So for example some dogs are socially sensitive or touch sensitive. That means that these dogs do not like social contact or being touched and will act to avoid these things. A strong sensitivity will override any drive. For example a dog who is scared is less likely to eat or play. If you can identify your dog's top three drives and sensitivities it will give you an idea of what drives his behavior from a personality perspective.

There are several recognizable forms of aggression. These forms or divisions are a way to differentiate between different motivations for the aggressive behavior. Some forms of aggression are purely fear motivated while others are motivated by hunting instincts while others are the result of a personality problem. Some dogs defend a place or an object and others have medical problems that contribute to anti-social behavior. It is not absolutely imperative that you label the form of aggression but the descriptions in the text will give you some clues as to why your dog behaves the way he does and offers suggestions as to how best to treat the problem.

Chapter 2
Preventing Aggression

Breeding

A significant factor in the development of canine aggression is genetic.

If you want an aggressive dog it is fairly easy to get one. All you have to do is start breeding dogs who are aggressive. If we breed dogs who are the most aggressive we will get very aggressive dogs very quickly and if we breed dogs who are not aggressive then we will get a significant reduction in incidents of aggression. Genetics can easily influence the structure and function of a brain which can contribute to the heightening or lowering of thresholds that affect aggressive behavior. Proper management of critical periods of development is vital but the first step is genetic. We as the domesticater of dogs need to pay a lot more attention to the reduction of aggression and ease of socialization. Dr. Ian Dunbar suggested at the 2000 C.A.P.P.D.T. educational conference that perhaps dogs should not be bred until they are 10 years old. Aggressive dogs don't tend to live that long and it gives us plenty of time to see what the dog is really like. I totally agree although perhaps 5 years of age is acceptable, especially for breeds with a life span of 7 years. That is another monstrosity but it is another story.

Many pure breed breeders, back yard breeders, accidental breedings and puppy mills alike are producing animals without regard for temperament. The solution to this is breeding with an eye to workability, temperament and health over looks, as well as spaying / neutering and a ban on the sale of dogs in pet shops. Pet shop dogs are at significantly increased risk of developing aggression. Dogs must not be bred until they have waiting homes or else the breeders are prepared to perform early training and socialization properly. It also requires education programs so that owners understand how to choose a responsible breeder and a puppy from within a litter. Education must be provided to breeders and owners on proper training and socialization practices.

If you are contemplating purchasing a puppy from a breeder you must ensure that genetically and developmentally they are likely to be sound.

Warning. Many of the following exercises have the potential to be dangerous. Use your judgement and only perform them if you are comfortable with it. If you are not afraid of dogs at all then perhaps you should NOT perform these exercises. Be cautious and stop immediately if you become uneasy with the exercise for whatever reason.

Genetic soundness means ensuring that the puppies come from nonaggressive parents and previous litters have not developed aggression problems. You can ask for references from people who have adopted dogs from the breeder and I encourage you to do so but let's face it; they are only going to give you references that will say good things. So, more importantly you will want to meet both parents as well as any grown offspring and the grandparents if possible. Ask the breeder permission to evaluate the dogs and ask if the dogs have any history of defensiveness, especially with strangers. If they do then you should probably not adopt a dog from this breeder. Ask if they have been awarded a Canine Good Citizen certificate. This will indicate that the dog has been evaluated for handling and behavior in a highly distracting environment. This is a good sign. When you meet the parents do so one at a time rather than seeing them together. When you approach them look for signs of nervousness. If they are nervous see how long it takes them to get over it. If they have not warmed up to you within a minute or two of your introduction then do not adopt a puppy that was born from that dog. You also want to see signs of social drive. The dog should approach you and be curious of you. They should accept you and preferably seek attention. If they do not seem to care about your presence at all then this indicates that they are independent. For some people independent dogs are ideal but it does also indicate that they may not have the social buffer needed to keep tolerance thresholds at safe levels. Use your judgement. You want prosocial dogs. Offer the dog a treat to see how food driven he is. Ideally you want a food motivated dog. This will also allow him to warm up to you. Let the dog sniff your hand to get used to you and then offer a little scratch on the chest. Then ask the dog to sit. Pet him on the top of then head gently. Then run your hand down the dog's back. Hold each paw for a few seconds, gently. Look in each ear. Check the teeth. Then stand in front of the dog and look at him in the eyes. For all of these exercises you want to act gently and friendly. If at any time the dog demonstrates any antisocial behavior end the exercise immediately and do not adopt a dog from that breeder. What you are looking for is prosocial behavior through out. Most normal dogs do not like having their paws touched or their teeth checked but you should not see anything beyond mild withdrawal behaviors. Stiffening and growling are bad indications. You may or may not get the opportunity to check the following but if you can do so it would be useful. Have the dogs fed a bowl of food and remove the bowl as they eat. Get the dogs interested in a brand new toy. When they are very interested in it approach them to remove it. At any point if you become uneasy with the dog's response immediately stop the exercises. Once you have checked out the parents and any other offspring, siblings or grand parents and are satisfied that they are sound prosocial dogs you can make the assumption that the puppies are genetically as sound as you can determine.

Developmentally sound means that the breeder sends the dogs home at appropriate times and does active training and socialization with them before they go home. Ask open ended questions such as 'what training will you have performed on the puppies by the time I pick him up to bring him home?' Same goes for socialization. It is not adequate that housetraining be started and the fact that the puppies will live in a household rather than a kennel. They should be able to tell you in detail that they will be starting training and more importantly that they are systematically exposing the puppies to novel stimuli at a pace that each puppy can handle easily. They should assure you that they will cover the bases of various sounds, types of people, objects etc. and that they will do it at a pace that will allow the puppy to make every new experience a positive experience. Some breeders may want to give you general or vague answers. Most of the time this is just because they do not know how much detail you want. Again, dig deeper and ask open ended questions. Ask them to follow up on their answer with a detailed description of exactly how they will carry out what they have just told you they will do.

The next order of business is choosing the puppy. In some cases you will not get to choose. They may be accounted for prior to birth or the breeder may use her own puppy evaluation process to place the proper puppy with the proper family. The tough and competitive ones may be placed with owners that might seem too domineering for a more timid puppy. Ideally you should be able to choose yourself but many times you will not be able to. This is not necessarily an indication of a bad breeder but you should be informed on the process that is used and fully understand it yourself. A good breeder knows a lot about the puppies and you from their interview and impressions. Many good breeders will not trust an inexperienced owner to make the right decision about which puppy is the best match. When you can choose try to visit the breeder several times and perform the same temperament evaluations each time you visit. A single test date may not be indicative of the adult behavior of a dog.

The first step is to simply observe the puppies playing together. Look for the one that picks on everyone else. This will usually be the largest and usually a male. Put that puppy on the list as one to avoid for the average family. Now look for one that seems to get picked on the most. That will usually be the smallest one. Put that puppy on the list of puppies to avoid for the average family. All the other little fellows somewhere in between are the ones to choose between. Think of it as a spectrum. If you are loud and demonstrative you might want to choose closer to the end of the spectrum where the puppy who picks on everyone is. If you are quiet and timid then choose more on the other end of the spectrum.

Take each one away into a low distraction room or area. When he looks at you crouch down and pat your legs to encourage him to approach. What you are looking for here is prosocial behavior over antisocial or aloof behavior. Now scurry away from the puppy and encourage him to follow. Ideally you want him to follow enthusiastically.

Now, sit down on the ground and handle the puppy all over his body. Check the ears and teeth as well as the nails etc. Work calmly and deliberately. Most puppies will be concerned with this. Some will roll over and perhaps urinate in extreme cases. This dog might be on the sensitive side. Others will bite at your hands and perhaps growl in extreme cases. These dogs also might be too sensitive and actively defensive. The ones that take it well and perhaps lick at your hands are better choices.

Along the same lines hold the puppy in the laying down position for a few seconds. Ideally you want a dog who will allow you to hold them in a position for a few seconds without becoming too frustrated. Try this in a sitting position as well.

Next allow the puppy to have a toy that he really loves. Let him play with it for a few seconds and then try to remove it from him. Ideally you want a puppy who wants to share with you or who at least gives it up without extreme protest. Puppies who run away with the toy may be just playing or testing you, but dogs who growl or stiffen up are likely to be possessive down the road somewhere, unless this is dealt with. You do not want a project though.

Next, hold a treat or toy that the dog really loves away from him. If he continues to lunge and gets more and more frustrated that might mean this puppy will have a hard time with frustration management. If he does this but then calms down quickly or sits for the treat or toy this is a better sign. If a dog is too timid to even take the toy or treat this may be a sign of excessive sensitivity.

The final test is for startle reflex and bounce back. When the puppy is not looking at you drop a can with pennies in it to the ground about 5 feet from the puppy and observe. If the dog is not startled at all then he is what we call unflappable. We don't know what his bounce back is but we know at least at that time and place he does not startle easily and is not particularly noise sensitive. If he startles then we want to know how long it takes for him to get over it. If he startles and approaches it within a couple seconds then that indicated good bounce back. He may startle but if he can get over it and recover his composure quickly then this too is an okay sign. If on the other hand it takes several minutes to recover then this indicates at least at that time and place a noise sensitivity. This may be indicative of a generally easy to startle dog who is sensitive to novelty and has generally poor bounce back. Avoid this puppy. Avoid this test on puppies who are between 8 and 10 weeks of age as this is the fear period and simple startling events can be traumatizing in some cases. You don't want to be the cause of a life time tin can phobia or something like that.

One last point. If you can, bring a professional dog trainer with you to perform the evaluation. This process is driven by experience and there are too many shades of grey involved. If you have a professional do the tests for you the results will be better. This is money well spent.

Breed Choice

Breed choice is immensely important in the prevention of aggression. If you choose a breed that is unsuited to you the stress and frustration that result can lead to aggressive problems. If you have children there are breeds you should not consider. I will be very courageous here and suggest that you not get the following if you have children. This does not mean that there are none of these dogs that are okay with children or that there are not other breeds that might be included. Don't send me letters on this; I know that it is a generalization. This does not mean that I think these dogs are aggressive by nature either. In some cases the dog is just too heavy and active or enthusiastic to safety interact with children. Dalmations, Pit Bulls, Chinese Shar Peis, Chow Chows, Akitas, Rottweillers, Komondors. I apologize if one of these is your favorite breed but I have seen too much for you to convince me otherwise. If you are sedentary do not choose a breed that requires lots of mental and physical stimulation (e.g., border collies, Jack Russell Terriers). Terriers in general are feisty and reactive. Guarding breeds tend toward aggressive responses as well. Research the breed you are interested in before you adopt a dog.

Why You Should NEVER Buy a Dog From a Pet Shop

Dogs bought in pet shops are significantly over represented in statistics on behavior problems. "In particular, dominance-type aggression and social fears were significantly more prevalent than expected among dogs acquired from pet shops,..." [Serpell,91] "The fact that dogs acquired from pet shops rated poorly in terms of behavior problems is of interest, since pet shop puppies are often the result of mass production in so-called puppy-farms or puppy-mills with little regard for their temperamental charecteristics...Such animals may also undergo inadequate early socialization and a range of abnormal or traumatic early experiences that could predispose them to develop inappropriate adult behaviour." [Serpell,91] *Never buy a dog from a pet shop.* Many pet shops do not sell dogs and some of them help Humane Societies by performing adoptions for homeless dogs. Please support the adoption locations and boycott ones that sell puppy mill dogs. If they tell you their dogs come from "local breeders" move on. A reputable breeder would never sell a dog to a pet shop. Papers mean nothing. It's a formality of paperwork and says absolutely nothing of quality or temperament. In one undercover operation a kitten was able to be registered as a pure bred Golden Retriever. Aggression problems will become significantly less pronounced when and if the sale of dogs in pet shops is banned, as is the case in some countries. Norway has very little aggression problems and they do not sell dogs in pet shops.

Puppy Kindergarten Classes

Puppy classes are very important. If you can get your dog into two classes so that he goes two times weekly rather than just once that would be even better. Once he has finished with puppy classes get him immediately into basic good manners class. Then, get him into agility class or some other canine sport. Continuous (but sensitive) interaction with strange people, other dogs, and different places with different activities will do wonders for socialization. I even suggest getting into puppy classes as soon as 10 weeks of age. Be sure the class uses ONLY positive methods. No reprimands. No choke chains. No leash corrections. Clicker training is one of the best types of training available. Sit in on a class before you go with your dog so you can be sure it is okay. Never let anyone do anything to your dog that you are not completely comfortable with. It is easy to allow a "professional" to be nasty to your dog in front of a class but you must not allow this. No good professional will be harsh with your dog. They will work harder to motivate him through the use of rewards. Remember to observe your dog for signs that his personal space is being invaded. When it comes to dogs playing with other dogs you must walk a tight rope. On the one hand you want to allow your dog to learn how to communicate with other dogs and this requires rough interaction. If you interfere too much with this learning process your dog may grow up sheltered and unable to communicate effectively with other dogs. This can lead to habitual defensive behavior. On the other hand you do not want your dog to be traumatized. Even one really bad experience can signal the beginning of a life long habit of defensiveness. Do not interfere in puppy play unless you absolutely have to. If play gets out of hand and too aroused remove the dog who is "on top". If the dog being picked on wants more and charges for the one you pulled off then everything is okay. Let them play more, perhaps after a very short settling down period. If on the other hand he stays away let him have his space. So many good things can happen with good group classes. The dog learns how to understand some english, gets socialized, socially stimulated, mentally stimulated, physically stimulated and gets used to doing what he is told. These dogs are less likely to become aggressive later in life. They have active cerebral cortexes. They think better.

Socialization

"Brains grow in two ways: they get bigger, and they change shape. How much they grow and which way they change shape depends on the kinds of environmental stimulation they receive during their first sixteen weeks." [Coppinger,111]

"At birth a puppy has essentially all the brain cells it is ever going to have during its whole life.

If the puppy brain has essentially the same number of cells as the adult brain, how can it grow ten times bigger? The answer is that brain growth is almost entirely in the connections between the cells. Of all the brain cells present at birth, a huge number are not connected or wired together. What takes place during puppy development is the wiring pattern of nerve cells. Some nerves make their connections spontaneously, driven by internal signals. Some nerves actually "look" for a muscle to attach to. Other connections are motivated by external signals. External to the brain that is." [Coppinger,111]

"A puppy that is raised in an impoverished environment has a smaller brain. ... Even if the impoverished pup gets taken to an enriched environment as an adult, it cannot learn to cope with that environment because it does not have the necessary cell connections. Once the dog gets to sixteen weeks it has made (or has not made) just about all the social connections it is ever going to make." [Coppinger,112,113]

Basic Socialization Program

Breeding practices are for the potential dog. Once you have a product (the actual dog) the single most important element in raising the puppy is socialization. The graph below describes the opposing influences of the dog's drive to explore and encounter novel stimuli and the tendency (growing sensitivity) to avoid novel stimuli. This shows you visually the window of opportunity in which your dog must be exposed to the things that he will be required to interact with throughout his life.

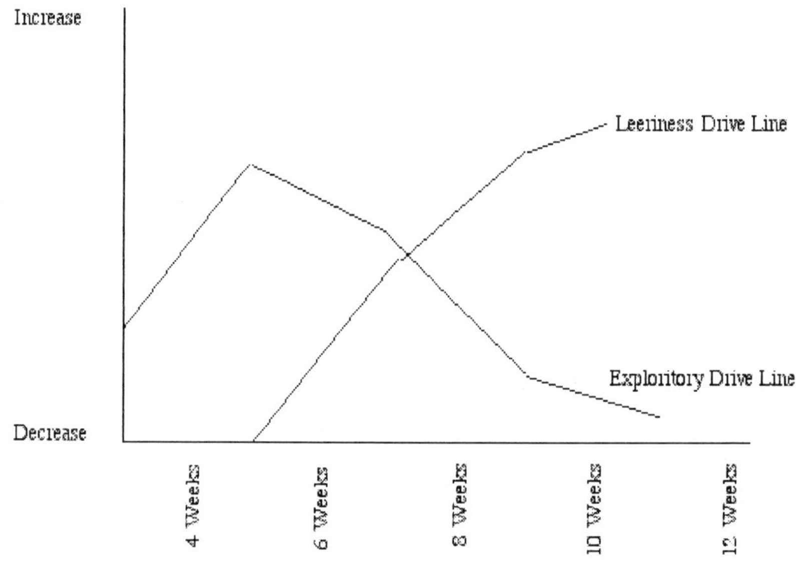

The most likely theory on why there exists a window of opportunity is that in the wild canids must be leery of novel stimuli so that they can avoid danger. If there were no opposing mechanism the canid would fear all things. The way around this is for puppies, while under the protection of the pack or their mother, to explore situations that he will need to interact with through out his life. This is not difficult in the wild since there is a limited number of stimuli that the canid will have to deal with. In our world life is more variable. As the puppy matures leeriness grows. At this point the canid will have a solid familiarity with what he needs to interact with throughout life. It is an ingenious system. The cycle of socialization works as such very well in the wild. In our society a dog is exposed to so many novel stimuli that it is close to impossible to work within these boundaries. That is why socialization is so important. If you miss the critical period you are playing catch up for the rest of the dog's life. So if you missed the boat regarding socialization the dog is at more risk of developing a fear based aggression.

Dr. Ian Dunbar wrote "A spoonful of prevention is worth truckloads of cure." [Dunbar, Dog Behavior, 1999] No one likes deadlines but your puppy has a brief window of opportunity during early puppyhood in which he must be exposed in a *sensitive and positive* way to the world so that he will grow up happy and well adjusted. Without proper socialization your dog will be at risk for various behavior problems including aggression. Many serious and difficult to modify behavior problems can be traced back to improper or inadequate socialization. The value of biting the bullet and putting a lot of work into socializing your puppy now cannot be over stated. Hopefully your breeder will have started the socialization process by exposing the puppy to noises, people, children, other dogs and other environmental stimuli. Now it is up to you to continue the process.

As much as I want you to know that undersocialization is a huge problem you have to understand that in a given day a dog can only handle so many new things even if they were all good. Dogs can become stressed and exhausted with socialization activities which can backfire on you. Keep the socialization moderate and watch your dog carefully for signs that he is being overwhelmed. Keep socialization steady. Get out into the world each day rather than massive outings on weekends only. Above all else make every new experience a good experience.

The Program

Negative associations last a life time. First impressions are extremely important and that is what socialization is all about. You want every experience your dog has to be a good one but especially that first experience.

7 to 12 Weeks of Age

When you bring your puppy home allow him his first day to ease into his new home then *gradually and sensitively* start exposing him to the world.

Aim for introducing your puppy to as many different kinds of ***people*** as possible. Invite friends, relatives and co-workers over to visit your puppy. Puppies do not generalize well so you must cover a wide range of things. A man is one thing but a man with a beard is a different thing. Try to cover as many ethnic groups as possible. Make sure both genders are covered. Cover both large and small people. Some very old and many very young. Be sure to have children interact with your puppy but make sure the process is enjoyable for your puppy. Some with hats and others without. Some loudish and some timid. It is important to cover people who are nervous of dogs and act hesitant so that later on your dog is not freaked out by this bizarre behavior. Try to cover uniforms if you can. Introduce your puppy to the mail man, fire fighters and police officers and have them give him treats. This can save your dog's life later, in as simple a context as a police officer reaching into your car to get your driver's license! It is better to spread people out than to bring them all over at once. Coach each person how to lure, or if your dog is ready, request a sit to greet people and then hand the dog a treat or play with a toy. No rough play. If at any time your puppy growls do not laugh. This is not funny and laughing could be the reinforcement that starts a lifelong problem. If this happens completely ignore the puppy. At the same time as he learns that all these things are good he will be learning what behaviors get him those good things. Make sure that appropriate behavior gets him these things but inappropriate behavior does not. Prevention is that simple.

Aim to introduce your puppy to as many novel ***things*** as possible also. Umbrellas, desk drawers, canes, walkers, wheel chairs, shopping carts etc. Play tapes of crying children, and allow him to smell diapers now if you think you may ever have children. Cover as many things as possible.

It would also be a good idea to work on ***handling*** exercises. This will socialize your puppy to things he may have to endure later. Better to get him used to this now. Every few days put a T-shirt onto the dog, give him some treats and then after you remove the shirt walk away and ignore him for a few minutes. He may have to wear a coat later in life, wear bandaging that resembles a shirt or have children dress him up later in life. Better to cover this base now. Gradually introduce handling of paws and use of nail clippers now. Generally dogs do not like having their paws touched. In an evolutionary context having one's paws touched is taboo, so you must convince him that it is okay. Pair this process with treats and fun. Take it slowly and do not overwhelm him. While you are at it bring him into the vet several times just to say hello to the staff and get a treat from them. If you do this carry him so the risk of infection is reduced. Perform little vet exams on him at home to get him used to that process, or even pay for a few minutes of the vet tech's time, so that it can be done by a professional.

If you will be showing or competing or if you simply know that your dog will have a life-style in which he will be around ***other dogs*** on a regular basis, and you want him to be well adjusted with them, now is the time to allow him to interact with other dogs. The problem is that immunity is more tenuous at this time. As maternal immunity wanes and vaccination immunity ebbs over the next 2 months or so there is a greater risk of infection. Many veterinarians will suggest isolating your puppy until either the second or in some cases well after the third shot. It will be your decision as to how isolated your dog will be. Make a decision relevant to your dog's life-style. We know infection is dangerous and we know isolation is dangerous. Most vets will agree that they euthanize more dogs for isolation-related behavioral problems than they do infected puppies. Even puppies who are not euthanized due to infection but suffer a prolonged illness are at risk for behavior problems, probably due to the isolation associated with treatment and recovery. You must make an informed decision regarding which side to err on. As mentioned, if your dog's life-style will require him to be well adjusted around other dogs he will have to be socialized toward them. If you decide to socialize him to other dogs prior to vaccination completion, be safe. Many puppy classes are now offering classes for 8 - 14 week old puppies. These classes should be requiring that all puppies be in apparent good condition and sanitization practices will be strict. Puppies are carried into class and shoes are left out of the training room. This class will be a great place for your puppy to learn affiliative behaviors; how to communicate in doggie language. If you wait until 14 to 16 weeks your puppy will miss out on some valuable lessons. There are no guarantees as to how effective socialization will be with any dog but it improves the odds. Other options are having dogs of friends or relatives who are up on their shots and who are well socialized themselves visit your place. Leave footwear out of the puppy's reach. It is important that the visiting dog be well socialized, especially to puppies. Don't assume this. Many if not most adult dogs are intolerant of puppies. Inappropriate behavior on the part of the adult may traumatize the puppy. Do not be too quick to step into such incidents. Your puppy needs to learn to be polite, and the well adjusted adult will be tolerant but will teach the occasional lesson. These lessons can be very valuable. If the adult is leery of the puppy and does not want to interact do not force the meeting.

12 - 16 Weeks of Age

If you chose not to expose your puppy to other dogs until shots are well under way due to immunity issues, now is the time to get into puppy class. There you will learn about dog training and your dog will learn how to behave on cue. He will also be exposed to novel people, dogs and other novel things.

Continue to maintain a high level of socialization toward novel people, dogs, places and things. Go to a mall and stand there so that your puppy can experience crowds. Manage your position so as to make it a pleasant experience for the puppy. If he acts fearful at any point outwardly ignore it but move away from the situation. Do not console him as this will make the problem worse. Allow people to meet your puppy. It would be a good idea to hand them a treat and request that they ask your puppy to sit before he can have the treat. Visit people parks and well run dog parks frequently. The work you put into this now will pay off for the rest of your dog's life.

16 Weeks to 1 Year of Age

Socialization must be maintained, especially in the first year. Continue to expose your dog to novel people, dogs and places on a regular basis. Doing this is as close as one can come to a guarantee that the puppy will grow into a well adjusted adult. Basic good manners classes or obedience classes are a great idea at this point. So are competitive sports. Choose a sport based on what your dog was bred for and on what seems fun to you. This will be a great bonding experience and will keep your dog in touch with the rest of the world. Make sure to get the okay from your vet before starting any exercise program. Some large breeds should wait until they are a bit older.

1 Year of Age On

Stay in touch with the rest of the world. Continue to get out there into it. Continue group training classes and continue to make novel experiences an enjoyable experience for your dog.

Life Time NILIF program

NILIF stands for Nothing In Life Is Free. Refer to the NILIF section in Chapter 4 for more details. Dogs without jobs can develop unrealistic expectations about their boundaries and responsibilities. It is important that puppies be raised with consistent adherence to the principle of working for all good things in life. Your puppy can have petting, praise, eye contact, food, treats, toys, tugging etc. but first he must say please by sitting and waiting patiently. All good things are contingent on deferential obedience (manners!). Give your dog a job he can enjoy. This practice will get your dog used to being told what to do, and that it pays off.

Possession Sharing

Dogs are possessive animals. They do not understand the concept of ownership but they do know what they value and that they want it. They will also find it very frustrating and threatening to have something they value removed from them unless you prepare them properly before hand. Your goal will be to habituate the puppy to having possessions removed from him. You will teach him that sharing is actually a good thing. Frequently when your dog is engrossed in munching on a valued toy approach and remove the item from the dog. Immediately upon removing it offer him a treat and then return the object to him. The treat should be a very highly valued one. Fried liver is a good one usually. Keep the treats hidden and surprise him with it. You do not want to start a habit of bribing the dog for what you want otherwise he will learn to differentiate when reinforcement is available and when it is not and he will only tolerate or perform when the bribe is present. So, surprise him with it as a reward for relinquishing the object. Try to vary the objects you remove. You can also put a command such as "leave it" or "drop" but sometimes simply remove the object. You will know you are doing it right and enough when the puppy seems pleased to relinquish objects and even voluntarily does so as you approach because it is just so worth his while. This exercise is never over. Throughout the dog's life when you remove something from him try to have a reward available for that.

Preventing Personal Space Issues from Becoming Personal Safety Issues

Dogs have personal space just as people do. Personal space is that fluctuating space around a dog that, if violated makes the dog feel uncomfortable. The amount of personal space a dog has will depend on:

- The way the dog feels in terms of health and mood
- The relative familiarity of the stimulus
- The presence or absence of a safety history with the stimulus

- The relative familiarity of the environment
- Other distractions present at the time
- Genetics
- How much he *likes* the person who is invading his space

When a dog's personal space is violated the dog feels anxious or frustrated and presents behavioral expressions of defensiveness. Initially these signs include cut off behaviors. The dog may also attempt to leave the area. With repeated violation of the dog's personal space the dog becomes more actively defensive. Two things happen. He starts to anticipate the need to become defensive which creates a trigger situation for habitual active defensiveness. The second thing is that he learns from each situation what works best and what does not work toward the goal of relieving the discomfort. Most people are under the belief that dogs do not have personal space or that they should tolerate or enjoy invasion of their personal space. Most people also do not recognize more subtle or passive defensive behaviors such as cut off behaviors or the significance of a dog leaving the area. This leads to the continuation of this story. Cut off behaviors and leaving fail to bring about comfort (relief) and the discomfort raises as options diminish. Over time the dog starts using more active defensive behaviors. It is not until one day the dog snaps at or bites someone that the owner realizes there may be a problem. Denial plays a role as does a simple lack of knowledge in the psychology of canine defensive behavior.

Personal space issues become personal safety issues when mere discomfort becomes fear. When a dog develops a personal safety issue with some stimulus it is extremely difficult if possible at all to take it back to a personal space issue. A dog who feels a personal safety issue will defend himself, as simple as that. The next step is generalization. The dog starts making associations with various context-setting stimuli that occur when the anxiety or frustration are triggered. Soon the stimuli that comprise these associations become triggers also. Soon it becomes very difficult to identify the original triggers and the aggressiveness becomes less predictable.

This downward spiral is significant because it is the genesis of most aggressive problems in pet dogs. Your goal will be to:

- Develop a solid safety history for your dog with as many stimuli as you can control
- Protect your dog's personal space
- Systematically desensitize and counter condition that personal space to reduce it

To do this you will first have to:

- Give up the belief that dogs should enjoy handling or contact with everything and everyone
- Give up the notion that dogs should just "cope" or "get over it"

Then you will have to resolve:

- To ensuring that your dog's personal space is not violated
- To make any contact with a stimulus voluntary and not forced either physically or psychologically
- To make your dog's first experience with something a very pleasant experience
- To make voluntary entrance of a novel or fear eliciting stimulus very pleasant and worth the dog's while

The result of these resolutions will be sensitive but heavy socialization. In every day life you will have to pay attention to your dog's body language. If he looks leery or nervous you must get him out of that situation. You do not want to add either punishment or reinforcement to the dog's aversion responses so it is imperative that you balance extricating the dog with providing as little reinforcement as possible to the event. In other words just get the dog out of the situation with as little fuss as possible.

Handleablility Exercises

If you can convince your dog now that handling is a good thing you will be less likely to have problems with it later. This is not to say that all dogs will come to like handling. Some may not, no matter what you do. The puppy should be exposed to all kinds of handling including vet check-up style handling, grooming handling, having to put on boots and a jacket. Most puppies are squirmy but are not terribly upset with being touched. Make it a regular event to perform a physical exam, or put on a shirt and footwear. Give out lots of treats and make this a fun time. Act upbeat and smile. You have to take it slow with some dogs. Pick up a paw and give a treat. Hold it slightly longer each time. Let him sniff the nail clippers and give a treat. Then touch his nail with the clippers and give a treat. Then squeeze the clippers near his nail and give a treat. Then clip a little piece of nail and give 4 treats. Take each type of handling in this slow gradual fashion and pair them all with treats, fun and games. For large and giant breeds, I recommend the type of nail-clippers with a guard. They only allow a very small amount of nail to be clipped at a time, and the guard allows the process to go much more quickly and easily, with very little stress involved. Desensitization is still necessary and recommended, but the chances of injury are much reduced, which helps to build the safety history.

Food Bowl Exercises

Most people do all the wrong things with food and their dog when the dog is a puppy and the natural progression results in food bowl guarding. Do not promote the practice of a dog eating in isolation. One suggestion is to not even have a food bowl for the first several weeks of having your puppy. This would solve more problems than simply food bowl guarding. In that case hand feed the dog his meals in return for good behavior. You could also offer some of it in a Buster Cube for mental stimulation and as part of chew toy training. Here is what you do:

Step #1. Prepare the dog's allotment of food for the day and put it into a zip lock bag ready for use.

Step #2. Offer some of the food in a Kong or Buster Cube as part of chew toy training.

Step #3. The rest of the food should be offered a piece at a time for obedience. Any obedience or signs of deference should be rewarded. Anything else he does that you like and want to see more of reward.

Step #4. After several weeks, introduce a bowl. Request the dog sit and when he does place a few pieces into the bowl. Make sure you give the release command before he goes for the food. Try to set him up for success. Release him before he initiates going at the food. If he goes before you released him snatch the food and remind him to sit. A few of these and he will start to learn that he can have his food but only when he is released. Food is contingent upon manners. If you find that you are doing a lot of snatching the food away you may be causing frustration, something we want to avoid. In this case you were moving too quickly. Expect shorter durations before you release and build up gradually.

Step #5. Another thing you can do in conjunction with step #4 is to feed the dog while the bowl is in your lap. Just sit down with the bowl on your lap and drop in a small bundle of food. Wait until he finishes the first batch before you offer some more.

Step #6. Occasionally reach toward the bowl while he is eating and drop in a very yummy treat.

Step #7. Occasionally reach for and take hold of the bowl while he eats and slip a yummy treat in.

Step #8. Occasionally reach for and pick up the bowl, offer a very yummy treat and place the bowl back down while he eats.

Step #9. Occasionally walk over and pet the dog while he eats and slip him a very special treat for his trouble.

Step #10. A few times per week hand feed him a meal.

Step #11. Hand feed a meal once weekly for the dog's life.

Take Home Message

Be very careful where you get your dog. Never get him from a pet shop or a breeder who is not willing to work with you to determine whether a puppy is the right puppy for you. Choose the breed to match your personality. Meet the parents of the puppy if you can and determine that they are friendly. Then meet the puppies and pick the one that most suites your personality. If you are big and assertive do not take the sensitive pup and if you are the sensitive type avoid the really bold one but also the very nervous one.

If you rescue a dog from a shelter your safest bet is the older dog who's personality is somewhat set. In that case pay attention to any reports written by staff or explained to you. Also meet the dog yourself. If he seems okay then you are set.

Once you get your puppy go through all of the exercises in the text. If you work really hard on this now you will be far less likely to have problems with defensive behavior later on.

Remember the key points of training the dog really well and then using that training all the time in order that the dog has a job he can perform in return for the good things in life. If you can get him used to working for a living he will be more likely to take direction well later on.

Chapter 3
Diagnosing Aggression

Diagnostics

Medical Rule Outs

The first step in diagnosing an aggression problem is to rule out common medical conditions that may be causing or contributing to the aggressive behavior. Until medical causes have been ruled out you cannot make a behavioral diagnosis. A brief physical exam in not enough. Unfortunately many veterinarians are not familiar with finding medical sources for aggressive behavior. Find a veterinarian who is up on this topic. The dog will require bloodwork and possibly other diagnostics.

If you can rule out medical causes you can start behavioral diagnostics. Once you have a behavioral diagnosis you can make a second appointment to discuss medication. Most medications require blood work and possibly other tests to be complete to determine appropriateness and safety for medication, so the first visit will have been valuable even if no medical problems were found.

Aggression Diagnosis

#1. Target

The first part of your diagnosis will include identification of the target. Is the target human, dog or other animals? ***HOMEWORK*** List all targets now.

#2. Function (Triggers, Responses & Consequences)

The function of a behavior is the definition of the factors involved in the presentation of the behavior. Generally these factors will be what triggers or provokes what behavior and what drives it or reinforces it.

Functional Analysis

Functional analysis involves defining the operant variable involved in the behavior. It serves to provide as objective a perspective on the behavior as possible which serves to provide you with as rational a basis for designing a treatment plan as possible. It also offers valuable information for evaluating the relative success of the treatment plan.

ABCs of Aggression

The first step in a functional analysis is to define the ABCs of the behavior.

ABC stands for:

- Antecedent (another word for cue or trigger)
- Behavior (the behavior in question)
- Consequence (the reinforcement that drives the behavior)

The antecedent is what happens right before the behavior. Every stimulus in the environment can be the antecedent. If a dog bites someone I want to have a very clear idea of what provoked or triggered the behavior. In this hypothetical case we want to know what was happening immediately before the dog bit. We want to be precise and not take things for granted. Lets say a male stranger approached the dog when the owner was present and made eye contact with the dog. The man has facial hair and was particularly tall. The dog was on leash and the owner tightened the leash as the stranger approached. This would constitute the antecedent for the behavior in question. ***HOMEWORK*** Make a list of antecedents for your problem now. Note: do NOT purposely cause your dog to respond aggressively! This exercise can be done from memory... it's not necessary or advisable to cause an aggressive episode, as this is very reinforcing for the dog, and can be habit-forming.

The behavior may seem obvious but we need to be precise with our description of the behavior. In this case the dog bit but he also lowered his head as the stranger approached, his ears went back and when the stranger got within 5 feet he initiated a low growl. As the stranger got closer the dog backed up one step and started to snarl a bit. Once the stranger was right in front of the dog and made eye contact the dog bit him on the leg with a level 3 bite (described below). This description would constitute the behavior. You will note that their is overlap. This is because as time goes on there will be new antecedents and new behaviors. ***HOMEWORK*** Describe each antecedent and resultant behavior as described above for your problem now.

The consequence is everything that happens immediately following the behavior. In this case the stranger recoiled and stepped away from the dog. The owner acted apologetic to the stranger and was obviously stimulated. Once she apologized in an animated way to the stranger she took the dog away from the situation. This would constitute the consequences for the behavior in question. ***HOMEWORK*** Describe the consequences for your problem now.

Now you have a detailed list of each trigger situation, the corresponding behavioral response and the consequences that occur after the behavior. If you have a long history of many incidents like this you will be able to weed out the coincidental factors. For example if the common denominator trigger was strangers making eye contact while the owner tightened the leash and some victims were tall while others were not you will have a better understanding of the actual triggers; strangers making eye contact, not necessarily tall strangers making eye contact.

Likewise if you are able to weed out coincidental consequences you will have a more concise or defined list of consequences.

The problem of course is that you require a long history of problem behavior to get this information which is not always the case. You also want to have some control over the situation rather than having a trail of bitten victims. This is the point at which you bring diagnostics to the next level. You will isolate individual triggers and consequences and present them in a safe and controlled manner to further define what the actual triggers and consequences are.

WARNING: For dog owners I suggest that you have a professional perform the following diagnostics. Provoking a dog to aggress costs you and so you had better get useful information from it. As an inexperienced dog owner you are unlikely to get really useful information from these exercises but you may likely cause a set back for the dog. The following diagnostics are described for the benefit of practicing dog behavior counselors or students of behavioral counseling. Provoking aggressive responses is dangerous and should not be carried out unless the information it is likely to offer is very valuable. For dog owners who will not be receiving professional dog behavior counselling for one reason or another I suggest that you merely look closely at the history and define the triggers and consequences as best you can from that rather than setting up rule outs as described below.

Trigger Definition

You will have to be extremely careful when isolating and defining triggers. You will be provoking the dog to feel defensive and this is not only risky but very difficult on the dog. If you are going to expose the dog to this it has to be for a valid reason. You will have to work efficiently so as to minimize the rehearsal of habitual defensiveness. You must be sure that you can control the dog. If you think you might not be able to then do not perform the tests.

It is important to mention that not all professional dog behavior counselors perform these techniques. Many counselors feel that the benefit does not necessarily out weigh the detriment. I include explanation of the methods here for instruction purposes. This does not mean that you must perform these techniques in any or every case. I have used it on occasion and have been pleased with the information that it yields but there are many cases in which I found it unnecessary. Use your judgement. If you really feel you need to further define the triggers or consequences make judicial use of these techniques.

The methodology of the tests will be to isolate for an individual trigger stimulus and test the dog's responses to that alone. Another method that works better in certain circumstances is to remove one trigger stimulus and test the remaining combination with the dog's responses. Through isolating in this way you will hopefully be able to determine which exact triggering stimuli are the most problematic. Keep in mind that the dog's mood or stress level or even hunger can effect his thresholds of reactivity. If he is in a really bad mood one day then he will be easily set off. Keep this in mind and within the limitations of the system attempt to gain a better understanding of what it is exactly that sets the dog off. In the hypothetical case discussed above lets say the owner tried introducing males and females and found it was primarily males that were the problem. Then lets say the owner tested facial hair vs. no facial hair and found that it might have a slight difference but not really significant. Then lets say she tested loose leash vs. tight leash and found that when she tightened the leash the dog was much more reactive. As you can see these tests might not all be definitive but the counselor and owner sure learned a lot. They learned that the dog has a problem with male strangers and that by tightening the leash she was either conveying her own fear which aroused the dog or she was removing the dog's flight option. The last two are assumptions but either way in this case depending on how things go they have a ready solution to her problem. Perhaps if she now ensures that she never tightens the lead when strangers approach and she is careful not to let strange men invade the dog's personal space she will have a good handle on the problem She could of course go farther and attempt to rehabilitate the dog's feelings about male strangers.

It is important that you address any triggers that the dog may experience at some point. Just because you can avoid a trigger does not mean it might not happen. Address each and every trigger that your dog may come into contact with.

Consequence Definition

Defining consequences is exactly the same. To define the exact consequences that drive or reinforce the behavior rather than just going with the exhaustive list it will be easier to know what not to allow to happen and hence to remove the reinforcement. Many forms of reinforcement you cannot effect. For example any behavior which has become habitual such as many forms of aggression are self reinforcing. The chemical brain bath that takes place when a dog aggresses is highly physiologically addictive and reinforcing. Another confounding factor is that removing a dog from an aggressive incident promotes relief which is highly reinforcing. On the other hand remaining allows the dog to rehears the behavior and become more habitually defensive. Plus, someone could get hurt. None of this is any good. Yet another confounding factor is that behavior that has been successful is resistant to change. If it has been reinforced on a continuous basis then it will be more likely to extinguish but if it has been on any form of variable reinforcement schedule (which is most likely in real life) then it will not extinguish quickly. It may even get worse before it gets better. Never the less you will want to get a better understanding of what is going on immediately after the incident that provides reinforcement and keeps the response (behavior) alive. We already mentioned that intrinsic reinforcement takes place. That is a given then. Isolate and test individual stimuli as with defining triggers. The difference with this will be that you will have to observe the behavior as it evolves through several trials. You may get an extinction burst which is an indication that the removal of that stimulus is extinguishing the behavior. This is tricky because you will have to use your judgement regarding the effect the isolation trials are having on the behavior. This test is basically using extinction to infer driving consequences. Your best bet is to appreciate that many things can reinforce a behavior including things that you do not think of as rewards. For example if you punish a dog research indicates that after a while punishment causes the release of analgesic chemicals into the dog's body which are physiologically addictive and reinforcing. A smack or yell may actually cause I high level reinforcement. Removing a dog from the situation reinforces also. Once you have taken a very critical and in-depth look at the consequence list you may want to only test the most likely candidates. On top of that you may also want to assume certain stimuli are reinforcing and note them. This can be a tricky diagnostic to interpret without a lot of experience so use your judgement and common sense (as well as a little research) and identify as best you can what is driving the behavior.

#3. Severity

The severity of the problem is best indicated by the level of response the dog delivers. Dogs are predators. They can bite hard enough to crush bone. This means they have the artillery to do amazing damage and that they live in family units. Aggression and biting each other as hard as they could would be a very expensive proposition in terms of survival of the pack and the species. Dogs have evolved a mechanism for ritualizing aggression so that they can maximize the benefits of aggression and minimize the expense (damage). Puppies are born biting with as little inhibition as they will ever have. Fortunately they have weak jaws. Evolution has also provided them with baby teeth that are needle sharp. Why? So that they will get feed back on how hard they bite one another and hence learn to inhibit the strength of their bite. This will be the basis of the ritualized use of aggression. Dogs or other canids will learn this lesson with their needle sharp baby teeth by the time they get in their adult teeth. A puppy with baby teeth is wired up to learn bite inhibition. They are little biting machines. Therefor you can appreciate that it is difficult to teach it to adults. You want to know the level of inhibition your dog has learned to this point so that you will know if you need to try to teach that before anything else and so you know the risk you and others face. It is important to note also that bite strength may have a significant genetic component and be resistant to modification. Some dogs will bite hard no matter how much feedback they get and will not soften with bite inhibition exercises. These hard biters may have a serotonin deficiency. A 5-HTP supplement or a tricyclic antidepressant may be a more valuable strategy in softening the mouth or beginning to teach bite inhibition. It's also worth noting that certain breeds are predisposed for a soft bite, particularly the giant breeds and bird dogs. This doesn't mean that no giant breed or bird dog bites hard. It simply means that their bite tends to be much more inhibited than some other breed's.

There is a standardized system of classifying 'biters' which helps us determine level of bite inhibition. There is a separate system for dog to human bites and dog to dog bites. Each system has six levels. Next to the level number will be a brief description of the corresponding behaviors and then a description of the human equivalent. I have modified the original system slightly.

Dog - Human Bite Levels:

- **Level 1**: Growls, shows teeth, barks, stares, snaps, no contact (Human equivalent; argument or warning)
- **Level 2**: Single bite, saliva, no puncture (Human equivalent; push/shove)
- **Level 3**: Single bite,1 to 4 punctures, 1/2 as deep or less as dog's canine (Human equivalent; assault, punch)
- **Level 4**: Single bite,1 to 4 punctures, greater than 1/2 as deep as dog's canine or shakes, there will be bruising evident within 2 days for very hard bites (Human equivalent; assault with bodily harm)
- **Level 5**: Multiple bites, greater than 1/2 as deep as dog's canine or shakes. Mauling. (Human equivalent; same)
- **Level 6**: Fatality (Human equivalent; same)

Dogs falling in levels 1 through 3 may demonstrate some level of bite inhibition. If he has not bitten yet then you may not yet know if he has an inhibited bite or not. He may just have not yet been provoked to bite. This of course does not mean that he bites lightly or hard. You simply do not yet know. In this case you need to look into the history of the dog. If he was removed from the litter prior to 7 weeks he may not have gotten enough time with littermates and parents and learned the lessons associated with bite inhibition. If a puppy does not mouth humans when young then we simply do not know what state his mouth hardness is in. He has not had the opportunity to learn bite inhibition. He may have a naturally soft mouth or it might be hard. It will only be tested when he is provoked to bite. If the owners did not give feedback for hard biting when the dog is a puppy because they find it embarrassing to say something or for other reasons, then this dog may not know that humans have sensitive skin. These level 1 through 3 dogs may be relatively easy dogs to work with because they have inhibited bite.

Dogs labeled level 4 lack bite inhibition and are dangerous. This will be a relatively difficult dog to work with, given the risk. Teaching bite inhibition should be attempted prior to any anti-aggression exercises.

Level 5 and level 6 biters are extremely dangerous. Many behaviorists and trainers will not work with level 5 or 6 biters as the risk is too high. If a dog has mauled or killed someone within the family it is recommended that this dog be euthanized. The psychological trauma the family faces will not be healed with this dog still around. On top of that the prognosis is very poor. You may have noticed shaking on the list. A dog who shakes what he bites may be demonstrating predatory behavior. Some breeds such as the pit bull type dogs have been bred to hang on and grind their teeth or shake. This is a product of breeding. This is the exception to the rule. By the way, there is no evidence to suggest that pit bulls lock their jaws when they bite. That is a myth. They have been bred to hang on and this has given way to the lock jaw myth. This problem is exacerbated by those owners who teach the dog to carry weights to build strength and endurance. Other forms of bites reserved for these upper levels involve multiple deep bites and/or those that result in mauling or death to the target.

Keep in mind also that bite levels are relative. A Pit bull at a level 4 is one thing while a toy poodle at level 4 is another thing.

Dog / Dog Bite Levels:

- **Level 1**: Growls or snap, no contact (Human equivalent; argument or warning)
- **Level 2**: Single bite, bruise/scrape (Human equivalent; push/shove)
- **Level 3**: Single bite, bite to back, head or neck, 1 to 4 punctures 1/2 as deep or less as dog's canine (Human equivalent; assault, punch)
- **Level 4**: Multiple bites or single bite but more than 1/2 as deep as dog's canine tooth or bites feet, legs or abdomen (Human equivalent; assault with bodily harm)
- **Level 5**: Multiple bites, maims/mutilates (Human equivalent; same)
- **Level 6**: Fatality (Human equivalent; same)

Dogs falling into level 1 through 3 demonstrate some level of bite inhibition. Those falling under level 4 either bite several times and/or they bite very taboo areas such as the abdomen or feet. These dogs demonstrate a lack of bite inhibition and are very dangerous. If a wild canid chooses to kill another, which is rare and abnormal, he will often crush his opponents feet and while the other canid limps around unable to fight back he will move in for the kill. This is why dogs are so leery of having their paws touched. As a canid you can get bitten pretty hard on the neck or head and it causes little or no damage but it is easy to cause life threatening wounds to the feet and abdomen. Consequently biting another canid there is strictly against the unwritten canine rules. So if a dog does this he is showing a serious lack of inhibition much like the those humans who rape and may be mentally ill. A dog who maims or kills other dogs shows no inhibition and is very dangerous. There are complexities of course. The phenomenon called predatory drift can occur where normal dog on dog interaction or even inhibited aggressive interactions go wrong. Usually this involves a large dog and smaller dog. What happens is they are interacting and then the smaller dog's behavior stimulates the predatory drive of the bigger dog who then responds accordingly. These dogs will sometimes maul the smaller dog. The bigger dog may be normally very inhibited and not aggressive. If the problem you are facing involves a small dog and big dog together you will have to explore predatory drift as a possible cause so that the attacking dog does not get mislabeled.

Prognosis

Prognosis (expected success or failure) is a very difficult determination to be made and must be considered in the light of various factors. This is really a task best left to a professional with years of experience. Some of the relevant factors will be listed below and briefly commented on. This should give you an indication of the prognosis as you relate the information to the problem you are tackling.

Dog - Human Prognosticators

Goals of treatment. If your goal is to have the dog love everyone no matter what then you are probably doomed to fail and the prognosis will be poor. If your goal is to get to a point where you can manage situations adequately so that no one gets hurt then you have a better chance, and depending on other factors your prognosis may be good. Be realistic about your goals.

Severity of bite. If the dog bites at a level 4 the best prognosis you will probably be able to get is moderate. If the dog's bite is a level 5 or 6 the prognosis is poor. This represents a huge risk and euthanasia should be very seriously considered.

Predictability. If you are able to easily predict the trigger stimuli then this bodes well, but the less able you are to predict the triggers the worse the prognosis gets.

Controllability. If you are able to maintain control of your dog either verbally or physically if needed, then this bodes well for the risk and hence prognosis, but the less control you have over the dog the worse the prognosis gets.

Training. If the dog is well trained and biddable then this is a bonus. If not then you will have a fair amount of work to do and the prognosis will be effected by this and the trainability also.

Trainability. If the dog is food motivated and attentive (easily trainable) then this a great indicator of success. If the dog is not motivated by food but perhaps by social contact or a toy then this is also good. Food is just easier to work with in many cases. If the dog is hyperactive or otherwise difficult (perhaps attention and focus are lacking), to get the attention of and focus out of then this will make retraining very difficult and hence bring the prognosis down.

Social Drive. If the dog always wants to be with you and is very socially driven this is a good sign. If the dog is more toward being independent and aloof this indicates a lack of social buffer and suggests a more poor prognosis.

Children. If there are young children in the house and the trigger stimuli are even remotely associated with anything the children could be involved in, then the risk is extremely high and the dog should probably not remain in that household. If there are older children in the household, prognosis may get a bit better depending on the trigger stimuli and the maturity of the children. If the trigger stimuli involve children and there are children in the neighborhood the risk is significant.

Elderly or mobility impaired. If there are elderly or mobility impaired people in the household and the trigger stimuli are anywhere remotely associated with what these people may do, then the prognosis is very poor if the dog remains in that household. These people are at risk because they are unlikely to be able to defend themselves and because many aggressive dogs seem to go after those who cannot defend themselves. These two groups must be separated; someone must go.

Size of dog. If the dog is a toy breed the prognosis is much better because toy breeds are less likely to do very serious harm. Don't get me wrong; a level 4 bite from a toy breed is a painful experience. The bigger the dog is the worse the prognosis gets and there is a huge dip in prognosis as soon as the dog gets to about 40 pounds.

Breed. I'm sorry to say this but lets face facts. Some breeds are more dangerous than others. If the dog is a pit bull type breed, the prognosis is going to be much lower than if the breed is a collie. Yes there are very dangerous collies and very nice pit bulls, but pit bulls are very easily arousable, they arouse immediately, they do not calm down quickly and they do not show precursor aggressive displays as identifiable as most other dogs. Other potentially problematic breeds include the Chow Chow, Rottweiller, Dalmation, Komondor and Chinese Shar Pei. These breeds possess peculiar temperament qualities which can affect the prognosis.

Money. Another unfortunate prognosticator. If you cannot afford a behaviorist, veterinary tests, equipment etc. you will be less likely to succeed. This is not necessarily the case, but it can be the deciding factor in some cases.

Time. If you do not have the time to dedicate to training each day and working on treatment plans, then the likelihood of success is very low.

Commitment. If you are not completely committed to managing the dog's behavior in every situation, then the risk is higher and prognosis lower. You need to be closely tuned into your dog's mental state at every given moment, and observant for potential problems. You must be able to handle tense situations and maintain this vigilance for the lifetime of the dog. If you are not able to commit yourself to management and training for the dog's lifetime, then the risk is higher and the prognosis lower.

Compliance. You may be committed to working with an aggressive dog, but if you are unable to appreciate the importance of each step in the retraining and fail to comply with the steps fully, the prognosis will be significantly lower.

Genetics. If a major portion of the problem is an untreatable illness or injury, or if the majority of the problem is a genetic or neurologic one, then the prognosis will be poor.

Duration. If the problem has been ongoing for a long time and getting worse, then the prognosis is poor. If you have a hard time identifying the triggers, this indicates generalization is occurring which will reflect poorly on the prognosis.

Dog - Dog Prognosticators

Many of the same prognosticators for dog to human aggression cases will be relevant to dog to dog aggression cases. Some dog to dog specific prognosticators are as follows:

Interhousehold aggression. If the dogs live together, then the prognosis will not be as good as if they did not live together. Likewise if they live together and the areas bitten are the feet or abdomen, then prognosis is extremely poor and one of the dogs should be given up, if you cannot maintain them separately at all times. This is not an easy decision to make, and management of these sorts of situations is often a daunting task. In many cases, it's simply not a feasible prospect.

Owner mediated aggression. If dogs living together are in constant conflict and the owner has been a major influence, and he or she is able to modify their own behavior the prognosis is better than if the conflict is completely between the dogs, or the owner is unwilling or unable to admit their participation if any.

Predatory drift. If the problem relates to predatory drift, and involves a big dog chasing and injuring small dogs, then this is largely instinctual and the prognosis will be poor.

If the bite level is high, then the prognosis will be poor unless contact between dogs can be highly controlled or negated all together.

If your goal is for your dog to love all other dogs, the prognosis will be lower than if your goal is mere tolerance and self control.

Take Home Message

Diagnosing aggression involves identifying a few characteristics of the behavior problem. The target simply means identifying whether the dog is aggressive toward people and/or other dogs. Function is tricky. You want to identify the common characteristics of what provokes a reaction from your dog. Try to be as specific as possible. Try to narrow it down to the most fundamental triggers. For example don't write strangers if it really is only male strangers. If it's male strangers, then is it all male strangers or is there some other element that will allow you to narrow it down? Is it all male strangers or only the ones with facial hair, or who are tall? Be as specific as possible. List all of the things that happen before, during and after the events to give you an idea of what causes the dog to become upset, and what possible consequences are rewarding the behavior. The severity is fairly objective. Follow the chart in the text. If there were punctures then have a doctor determine the depth. If this was in the past and the depth was not determined for sure then take an educated guess. Was there a lot of pressure and significant bruising or was it only enough pressure to break skin? Was the damage primarily from the pressure of the jaws or was is more from ripping as the target pulls away?

Review chapter one and see if you recognize any of the inventory descriptions. This will help guide you in designing a treatment plan.

Regarding prognosis. If the risk is high then the prognosis is not good. If you cannot maintain control of the dog and he is a level 4 or higher biter, the prognosis is not good. If the dog ever comes in contact with children the prognosis is not good, either. Even if his problem is not with children, aggression generalizes and mutates quickly. It might become a problem in the near future. Assess the risk and your abilities and commitment very carefully to determine prognosis.

Chapter 4

Treating Aggression

I am here to tell you there are no magic wands. There are NO cures for aggression, because aggressive behavior is highly prone to habitualization. Habits are very hard to break, and it is very easy to "fall back into" those old habits, when new behaviors don't bring relief. Dogs that are aggressive will always tend toward aggression. There are no easy answers. "Treatment" will largely involve managing your dog and his environment so as to prevent problems. Another part will be training that will promote verbal control. Yet another part may involve medication. Another part will include improving the dog's life-style. Yet another part involves sophisticated behavior modification techniques. In the end you will be throwing everything you can at this problem and you will NEVER be able to consider the patient "cured". Below will be a discussion, not on how to cure your dog, but rather on how to deal with your problem.

First we'll discuss how dogs learn and hence how we can change behavior. Then we will get into step by step instructions on what you can do to manage an aggressive dog and, hopefully, modify behavior along the way.

Learning Theory 101

Operant Conditioning

"One cannot choose to either employ or ignore the empirically established rules of learning. Much like the law of gravity, the laws of learning are always in effect. Thus, the question is not whether to use the laws of learning, but rather how to use them effectively." [Spreat and Spreat, Learning Principles, 1982]

Operant conditioning is what happens when an animal learns an association between a behavior and it's consequences. We know learning has taken place when behavior changes. There are four ways of operantly conditioning which are illustrated in the diagram below:

	Start	End
Good Things	Positive Reinforcement Start Good Things Increase frequency	Negative Punishment End Good Things Decrease Frequency
Bad Things	Positive Punishment Start Bad Things Decrease Frequency	Negative Reinforcement End Bad Things Increase Frequency

A behavior can be affected by providing consequences. Thorndike's Law of Effect states that if a consequence is pleasant, then the preceding behavior becomes more likely; and if the a consequence is unpleasant, then the preceding behavior becomes less likely. Consequences always exist for behaviors. Consequences are provided by both internal and external sources. If a dog eats a poisonous plant and vomits, the behavior of eating that plant will decrease in frequency. If a dog growls and people step away (and if that was the dog's goal) then the incidence of growling will increase in frequency. Keep in mind that whether a consequence is viewed as "pleasant" or "unpleasant" depends entirely on the perspective of the animal performing the behavior. If the dog wants you to leave him alone and you go away then the behavior used to achieve the goal will have been positively reinforced. On the other hand if the dog wanted you to stay put or pet him then walking away would not be positively reinforcing. It may have been negatively punished actually. It all comes down to what the dog wants, and whether he gets it as a result of the behavior or not. Operant behavior is goal-oriented.

Whether something is reinforced or punished is not determined by how you feel or what you think about the stimulus that was presented or removed. The only way to tell if something was reinforced or punished is to observe the frequency of the behavior; whether it increases in frequency or decreases in frequency. Try to stay focused on the effect your actions have on the actual behavior, rather than on whether you think something should or should not have been reinforcing or punishing.

Positive Reinforcement (PR)

PR involves the presentation of a good thing to the animal. If you present something that the dog experiences as good then the behavior he was performing immediately before he got it will become more likely. Behavior is efficient. Dogs do what works to get good things. They can be counted on to maximize reinforcers, as they are opportunists.

Timing is important. The behavior the dog was performing when he got the reinforcement will increase in frequency, so if your dog does something you want to reward, and you wait 3 seconds to reward him, who knows what you rewarded? He may have done a dozen things in that amount of time, and one or two of them would have been reinforced and, neither of those will have anything to do with the behavior that was to be reinforced. What is reinforced is what you get; not necessarily what you think you reinforced. You may also think you are punishing a behavior but it does not matter what you think. It only matters what the animal thinks and if he took it as positive reinforcement then that is all there is to it. For example a lot of people think yelling at and pushing a dog away who is jumping up for attention is punishing but in fact it is usually reinforcing, because the dog is seeking attention when he jumps. Yelling and pushing are attention. The behavior increases in frequency and people invariably fail to recognize this because they feel that their actions should have been punishing, and this blocks their accurate assessment of the effects of their actions. Another example: once a dog has habituated to punishment his body releases surges of stress fighting hormones when he is punished. These chemicals are highly physiologically addictive and pleasure causing. The owner usually fails to note the increase in behavior because he is "sure" it should be punishing, when in fact, the punishment is highly reinforcing. Observe the actual effect on the behavior to determine whether it is reinforced or not.

Negative Punishment (NP)

NP involves removal of something good from the animal. If a dog wants your attention or support, then walking away from him when he does something undesirable will decrease the frequency of that behavior. If you hold a treat in front of a dog's nose as if he will soon get it and then when he performs some undesirable behavior you snatch it away (or better yet give it to another dog or eat it yourself), the behavior should decrease in frequency. The behavior did not work for him to maintain the hope of keeping or achieving the reinforcer. Another form of negative punishment you can use to decrease the frequency of aggressive or controlling behaviors is the time-out. To perform a time out the dog is put into a time-out room for a few minutes or if that is not possible then in a down stay while stepping on the leash without interacting with him. Yet another example is when your dog does something that you don't like and (if he finds your presence pleasant) you simply walk away; and the incidence of that behavior decreases in frequency.

Positive Punishment (PP)

PP involves the presentation of something the animal considers bad. If you shock or kick or severely reprimand a dog, the behavior he was just performing is likely to decrease in frequency. Dogs can be counted on to minimize punishers and hence will give up behaviors that lead to them, unless there exists a reinforcement that outweighs the unpleasant experience.

Negative Reinforcement (NR)

NR involves removal of something the animal considers bad. The application of NR infers PP since to remove bad things they must have been presented to begin with. If you strangle a dog on the end of a choke chain until he stops pulling you are administering NR and once the animal experiences this a few times the incidence of pulling will decrease in frequency unless there is a reinforcement that outweighs the bad experience.

The Problem with PP and NR (Bad Things)

You may have noticed the rider "unless there is a reinforcement that outweighs the bad experience" attached to PP and NR. That is because reinforcement is what drives behavior. Dogs will attempt to minimize bad things, (they will try to work around them to gain access to the reinforcement) but unless the reinforcement for a behavior is effected dogs will continue to attempt to work around bad things to get to it. Manipulation of good things is the key to affecting behavior efficiently.

That is not the only problem with making use of "bad things" in training. While operant conditioning is taking place, so too is classical conditioning. When a dog experiences a good thing or a bad thing he will associate that with the stimuli present at that time. You will be one of those stimuli. If you make use of bad things in training, your dog will associate you with bad things. When it comes to dealing with aggressive behavior, the dog is already uncomfortable with a stimulus. If you operantly condition the dog with PP or NR when he responds poorly to the stimulus, then he will also be classically conditioned to associate the stimulus with an unpleasant experience. This is one reason why the use of "bad things" in training cases of aggression is more likely to increase aggressive behavior rather than decrease it. The dog becomes more uncomfortable with the stimulus and feels a greater need to defend himself. And, lastly, punishment tends to suppress behavior, rather than remove it from the dog's repertoire. This means that the behavior is still present; it's just not surfacing at this point in time. A dog who has been treated for aggression with PP and NR can not really be trusted because the root cause has not been dealt with. Suppression through fear is untrustworthy!

Another problem with using PP is that you walk a thin line that you realistically cannot hope to maintain. A dog will either view a stimulus as punishing or reinforcing, and you might be surprised to find out what some dogs find reinforcing. If he views your attempt at punishment to be reinforcing you risk increasing the frequency of the behavior. If on the other hand he views it as punishing, then it will have to be sufficiently punishing to convince the dog that with a cost / benefit analysis he is better off to decrease the behavior. That level of punishment may also traumatize the dog. If you deliver too harsh a punishment, the dog will activate defensive mechanisms, and if it is not harsh enough he will habituate to it. Walking that fine line is about as close to impossible as you can get. It would be remarkable to get a professional to get just one punishment just right and exponentially remarkable to get more than one correct. Even highly experienced trainers cannot hope to execute punishment effectively, because every dog is different, with different drives and sensitivities, as well as having breed and size differences. Certainly average dog owners cannot. It's a recipe for disaster to suggest or to use positive punishment with defensive dogs. The consequences of missing that mark are high. It makes much more sense to just focus on positive reinforcement and increase the frequency of a behavior that is incompatible with aggression.

Another problem related to the use of punishment: after repeated punishments, a dog starts to respond differently to them physiologically. When punished, these dogs will release several stress fighting chemicals into the blood stream. These chemicals such as cortisol, endorphins and adrenalin are highly reinforcing because of the euphoric and analgesic feelings they produce in the animal. That means that after a few punishment deliveries, the punishment can start to act as a high level reinforcer. In many cases, the person will not recognize this effect. At best they will simply recognize that it does not seem to be working. But PP is so reinforcing for people who use it, to do that people rarely recognize that it is not working. Violence begins where knowledge ends. I doubt the assertion very much that it is the only thing that works, inferring that he has "tried everything". It is pretty unlikely that he has tried everything. So you are left with a situation in which the dog is reinforced for a behavior and the owner continues to punish and punish, totally oblivious to the fact that it is causing more harm than good. There is just too much stacked against the use of PP and NR to make it effective.

The final problem with the use of bad things in training dogs is that it is just unethical. Dogs did not ask to be adopted into your home; you chose to adopt the dog; and no living thing deserves to be treated abusively. Even if PP and NR worked, that is not the point. The end does not justify the means. It is not right to hit, strangle, choke, yell at or otherwise intentionally cause unpleasant feelings within a being whom, by the way YOU have chosen as a social companion. This is your friend. This is an animal whom you have put into a foreign world (read The Culture Clash by Jean Donaldson). He is having some adjustment problems. Please do not harm your friend. If you can find no way to solve your problem except to suppress through fear, then just euthanize the dog. It's more of an insult to abuse him. If you love your dog then be creative, get help and figure out a way to get what you can live with, without abuse. Please, I implore you!

The Beauty of PR and to a Lesser Extent NP (Good Things)

Reinforcement drives behavior, and the beauty of making use of good things to affect behavior is that you get to be the good guy. The dog forms a pleasant association with any stimuli present at the time, and it gets at the cause for the dog's use of aggression. You have the ability to control many reinforcers. You can present and remove good things quite easily, and this puts you in a position to get the dog's attention and change his behavior efficiently.

Differential Reinforcement Schedules

Differential reinforcement is all about increasing the probability or frequency of behavior. It is best used in correlation with proofing or systematic desensitization. There are several schedules of reinforcement. If you reinforce a behavior every single time, you would say it was on a continuous schedule of reinforcement. If it is not reinforced every time, you would say it is on a variable reinforcement schedule. When you differentially reinforce you choose which behaviors to reinforce and which not to. This is the most powerful tool at your disposal when dealing with aggression!!! You increase one behavior set and decrease another by taking control of the reinforcers and manipulating them. This is what training is all about.

There are several ways to use differential reinforcement. Some of them will be discussed below. Each has a more appropriate application for certain circumstances than others.

Differential Reinforcement of Incompatible Behaviors (DRI)

DRI involves reinforcing a behavior that is mutually exclusive to the undesirable behavior. For example, a dog cannot be jumping up on you if he is sitting. Sitting is mutually exclusive or incompatible with jumping up. So, you encourage sitting to discourage jumping up. Dogs who lunge at other dogs while on leash or strangers that walk by are prime candidates for DRI training. The dog cannot lunge if he heels nicely while walking or sits while not walking. If the dog is set up for success by starting at a distance he can handle, and then is taught to sit and heel, you can start working on making heel or sit very much worth his while (by heavily reinforcing them) and the lunging not worth while (by not reinforcing them). Keep in mind that lunging is self reinforcing so you have to combine systematic desensitization or proofing; that is, you have to start at a point the dog can handle, and work your way up closer to the distraction. In this way you prevent access to the reinforcement, more so than you withhold it. Then you train a solid sit / heel. A dog who bites can be trained in some cases to carry an object in his mouth. If it is conditioned enough, the dog will be inhibited from giving up his job of carrying the item, in favor of snapping or biting.

Differential Reinforcement of Alternative Behaviors (DRA)

In some situations it is not practicable to come up with an incompatible behavior. In this case an alternative behavior can be chosen. They are not mutually exclusive but reinforcing the new, desirable behavior without the presence of the undesirable behavior will discourage the performance of the undesirable behavior. For example a dog that barks menacingly can be taught to down without barking. It is not impossible to bark while in this position but having a task to focus on can discourage the dog from engaging in the barking behavior. It is also entirely possible to teach a "chill" or "settle" command at home, simply by repeating this cue when the dog lies down, and then use that under circumstances that would cause the dog to react by barking. Remember to immediately reinforce the dog when he *stops* barking, on cue.

Differential Reinforcement of Other Behaviors (DRO)

DRO is often referred to as 'shaping the absence'. In this case there is no specific target behavior but rather the absence of a behavior is reinforced. In this case you reinforce anything except the behavior you want to diminish. This can be particularly useful in cases where you are having a hard time getting any other specific behavior. DRA focuses on a specific behavior while DRO focuses on any number of behaviors as long as it is not the undesirable one. For example, rather than teaching the dog an alternative behavior for barking, you simply wait until he hesitates in his barking, and reward. Then wait; reward the absence of barking. Wait a little longer, reward the absence.

Differential Reinforcement of Excellent Behaviors (DRE)

DRE simply means that you reinforce only the really exceptional behaviors and not the poor ones. You are looking for a breakthrough in commitment or the very quick and enthusiastic responses. Attitude is everything in aggression and so DRE refers to reinforcing only the ones that are committed to with excellent enthusiasm and attitude. This is how you produce the really great behaviors.

Antecedent Control

Remember we discussed the ABC of behavior: Antecedent, Behavior, Consequence. Much of what you have learned so far has had to do with consequences. In many cases, manipulation of the antecedents can affect the behavior. If the trigger is something that can be eliminated then this alone may help. For example, if the use of a choke chain collar or scruffing and shaking the dog as punishment are provoking aggressive responses, then by all means get rid of the choke chain and do not physically punish the dog. Another common antecedent problem involves arousal. If the dog is worked into a highly aroused state by some activity and this leads to aggressiveness, then ceasing to perform that activity may be an acceptable stop gap for the undesirable behavior.

Learned Irrelevance

Learned irrelevance is like an extinction procedure. If a behavior produces no consequences when consequences were expected, the expectation is disconfirmed, and new adaptive learning takes place. If you say sit, sit, sit, sit to a dog when you are trying to train him to sit, or if he fails to sit upon request some time and you continue to deliver the cue without any consequence, in both cases the cue "sit" is likely to become irrelevant to the dog. The meaning will be gone because it fails to become or remain meaningful. Consequences provide meaning, and if no consequences are forthcoming the cue leads to no further learning (except perhaps that they have learned that it means nothing). As it pertains to aggressive displays, learned irrelevance can be tricky; because if the exposure is intense, the dog will not wait for the chance to confirm or refute (disconfirm) his expectation. He will react, and in doing so, be intrinsically reinforced. The event will not be irrelevant if the dog is reinforced. That is where it becomes necessary to systematically and gradually increase intensity of exposure so that the dog gets a chance to have his expectation disconfirmed. Learned irrelevance is not a technique you will consciously set up. It is a form of operant learning that will take place while you perform proofing and differential reinforcement. It is part of the puzzle of mechanisms that take place, which that lead to more adaptive behaviors.

Proofing

Proofing is about improving the reliability of a behavior you are training in increasing levels of context change. It is about teaching the dog to generalize the response in increasing distraction levels or for extended durations or distances. Dogs do not tend to generalize very well so we must teach them that the word sit means to sit; not just in your living room, but also in the yard and on the sidewalk and when in crowds etc. The process of proofing involves very gradually increasing the intensity of exposure to distracting environments. It also involves exposing the dog gradually to different forms of distraction so that he generalizes the behavior he is supposed to perform. To proof a response, you must set the dog up for success. Never bring on so much distraction that he will fail to perform. It is a balancing act. Proofing procedures set you up for training learned irrelevance also. A trick to remember is that when you do raise the level of distraction a little bit, relax other variables temporarily. Other variables include the distance you require the dog to perform the behavior from you, or especially the duration he is expected to hold the behavior for. Once you achieve a bit of success at the new level you can start raising duration and distance. The schedule of reinforcement should be relaxed also. Start by convincing the dog to continue performing in the face of increased distraction by continually reinforcing the first few. Then put the reinforcement on a differential schedule again. Reward especially for the breakthrough moments. When you can see a particularly enthusiastic response, or you see a committed response, or one that he maintains when something more distracting accidentally happens, reward these breakthrough moments.

Proofing is very much similar in process to systematic desensitization which will be discussed under classical conditioning below. The focus in proofing is operant rather than classical. In this case you will be training an alternative behavioral choice rather than attempting to change a reflexive emotional response, although that usually tags along for the ride so that both occur.

Clicker Training

Clicker training is a term given to the use of operant conditioning with the use of what is variously called an event marker, conditioned positive reinforcer or a reward mark. All of these terms are correct. The clicker is a little device that when pressed makes a click-click sound. Through classical conditioning, which is discussed next, the sound of the click is paired with the delivery of a primary reinforcer repeatedly until the dog responds toward the click in a similar way as he responds to the treat, game or other reinforcer. You click, treat, repeat several times and the dog will anticipate the coming reinforcer when he hears the click. This allows you to reinforce a behavior quickly and efficiently. By using a clicker you can reinforce a dog at a distance or for a behavior that only happens for a spit second. You can also reinforce without the distraction of your approaching the dog. To condition the clicker you merely take a few days to do several sessions of clicking the clicker followed by the delivery of a treat each time. Repeat several times until when you click, the dog looks eagerly to you for the treat. Now the clicker is "loaded". You will always follow the click with a treat. I would urge you to get a good book on clicker training such as Clicker Training for Dogs by Karen Pryor. The clicker is particularly useful for what is called free shaping behavior. Free shaping refers to reinforcing an approximation to the behavior you want to eventually see (called the terminal behavior) and then once the dog is performing the behavior regularly, you hold back the clicks and treats until you get a behavior a little closer to the terminal behavior. Then a little closer. On and on until you get the terminal behavior. Then you put the command on it to put it on cue and you have trained a behavior without even touching the dog or even luring him into position. This low level of invasiveness and highly effective training method makes clicker training well suited to rehabilitating aggressive dogs. Dogs who are free shaped actually learn to think better than dogs trained in other ways. They have to think to get the treats. It does not require as much thinking and problem solving to target a treat that is maneuvered to make the dog move. It required no thinking at all to allow someone to force you into position. This high level of cognitive activity has the added bonus of focusing the dogs attention and hence activating the cerebral cortex, which as we have learned helps inhibit emotional reactivity. Free shaping can be a fun process and it can very easily applied to retraining aggressive dogs.

Classical Conditioning

Classical conditioning is what happens when an animal learns an association between two stimuli. Classical conditioning is all about anticipation. Describing classical conditioning in scientific terms can become a little wordy and difficult to understand so I will keep it as simple as possible You may wish to reread this section more than once. When I was first learning these principles I had to reread articles so many times my head started to hurt as I wrapped my mind around these concepts. When a *neutral stimulus* is presented prior to an *unconditioned stimulus* US (a stimulus that does not require learning to produce a response, e.g. liver treat) repeatedly the animal who is being conditioned will start to associate the two. He will anticipate the presentation of the US when the previously neutral stimulus is presented. When this association forms, the neutral stimulus is no longer neutral because it now has significance in that the animal anticipates the US when it is presented. At that point we call it a *conditioned stimulus* CS. How do we know that the animal has associated the two stimuli? Through the dog's responses. Classical conditioning affects the reflexive actions of glands and smooth muscles. The responses are *involuntary*. This is in contrast to operant conditioning in which the conditioning affects *voluntary* responses and specifically striped muscles. Classical conditioning *elicits* responses whereas operant conditioning *emits* responses. Drooling is an example of a reflexive and involuntary response. If you present a dog with a liver treat (unconditioned stimulus US) he will most likely drool (unconditioned response UR). Now if you ring a bell (neutral stimulus NS) and then present the liver treat (US) repeatedly the dog will become conditioned to anticipate the liver treat (US) when he hears the bell (NS). When this happens the dog will drool when presented with the bell only. Now the drool is a conditioned response (CR) and the bell is no longer a neutral stimulus but rather a conditioned stimulus (CS). The process is illustrated below.

Step #1 US (Treat) > UR (drooling)

Step #2 NS (Bell) > No Response

Step #3 NS (Bell > US (Treat) > UR (Drooling)

Step #4 Repeat step #3 as many times as necessary until step #5 occurs

Step #5 CS (Bell) > CR (Drooling)

What is the relevance of classical conditioning when attempting to modify behavior including aggressive behavior? Classical conditioning is used to change the reflexive elements of emotional responses. Emotional responses comprise a series of neural and glandular actions that put into place a whole cascade of chemical reactions. Emotions are complex processes with varying levels reflexiveness. It would seem from the research that emotions can be created and changed with both voluntary and involuntary processes. Associations can be manipulated such that the reflexive elements of emotional responses are involuntarily altered. Conditioned fear responses and elation are the most alterable emotional responses open to the effects of classical conditioning. We can classically move an emotional response from one direction to the other. For our purposes, our goal with classical conditioning will be to pair a feared stimulus with an elation-eliciting stimulus such that, eventually, when the animal is presented with the previously fear-eliciting stimulus, the animal responds with elation. Theoretically that is the goal. There are many limiting factors with this form of learning, though and the intensity of the fear elicited can block attempts to recondition the emotion.

It is important to note that, theoretically, the difference between operant and classical conditioning is clear; but in real life there is significant overlap. Often both kinds of conditioning are occurring at the same time. They are distinct but occur simultaneously. We can discuss how each is taking place, but when we treat a behavior problem we will usually be using both kinds of conditioning at the same time. The distinction is more for academic purposes and allows us to better appreciate the theory behind why dogs learn certain things and how we can go about changing their behavior. For example if you have a dog who is fearful of children and you bring a child to100 feet away from the dog where he is not yet overly concerned about it, and you pair the presence of the child (bell) with treats (liver) or a game, both operant and classical conditioning will take place. You will make children predict treats and games (fun emotional stuff). Eventually the hope is that the child will provoke a pleasant conditioned response, rather than an unpleasant one. At the same time, you will be reinforcing behaviors associated with tolerance. Both will happen and that is what we are after.

Another important point is that classical conditioning is difficult to achieve and maintain in the real world when you are dealing with a complex set of emotional responses such as those experienced by dogs who behave aggressively. A dog who responds to something with fear and the (flight or fight mechanism is triggered) will be resistant to change his emotional response. Is there anything you are deathly afraid of? Lets say that a bank robber pointing a gun at your head provokes a fear response. What could we pair with that event to make your emotional response change to that of comfort? How many times would we have to present them together before your emotional response would change? Do you think that a big part of your eventual progress would be from the repeated exposure without negative consequences (learned irrelevance), as opposed to the pairing of a "bad" thing with a "good thing" (called counterconditioning; discussed below)? And if it is just a matter of pairing good with bad, then who is to say that the bad will come to represent something good, rather than having the good come to represent something bad? The answer probably has to do with which is more powerful; the good thing or the bad thing. These are tough questions and I do not ask them to discourage the use of classical conditioning but rather because these questions are not adequately dealt with in the literature and research and this leads to mistaken views as to what works and what does not. The dog training literature considers emotion an involuntary reflex which leaves us with a problem. It may very well be the case that classical conditioning is not the primary form of conditioning occurring here. This phenomenon may turn out to be learned irrelevance rather than counter conditioning. The jury is still out. I say all of this because I mentioned that the emotional response must be dealt with in order to fully trust an aggressive dog. Now, I meant that but,... I now have to qualify it by stating that it can be extremely difficult to change that emotional response. We must try, but we must also work hard on operant conditioning, because stopping the behavior is the important thing. The take-home message here is that classical conditioning is used to change an emotional response, and without a change in emotional response, a dog is not truly trustworthy. It can be extremely difficult to change an emotional response to a significant degree when that emotional response is intense. Think about how hard it is to cure human phobias of flying for example. Therefore dogs who have been aggressive are unlikely to become totally trustworthy. The conclusion is that management of aggressive dogs will be a life long issue and both operant and classical conditioning are vitally important.

Counterconditioning

Counterconditioning is a classical conditioning concept. Counterconditioning counters conditioning that has previously taken place. It replaces the conditioned response. For your purposes it will replace a negatively conditioned response with a positively conditioned response. By pairing a stimulus that has come to provoke an unpleasant emotional response in the dog with a very pleasant US, you will hope to change the CR to one of positive anticipation rather than negative anticipation. The term counterconditioning has been used in the past to describe training a behavior that is mutually exclusive to the behavior you want to decrease, but this is not an accurate way to use the term counterconditioning. It is a classical conditioning term and the mistaken definition given is clearly an operant conditioning process. The process described is better defined by an operant conditioning term such as differential reinforcement of incompatible behaviors DRI.

To change an emotional response, you will have to pair a significantly valued stimulus with the object in question. Every dog is different. ***HOMEWORK*** Make a list of your dog's top 5 valued things from most valued at the top and in order. #1 will be your dog's most highly valued stimulus and #2 will be his second most valued stimulus and so on. The stimulus can be an activity, a game, a toy and yes a food. Make your list now and put it into your file.

Systematic Desensitization

Systematic desensitization is a classical conditioning concept and is a type of counterconditioning process. Systematic desensitization, on it's own, refers to the process of exposing the dog to a stimulus at such a low intensity of exposure through manipulation of distance and duration that the dog does not experience a sensitized response, and then allowing the dog to habituate to that intensity of exposure. Then once the dog has habituated to that intensity of exposure, the intensity is increased slightly and the dog is again allowed to habituate. Habituation is the process whereby the dog experiences a decline in the magnitude of the conditioned response after it has been elicited repeatedly. The dog is to habituate to a given level before being exposed to a higher level of intensity. The idea is that a dog who is exposed to a high level of intensity will not habituate because the sensitized response is too strong. What we need is a foot in the door. If we can reduce the intensity of contact we can get the dog to habituate to that, and then once that is done, we can intensify the contact and allow the dog to habituate to that level. Many times the process is excruciatingly slow and susceptible to setbacks.

Systematic desensitization is rarely ever used on it's own. Most commonly systematic desensitization is used in conjunction with the basic form of counterconditioning. By using a gradual process and by changing the CR at the same time, we have a powerful technique for affecting the behavior of a dog who is uncomfortable with a particular stimulus.

In the real world it can be tricky to gauge the comfort zone. Sometimes you will push a little too far and the dog will experience a sensitized response. In this case you will back off several levels and try again, this time going more slowly.

This also brings up the question of what to do when this happens. When this happens you must avoid reinforcing the behavior. That means that you will be using operant conditioning also. If the dog never responds poorly and you were able to present the pleasant stimulus every single time this will have been a classical conditioning exercise totally. If the dog responds poorly, which at some point (realistically) is going to happen, you will be making use of operant conditioning. You will continue the process as described, but technically, since you are presenting the pleasant stimulus some times and not all the time, you are rewarding differentially. That means both kinds of conditioning will be exploited. This is another example of how terms can be used in a sloppy manner sometimes. Systematic desensitization is a classical conditioning process but when you choose when to present the stimulus (treat, toy, game, whatever), then you are using a separate and different process altogether.

How to Use Systematic Desensitization and Counter Conditioning

Here is how you perform systematic desensitization and counter conditioning:

Lets say the dog is afraid of strangers. Lets say at 100 feet he notices the stranger but does not experience fear. At 50 feet he tenses up and focuses intensely on the stranger. At 20 feet he attempts to hide behind your leg. At 10 feet he barks and lunges. At 5 feet he bites if he can.

Step #1. Perform this exercise before a meal, and generally be boring when a stranger is not presented. Present the stranger at 100 feet, bring out your dog's favorite treats and continuously feed them to the dog for several seconds to a few minutes. Have the stranger leave and stop feeding treats to the dog; be boring again. Repeat this process several times per session, through many sessions. Do not move onto step two until the dog is clearly excited about the presentation of the trainer at that level of intensity. When you present the stranger and the dog immediately starts wagging his tail and looks to you for the treats then you are ready to move on to the next step. Step one may take a few days or several months. It is vital that you do not move on to the next step until the dog is clearly excited about the presentation of the stranger at that level of intensity.

Step #2. Present the stranger at 80 feet. You should show the dog the treats at 100 feet, but only start giving the treats when the stranger is presented at 80 feet. Repeat several times per session and through several sessions, until the dog is visibly excited about the presentation of the stranger at 80 feet. Repeat this gradual increase of intensity again at 70 feet and then at 60 feet. Then at 50 feet, then 40, then 30, then 25, then 20, then 15, then 10, then 5. Remember NEVER to move to an increase in intensity until the dog is happy about the level you are at.

Step #3. Now you will relax the level you are at by going back to 100 feet or so, but now helping the dog to generalize the lesson. That means take it back to low levels of intensity but present a different stranger. You should be able to work through a bit quicker this time around, but go as slow as necessary. Once you have worked through several different strangers, perhaps you could perform the exercises in a strange neighborhood or under slightly more distractions. When ever you add in a new element, relax the intensity and build back up. Do not move on to the next step until you have really generalized the lesson with the dog and he is excited about strangers in various contexts.

Step #4. It is more difficult and risky to move into striking distance so step three is very important. Step four will involve contact. Context is important. This is where more specific things can cause problems. Moving quickly or even really slowly can freak many dogs out. Staring at the dog can be scary. The increases in intensity must be carefully thought out. The stranger should face sideways to the dog and move at a predictable and regular speed. You may want to start by having the stranger walk to 10 feet or so and toss a treat to the dog. After several trials like this the intensity can be increased and the stranger can toss them from 5 feet and then 3 feet and then he can hand feed them to the dog. Go slowly and gradually with the increases in intensity. Once the dog thoroughly enjoys the strangers hand feeding him, the stranger can start acting a little more normally each time, until the dog is comfortable with strangers dealing with him in a normal fashion.

You do not have to set up all of the above exercises with people you know, although this entire process works better if you do start with known people. This gives the dog the opportunity to learn how the game is played, before introducing the "stranger element". You can find just the right spot where you have lots of room to work in and people walk by. Then you can perform the exercises with your dog as the strangers walk by. Just make sure that you are able to keep the proper distance and control the environment.

If you are blind sided by a stranger and you were not able to prevent the dog from triggering, say nothing and quickly move away from the situation. When you get far enough away that the dog can calm down, wait several minutes for the dog to calm down without you saying or doing anything. Do not even look at him. Once he is calm you may request a sit and reward for that, ending on a positive note. In that case make a mental note of the context in which the event occurred. You will have to go back to that and do exercises there to try to make up for that experience.

You must continue to perform these exercises way past the point at which you think the dog is now okay with strangers. One of the biggest problems with this process is that people give up before they should, or they move way too quickly. Even if the dog seems fine at some point, keep doing the exercises for a few more weeks. Then, after that, continue to take advantage of situations that occur naturally. Don't take your progress for granted. When you see strangers, pop out a few treats or a ball or whatever makes your dog happy. Continue to remind him how great strangers are.

The Problem with Systematic Desensitization and Counter Conditioning

The following problems exist with the use of ONLY classical conditioning processes in general and systematic desensitization and counter conditioning specifically is:

- The dog may learn reflexive behaviors, but does not learn to <u>think</u>
- The procedures require an extreme volume of well-timed exercises which are unrealistic

For example, Jean Donaldson (1998) suggests a classical conditioning tool called open bar / closed bar. To perform this exercise the owner would set the dog up such that he would be generally bored, then present the feared stimulus, give a cue such as "open bar" and start continually feeding the dog treats or playing or whatever, then the feared stimulus would be removed, the owner would cue it with "closed bar" and stop presenting good things. The owner would be instructed to continue carrying out the exercise repeatedly NO MATTER WHAT THE BEHAVIOR THE DOG PERFORMS. The goal is counterconditioning. Systematic desensitization can easily be added in by gradually increasing the exposure intensity. The owner is instructed to continue feeding the dog even if he continues to aggress. The theory here is that we must change the emotional response to achieve reliability. The dog will be unlikely to be performing any one particular behavior and so the positive reinforcement for aggression is unlikely to affect it. It is suggested that classical conditioning is prepotent over operant conditioning and so a few reinforced aggressive behaviors is the price to pay to make the dog come to LIKE the feared stimulus.

Theoretically this is great except for our two problems above. If an owner were willing to perform hundreds of these exercises over and over and over with perfect timing and management, then counter conditioning would probably take place. That would be great except almost no one is willing to commit to this amount of work. The experience of many behavior counselors is that those who would commit to this usually fail to follow through completely. In this case, the problem may potentially become worse through positive reinforcement of defensiveness. The argument offered against this is that no one particular behavior is reinforced repeatedly, but what is not accounted for is that a defensive *attitude* is reinforced repeatedly. Aggression is all about attitude and when you reinforce defensiveness you get more defensiveness.

Of course both of these problems can be circumvented by switching from counter conditioning to a system of differential reinforcement: reward behaviors that most closely approximate those that you're looking for, and raise your criteria gradually until you have replaced all of the defensive behaviors with appropriate ones. It's not advisable to use a strict system of counter conditioning, because of the problems outlined. It is much more efficient to start with counter conditioning, and then switch to differential reinforcement once you have got an initial partial happy response, like a tail-wag. In this case, you'll only be using counter conditioning for a short time, and so the practical aspects are maximized, while the shortcomings are minimized.

The other problem is that if you do manage to change a reflexive behavior the dog is unlikely to generalize it to other situations very well, because it involved no voluntary thought processes. If the dog learns to respond involuntarily to something, you lose out on the beneficial effects of having the dog learn to think about how to behave voluntarily, and, hence you get less reliability and generalization. We want our dogs thinking and choosing prosocial behaviors.

Once aggression becomes habitual it will always remain a default setting. If your dog gets stressed out and his thresholds shrink a bit and he goes limbic what behaviors would you expect? Habitual behavior. That's why it is important to use both classical and operant conditioning. You want to replace one habit with another.

By focusing on operant processes such as proofing, you get the gradual exposure effect. After all, proofing and systematic desensitization are very similar except for the focus we place on the type of learning. By differentially reinforcing for the right behaviors, and teaching the dog that the feared stimulus is irrelevant and not in fact dangerous at all, you teach the dog to think and problem-solve and you reinforce prosocial behavior. By focusing on operant conditioning you can also count on classical conditioning taking place without your specific intent. If you set him up to achieve success through operant conditioning the feared stimulus is likely to come to represent the opportunity for positive reinforcement IF he thinks and does the right thing. You thereby achieve habituation, but you achieve all the benefits of operant conditioning, too. Go operant and you buy one get the other for free.

Flooding

Flooding refers to exposing the dog to the stimulus at a high level of intensity, and not reducing the intensity until the dog has become exhausted with responding, and then finally habituates. It is not flooding unless the dog ceases responding to the stimulus with a sensitized response. It is only after that point has been reached that the dog will have a chance to habituate to the stimulus. This technique is a risky proposition and not frequently suggested anymore, since systematic desensitization was refined. The experience is likely to make the animal more fearful rather than less. It is not always possible to wait until the dog becomes physically and mentally exhausted. The level of discomfort this technique causes makes it an unethical choice in most cases.

A similar response prevention technique involves presenting the stimulus that provokes aggression, along with a stimulus that tends to over ride the aggressive response. For example some dogs are so motivated to play fetch that they will do so even when playing with or close to a stimulus that would normally provoke an aggressive response. It is difficult to say whether in any given case this will decrease the incidents of aggressiveness when the stimulus is not presented along with the game of fetch, but in some cases it may help. If a dog is very uncomfortable with having his hips touched, perhaps he would not mind so much if he was given a quick brush while playing tug of war or being fed a treat.

Pharmacological Intervention

The choice to use medication should be carefully made. Medication will not replace a behavior modification program. The most it can do in many cases is give you a foot in the door. Medication is most helpful with highly reactive dogs or dogs with high anxiety or fear levels. Many dogs are not suitable candidates for many medications. All animals should have a complete blood count (CBC) and serum biochemistry profile before treatment is initiated with any behavior altering medication. [Overall, 1997] Your veterinarian will perform a full physical exam and appropriate tests that will determine whether your dog is a suitable candidate for a particular medication. Clients should be given a complete list of potential adverse responses to the medication and they should be encouraged to contact the veterinarian with any concerns. [Overall, 1997] Expect to pay about double or more the fee of a regular visit for this consult with tests.

There are a wide variety of medications from which to choose. In many cases dosage is experimental, meaning your dog may start on a certain standard dose but it may have to be raised or lowered as needed. Do not make this decision yourself unless your veterinarian gives you the okay to do so.

What follows is a brief description of a few of the more common medications used with aggressive dogs.

Elavil (Amitriptyline Hydrochloride)

Elavil is a TCA (tricyclic antidepressant). TCAs inhibit prejunctional reuptake of norepinephrine and serotonin. This is what is primarily responsible for it's antidepressant properties. Side effects may include dry mouth, constipation, urinary retention, tachycardias and other arrhythmias, syncope associated with orthostatic hypotension, ataxia, disorientation and generalized depression and inappetence. [Overall, 1997] Use is contraindicated in dogs with a history of urinary retention or severe, uncontrolled cardiac arrhythmias. [Overall, 1997] Elavil is particularly helpful with fear and anxiety based aggression. It may be helpful with interpack aggression.The closer the dog is toward the fear and anxiety spectrum of aggressive behavior (without anger), the better this medication will work. The more the behavior is anger-motivated and reinforcement-based the less likely this medication is to work. If your dog is put on this medication you will have to be very observant and careful. If the behavior is reinforcement-based the lack of anxiety may remove some inhibition from the dog and aggressive behavior could get worse rather than better. The onset of action may take as long as 2 - 6 weeks. [Beaver,1999] Drug treatment should continue for at least 6 weeks before it is abandoned as a failure unless of course the aggression gets worse. [Beaver,1999]

Prozac (Fluoxetine)

Prozac is a specific serotonergic reuptake inhibitor far more potent than Clomicalm. [Overall,314] Prozac inhibits the reuptake of serotonin only, unlike Clomicalm or Elavil, which also inhibits reuptake of NE. Prozac can take up to 1 month or more before it takes effect. Prozac seems most effective in treating aggression characterized by severe impulsivity or profound aggression and inter-dog aggression. [Overall,314] It is also used for OCD. [Overall,314]

Paxil

Paxil is not licensed for use in the treatment of aggression in dogs, but it is being used for that purpose with some exceptional results. Paxil is similar to Prozac but is more advanced.

Clomicalm (Clomipramine Hydrochloride)

A recent major contribution to the treatment of anxiety based problems is the licensing of Clomicalm, the brand name for a drug containing clomipramine hydrochloride. Clomipramine is a tricyclic anti-depressant. Clomipramine blocks the re-uptake of serotonin and NE by neurons, thus increasing the serotonin and NE levels in the brain. Increased serotonin levels decrease the level of fear, stress and anxiety experienced by the dog. Clomipramine is metabolized in the body to desmethyl clomipramine, which increases NE levels in the brain. Increased NE levels cause the dog to be more receptive to behavior modification techniques. This medication can actually focus the dog, making learning easier. This medication is used in many human anxiety disorders.

ProQuiet (L-Tryptophan Supplement)

ProQuiet is a tryptophan supplement with complimentary and synergistic ingredients added that may help increase serotonin levels in the brain. What follows is information provided by the company.

"ProQuiet® The Safe and Gentle Calming Formula. ProQuiet is indicated for use when outside stress causes a pet to become overanxious, nervous or overly excited. It has been tested and is safe and effective for use as directed. ProQuiet is safe enough to use daily or can be used as needed in stressful situations. Because this calming formula is not a drug, your pet won't experience side effects such as drowsiness, lethargy or other health problems. Form: Chewable Flavored Tablet - savored by both dogs and cats. ProQuiet is available in 60 ct. bottles. Ingredients: L-Tryptophane, Taurine, Hops, Chamomile, Brewers Yeast, Vitamin B3, Vitamin B6, Ginger, Vitamin B12, and Folic Acid." [http://www.animalhealthoptions.com/f_products.html] This can be purchased through a veterinarian. If a veterinarian is not familiar with this new product here is the contact information for the manufacturer. Animal Health Options 500 Corporate Circle, Suite A Golden, CO 80401 (800) 845-8849 Fax: 303-271-0512 info@animalhealthoptions.com.

"Studies show that taking supplements of tryptophan or 5-HTP will increase the amount of serotonin available for use by neurons. (Note: Chronic stress, with its concomitant increases in cortisol, can inhibit the conversion of dietary tryptophan to 5-HTP, but not 5-HTP to 5-HT. This suggests an advantage of using 5-HTP instead of tryptophan for relieving problems associated with stress.)" [http://www.life-enhancement.com/displayart.asp?ID=208] "If low serotonergic function can lead to aggressive and violent behavior, can reversing a serotonin deficiency restore more normal behavior? Although this area has not been studied systematically, some evidence suggests that it may. Serotonergic function can be enhanced in two basic ways: by providing the metabolic precursors for serotonin or by preventing the inactivation of serotonin that is released into the synapse." [http://www.life-enhancement.com/displayart.asp?ID=208]

5-HTP (5-hydroxytryptophan)

This is a metabolite of the transformation from tryptophan to serotonin. That means it is one step closer to serotonin than is tryptophan. Tryptophan also has a limiting factor as described above whereas 5-HTP does not. 5-HTP can be purchased over the counter in Canada and the U.S. whereas tryptophan cannot be. 5-HTP should not be used in conjunction with other medications that effect serotonin activity unless the combined effect is taken into consideration by the prescribing veterinarian. Dosage is experimental. If the dosage is high the dog may be initially nauseous. If the dose is too low no effects will be achieved. One suggested dosage regime might be as follows:

Small breeds: start with 10mg three times daily, perhaps increasing gradually until results are achieved and decreasing or stopping the increase if the patient becomes nauseated.

Large breed: same as above but starting with 40mg three times daily. Be sure to check with a veterinarian for dosage to be sure.

5-HTP is not as yet a Generally Recognized As Safe (GRAS) ingredient according to the state regulatory agencies governing feed supplements while the ingredients used in ProQuiet are. This is not to mean the 5-HTP is not safe, it only means that manufacturers have just not as of yet sought this regulatory certification, and since 5-HTP is not a patentable chemical, they are unlikely to do so.

Surgical Intervention

Spaying and neutering is an often suggested remedy for various behavior problems including aggression.

Males

Neutering the male dog removes the source of circulating testosterone.

"Ben and Hart at the University of California carried out the most extensive surveys on the effects of castration on dogs and came up with these statistics:

Roaming: Reduced in 90% of cases, Rapid reduction in 45%, Gradual reduction in 45%, No effect in 10%

Intermale Aggression: Reduced in 60% of cases, Rapid reduction in 25%, Gradual reduction in 35%, No effect in 40%

Mounting People: Reduced in 60% of cases, Rapid reduction in 30%, Gradual reduction in 30%, Some decline in mounting bitches in heat too

Urine Marking in the House: Reduced in 50% of cases, Rapid reduction in 20%, Gradual reduction in 30%" [Fogle,53]

Testosterone has the effect of modulating sexually dimorphic behaviors as well as aggressive or reactive behaviors. "Testosterone acts as a modulator that makes dogs react more intensely. When an intact dog decides to react to something, he reacts more quickly, with greater intensity, and for a longer period of time." [Overall,96]

There is a two-fold explanation of the effects of androgens (specifically testosterone) upon behavior which bear upon the affects of castration and behavior: 1) prenatal androgenization of the testosterone sensitive neural substrate which mediate sexual and aggressive behavior and 2) reinforcement and sensitization of these substrates once they have been realized at puberty. [Lindsay,vol1,186] This is supported by the fact that testosterone can create male sexually dimorphic behaviors when injected into females, and, that male sexually dimorphic behaviors are not eliminated upon castration, even prepubertally. There are two significant surges of testosterone in the male canine system; one just before and just after birth which masculinizes the brain and essentially sets up the potential for associated behaviors, and another at puberty which further modulates these behaviors. Thereafter, the behaviors take on more of a learned component. This first androgenizing effect is not affected by castration which explains the inconclusive results of castration upon behavior. I would be remiss not to add into this model the high likelihood that many male sexually dimorphic behaviors may be fixed action patterns to some degree. Male urine marking for example is possibly a fixed action pattern, as may be mounting. Roaming is possibly instinctive as dogs must leave their families in search of nonfamilial mates. As with most canine behaviors it always comes down to a complex amalgam of genetics, biochemicals and learning. We can affect some chemicals by spay or neutering. We can affect learning to some degree and genetics to a lesser degree. This all leaves us with a tough set of behaviors to modify once it has been initiated.

"Testosterone titers start to rise by the time the male pup reaches 4 to 5 months, whereafter testosterone levels reach a maximum at 10 months of age and then fall to adult male levels by 18 months of age." [Dunbar,68] Raising testosterone levels at 4 to 5 months of age may be important in provoking other dogs to target them so that they will learn affiliative behaviors [Dunbar,68]. On the other hand, as circulating testosterone levels increase, associated behaviors become more learned and entrenched in the behavioral repertoire of the dog. This argues for neutering to be done at 6 months of age in order that affiliative behaviors may be learned through the targeting phenomenon, but so that affects of circulating testosterone are not present long enough to cause significant reinforcement histories for associated behaviors. One argument is that dogs who are expected to live with or otherwise interact with other dogs throughout their lives and who are also extra sensitive should be neutered early (say at 4 months), so that they are not targeted quite so heavily by other dogs. Waiting with these dogs can provoke interactions that lead to classical conditioning complications. If a dog is provoked to perform intermale aggression for example, he may learn from his interactions to anticipate a confrontation. This classical conditioning effect can influence the dog's behavior long after circulating testosterone is removed from the body. This beneficial effect must be weighed against the potentially negative ramifications of prepubertal neutering. Prepubertally neutered dogs show a significant increase in excitability and general activity level. [Lindsay,vol1,186] For some breeds and some owners this may not be a problem and prepubertal neutering may prevent otherwise difficult to avoid traumatic experiences with other dogs while allowing for maximal socialization. A cost-benefit assessment must be made in each case before the timing of neutering can be advised upon. It is also often suggested that puppies who show control complex aggression or simply high levels of controlling behaviors be neutered early. Research is mixed on the results of this. Until research comes up with an answer, early neutering at 4 to 5 months of age may be a wise choice.

Females

Spaying of the female dog removes the source of estrogen and progesterone. Estrogen and progesterone are increased or decreased in cycles. The biggest influence cycling fluctuations in estrogen and progesterones have on female dog behavior is pregnancy related behaviors. "While estrogen increases in the dog's body for a short length of time, progesterone remains in circulation, influencing the brain for two months after each estrous and can have a dramatic effect on canine behavior. The most common behaviors are those associated with pregnancy, nest building, guarding possessions and milk production." [Fogle,54] The most notable problem arises when the dog guards items maternally. Other problems can involve irritability, conflict with other dogs and energy reduction. "Guarding toys, dolls, rags, slippers or anything else that can be carried is another common behavioral consequence of the surge in progesterone." [Fogle,55] Possessive guarding in intact females that occurs in cycles is usually a hormonal guarding of the type described.

Female dogs are at increased risk of disease if they are allowed to experience their first heat. For this reason it is often suggested that a female dog be spayed prior to 6 months of age. It would appear that dogs who demonstrate control related aggression toward owners prior to 6 months of age are at risk for becoming more aggressive after ovariohysterectomy. If a dog demonstrates a significant propensity to control related aggression, it may be wise to avoid spaying these dogs. "When the female dogs neutered at or after puberty were compared to intact controls, several differences were noted. One difference was a significantly greater tendency for dominance aggression to be shown toward family members by the neutered females. What is not clear about the study is whether the surgery was performed in more of these dogs because aggression had already been identified as a problem, or whether there is a direct cause-effect relation. Ovariohysterectomized bitches also showed significantly more excitement in the car and less discriminate appetite than did the intact ones, even immediately post surgery." [Beaver,229] These observations are backed by Fogle, (Fogle,56) and Overall (Overall,97) ". It remains unclear exactly why some undesirable behavioral side effects occur. Inconclusive evidence exists that androgens may be implicated in dominance aggression in females." [Overall,97] Experiments performed on hamsters (Brain & Haug, 1992; Vom Saal, 1984, 1989) suggest that females positioned in the uterus between two males will be more aggressive than other females and this conflict behavior more resembles male conflict behavior. [Overall,97] We know that the male brain is exposed to testosterone prior to birth which masculinizes it. It is theorized that this masculinizing of bystander females results in aggressive tendencies in females, again adding to the debate of how important testosterone is in the development of aggression and other behaviors. Animals experimentally injected with testosterone, including females, tend to take on male sexually dimorphic behaviors. It would seem that testosterone may turn out to be very important one way or another in the development of aggressive behavior.

Foundational Program

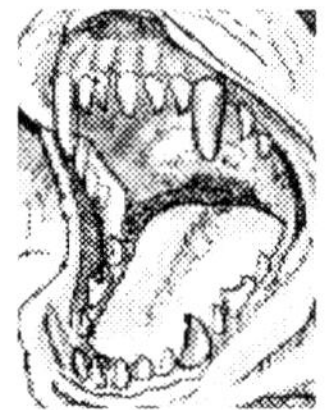

Take Control

First you need to accept that there is a problem and that it is worth dealing with. The very next thing you must do if you have an aggressive dog is vow to take control of the situation. You may never successfully retrain the dog, and you may never really trust him in certain circumstances again, but one way or another you must take control. Taking control means taking full responsibility for the risks and not denying, enabling, facilitating or procrastinating about it. From now on you must not only have complete control of your dog, but you must also demonstrate to the dog that you have complete control. You must set up for him the consistent expectation that he is to defer to your control. This may require a major shift in thinking and require major changes in the way you interact with your dog. I wish I could make it easier than this for you, but I cannot. You will have to take special precautions. You will have to use special equipment. You will have to train your dog. You will have to hand feed the dog etc. This will require a significant input of effort. There is no magic wand. The following subsections are explanations of how to take control of the situation.

Management

Management refers to manipulating the environment so as to prevent or control something. Take all precautions necessary to ensure the safety of you, your family, strangers, visitors and other animals. Whether you will be actively treating the dog or not, management will be a very important initial step.

If your dog cannot be supervised, be sure that he is confined where no other person or dog will be able to have access to him. Do not leave an aggressive dog in the yard while you are at work or inside the house. Children may enter the yard, or a utility person may come to read the meter. Avoid any situations in which he may come in contact with others without your presence and control.

You will have to be vigilant while on walks. You may have to be more assertive with people who approach your dog. Tell them (clearly and ahead of time, and even loudly if you have to) if you have to that they should not approach your dog. Please be up beat and happy while you do this. Otherwise you could train your dog to be more defensive. Dogs pick up on our apprehension, so do it in a warm happy way.

Your dog will almost certainly never be able to be off leash in public. Use a Gentle Leader always.

You will need a good understanding of what contexts trigger aggression in your dog. You will need to avoid these situations as the program progresses at whatever costs. Every time a behavior is performed, it becomes more deeply entrenched. Avoid provocation, even if it means no walks at all for the time being, or no toys at all for the time being, or no access to the bedroom. What ever provokes must be avoided until exposure to it plays a part in the treatment plan. One of the first components of a treatment consultation with a behaviorist will include a description of each aggressive context, and discussion on all of the creative ways in which the whole event could be prevented or subverted. ***HOMEWORK*** So sit down right now with your file and come up with ways to manage it so that you will not even have to face an aggressive incident. While you are at it, come up with a plan for what you will do when there is an aggressive incident in each of those contexts. Generally, ignoring it and walking away is the best way to handle it; even if it technically reinforces the behavior.

Equipment

Muzzle

The first and most obvious piece of safety equipment is a muzzle. Have the muzzle fitted by someone who knows how it should be fitted, and introduce the muzzle gradually. There are generally two kinds of muzzle. The first is the cage style. These are often metal, plastic or leather. These are used when the dog will wear the muzzle for longer than 1 hour or so, or when the dog will be exerting himself and needs to pant or if it is hot out. The other kind is the groomers muzzle which is usually nylon but could be leather. They are snug around the muzzle and only allow the dog to open his mouth enough to accept a very small treat. If the dog will be wearing the muzzle in cooler whether, without physical activity and for short periods of time, these are acceptable. With either kind the muzzle should be fitted by a professional (not usually a pet shop employee) and it should not be left on when the dog is not supervised. There are other muzzles that are essentially an elastic band around the muzzle. These will not prevent the dog from biting and all the rules of a tight muzzle must apply, no matter what the packaging says. These are not suggested for safety purposes. Here is how to introduce a muzzle:

Step #1. Keep fun, games, attention and treats to minimum otherwise, and bring them out along with the muzzle several times daily for a couple of days.

Step #2. Then hold a treat on your end of the muzzle such that he has to put his nose into the muzzle to get the treat.

Step #3. Do that several times and then let the muzzle remain on him while you feed multiple treats in a row, rapidly.

Step #4. Spread out the treats with a couple or few seconds in between each. Clasp the mechanism in the back and offer treats.

Step #5. Then wean off the treats by spreading them out more and substituting life rewards such as going outside or whatever else the dog finds rewarding. If you are pairing the muzzle with good things and not devaluing them by offering these things all the time he should be happy to wear the muzzle. When you bring it out he should be wagging his tail and getting excited. For dogs that are not completely predictable, or where triggers cannot totally be avoided, have the dog wear the cage style muzzle around the house. This will ensure the safety of people who may inadvertently push his buttons. Almost all dogs will have to at least wear their muzzle during treatment exercises.

Gentle Leader

A Gentle Leader is a head halter similar to the halter that a horse wears. It goes around the dog's muzzle and back of the neck. The leash attaches under the chin. This device is not a muzzle and does not keep a dog's mouth closed. They do not tighten around a dog's neck. These devises tend to calm dogs down and most importantly it offers you control. You can get a Gentle Leader through www.PAWSsitivesolutions.net or www.CourteousCanine.com. If there is any possibility that the dog will be exposed to a trigger stimulus in the house that you cannot prevent, the dog will wear the Gentle Leader with a ground line dragging while inside, and while you are there to supervise. This can be used, if necessary, to control the dog. It must be fitted properly. Ideally it should be fitted by a professional. Otherwise follow the instructions in the booklet or video that comes with it carefully. When the dog is out side of the house he will have to be on leash with his Gentle Leader and muzzle.

Try to run through the introduction process much the same way you would with a muzzle. Walks and other life rewards will help this become an acceptable device to many dogs. The manufacturer would have you believe that all dogs will come to like this devise rather quickly. The experience of many trainers is that many dogs take a significant amount of time to get used to them. Remember that until he is used to it, the distraction will make it difficult for him to concentrate on training. It would be a good idea to avoid exposing the dog to the problem contexts at this stage for that reason and because we do not want that context to become associated with anything else, like the head collar. Get the dog used to it first. Many dogs never really like wearing the GL being on but it can help tremendously. There is never to be a leash correction on a dog wearing this devise. It is used to guide the head when needed, and it would be dangerous to apply a leash correction with one of these devices in place. Do not allow a dog to run to the end of a leash when wearing the Gentle Leader, and try to avoid pulling the dog's head back; pull it to the side. Never use Gentle Leader with a retractable lead or long line.

Leash

Be sure it is strong enough to handle the dog. For most work you will simply need a 6 foot nylon, canvas, leather, hemp or cotton leash. Leather is the best choice, as leather is less likely to burn or cut your skin, if your dog should lunge suddenly.

Ground Line

Buy a standard thin leash and cut off the loop at the end. No loops or knots as these can get caught on things. The purpose of this tool is to drag on the ground when he is on or off leash. If he jumps up or lunges or if you just need some momentary control you simply step on the dragging rope and he cannot jump or lunge. It offers a better measure of control. This is not meant to be left on when the dog is alone and you should stand on the line so that the dog is not jolted when he jumps. It is to prevent not punish.

Prevent Rehearsal

Once you have identified the triggers it is vital that the dog not be exposed to the stimulus until it plays a part in treatment. Every time a dog responds aggressively they learn from the event; it becomes more entrenched and more difficult to modify. The initial fight or flight response is reflexive to some degree, but what follows is learned to a large extent. Behavior is a strategy, and if successful, it will become stronger. If it is not successful then either the target is put at risk or the behavior experiences an extinction burst. An extinction burst is what happens to a behavior when the reinforcement is not forthcoming. The animal will vary the behavior. Usually this means the behavior will become more frequent or more intense. This is a temporary state before the animal moves on to plan B, but if this variation works then that will be the new standard behavior. This is the double edged sword of allowing an aggressive response to occur. Either it works and continues to become stronger or it does not work and risks a more intense behavior being created. It is vital that you do what ever it takes to prevent having the dog face the situation that provokes the response so that you can avoid this consequence.

Prevention will require creativity. You have to do a bit of lateral thinking, also, to challenge the priorities you presently have. For example, we all want to bring our dog out for walks, but if going on walks provokes the dog then you may have to discontinue walks for a while altogether. If that is what it takes that is what must be done. If a toy causes problems then the toy is gone. If a food dish causes problems then it is gone. "How", you say? Well, if need be food can be given as treats for training, in a treat-dispensing ball, or just hidden around the house to encourage scavenging. For water you can try offering it in a different bowl each day and putting it in different places so he does not get too attached to a particular place or bowl. A good example of a common difficulty in being creative is a dog who guards the couch. Obviously the piece of advice you will always receive is don't let the dog on the couch. So are you going to go face to face in conflict with the dog when he wants to get up on the couch? No, because if you do, you have not prevented the conflict. It is not good enough to prevent the dog from getting up on that couch; you need to prevent conflict. The couch either goes into an off limits room or the dog does not even get access to that room unless walking through it on leash to go outside for example. Prevent conflict. Prevent the triggering of fear or anger responses. Prevent high levels of arousal or stimulation if this is a problem. You may have to go quite far out of your way to prevent these things. Yes, that's true. It may require the dog not getting things such as toys and walks for a little while. It may require restricting access to certain people for a while. These things are not easy. Reevaluate your commitment, and then move forward.

If your dog is provoked to become aggressive, stop the behavior and get him out of that situation. When you intervene in an aggressive incident, you run the risk of reinforcing it. Removing a dog from a situation like this may be reinforcing. But, the alternative to removing the dog is dangerous, and also reinforcing as the dog rehearses the behavior. Put a stop to it. You must be careful not to provoke a redirected aggression. The dog should have it's Gentle Leader and muzzle on, and be on-leash so merely walk away from the incident. If it is at home, step on the ground line if you must. If it is in a situation in which you are the target, just do not push it. Walk away slowly, or remain still and avoid making eye contact. Do not face a confrontation or accept a challenge. And after you stop shaking give some thought to how you can be creative and prevent that from happening again.

Leadership

Leadership does not mean domination. One of the primary tasks you will undertake in the rehabilitation of your aggressive dog will be for you to achieve and maintain a benevolent leadership role in your relationship with your dog. Dogs are very comfortable with the leader-follower role. They develop an expectation of their role in relationships, and as long as that role remains consistent, most dogs seem content. Structure and consistency is really all we are talking about here. This is NOT a rank reduction program. Being a leader does not mean using any form of aversive suppression or dominating your dog. The following sub sections will describe what it means to provide good leadership.

Establishing Safety History (TRUST)

Your absolute first step with an aggressive dog is to immediately initiate or rehabilitate a safety history. You develop a safety history by not allowing your dog to be exposed to stimuli that attacks his sensitivities. Have you ever known someone in your life who you did not have a safety history with? This means having a relationship fraught with mistrust due to actions (or INactions) taken by that person. To the extent that the person actively is associated with your sensitivities, you will mistrust that person and feel suspicious of them and their intensions. Perhaps a relative? This suspicion and mistrust makes you defensive and vigilant. It causes you stress. Is your defensiveness going to be reduced with the continued attacks on your sensitivities and continued mistrust? No. Absolutely not. Dogs are the same way. If they do not have a solid safety history in general, then they will be vigilant, distressed, mistrustful, suspicious, and, yes, defensive (read aggressive). Your first task will be to vow to rehabilitate this dog's safety history generally and specifically with you, the owner. Lacking a safety history causes lack of confidence and fear and a lowering of anger thresholds. Lack of a safety history leads to a pessimistic cognitive mind set (outlook on life), while a solid safety history promotes an optimistic cognitive mind set. Pessimism will lead to increased suspicion while optimism leads to tolerance and trust. You must vow that you will not allow your dog's sensitivities to be attacked and defensiveness engaged. This is rule number one; keep it in mind at all times. This means you must prevent sensitized responses and manage your dog's environment. If your dog cannot trust you, then you are wasting your time with all of the other treatment options.

Structure vs. Chaos

As mentioned, dogs learn from each event in their lives, including their social relations, and they use that knowledge to predict future events. With inconsistent outcomes, a dog will start to perform more control-seeking behaviors. This control-seeking is often aggressive by nature. Dogs need structure. They need clear and consistent boundaries, so that they do not feel the need to test those boundaries. You must provide your dog with regimented structure so that he will be able to get used to following instruction and looking to you, the owner, for guidance. The less control you have and the less structure you provide, the more your dog will simply adapt and use any behavior he feels at the time is appropriate. Those behaviors may be aggressive. Lack of structure is chaos. Again, this does not mean more punishment or harshness. If you use suppressive coercion your dog will simply adapt and learn how to work around you. (refer to The Third Way articles) The dog will appear manipulative, but he is just trying to find consistency he can count on. You must be able to reconcile love and gentleness with structure, consistency and firmness.

Many people feel sure that punitive methods "work". Fear inhibits aggression, which is part of why people feel that their actions are working. If you use fear to inhibit aggression, you may be likely to feel in the short term that it is working, but it is just a matter of time before this system falls completely apart; and when it does it will be a far worse problem than before. The safety history will be gone and unlikely to be rehabilitated. A life of fear and coercion has a way of twisting perception and creating a neurosis that prevents the animal from using data from the outside world around them to guide their behavior. Consequences will cease to operate on the dog's behavior as he increasingly takes cues from his twisted and neurotic perceptions of the world around him. After all, the outside world, including consequences, must be perceived and evaluated by the animal. These dogs who are treated with domination and punishment are a complete mess and become, in many cases, beyond rehabilitation. I tell you this because the dog training world has been inundated with dominance programs and pack theory, and I do not want you to take our discussion of such subjects as leadership and structure to mean anything like domination and punishment.

NILIF

The NILIF program is a way of providing structure to a dog's life. It builds confidence in the anxious dog, and promotes deference in the controlling dog. The basis of the NILIF program is that you will take control of all of the dog's controllable reinforcers, and make the dog work for them. The dog is to defer to you and sit for all good things in life. Before you give the dog his food, pet him, praise him, put on his collar, open the door, give treats etc. you should request a sit. For dogs who are controlling, you may request a sit, then down, then sit (doggie push ups). Remember this should be a fun game, not a boot camp. The first few times you do this with a controlling dog, you may get some reluctance. He has an expectation of being able to demand stuff, or at least get it for free, so that is what you will have to overcome. In many cases the dog's behavior will get worse before it get's better. This is another extinction burst. If this happens it is working. Keep it up.

Start with the food bowl. Prepare the food and then request a sit. Give him 5 seconds to comply. When the five seconds are up and he has not responded simply say "Oops" and put the food away. Skip that meal. At the next meal he will be more hungry and likely to be more receptive to commands. Same deal this time. Not many dogs will go more than 3 days without eating before they will sit for food. Please make sure he understands what you are asking for before you do this; and NO, I am not advocating starving dogs. All he has to do is sit, and it's his choice as to whether he wants to comply or not. Your dog has learned to make some problematic decisions independently, and so he must now learn to be a little less independent for a while so that he has a chance to learn appropriate independent behavior. Once he sits, give him the food. When he's doing well at this level, up the criteria: change the rules. He must sit now within 3 seconds. Once that is going well make it two seconds. You will soon have an enthusiastic and quick sit, on cue. He will be learning to look to you for cues. He will be learning to defer to your leadership. He will be learning that all good things come through you, and that if he wants them he will have to pay attention and do what he is told. This is a good way to begin hand feeding exercises and to teach games like eye contact / attention. The same thing goes with other good things in life. Your dog should be sitting for you a minimum of 20 times per day. If he does not want to comply, there is no conflict; you simply say "Oops" and walk away without giving him the thing he wants. No excuses. Guard against your own rationalizations. With the more anxious dog, you want to avoid the "Oops", so be gentle and set him up for success. This should be a fun experience for all dogs once they get the hang of it. After all, they will know what it takes to get what they want and that will not be growling and biting. The consistency inherent in this program will benefit all dogs.

When you instate the NILIF program you are taking control of the dog's reinforcers. These are your dog's most valued things. Since every dog is different your dog will have his own list of things he likes. The NILIF program will entail controlling all reinforcers possible, but knowing exactly what your dog's top reinforcers are will help you add "umph" to the program. You will want to use his very favorite things in life for the treatment plan. ***<u>HOMEWORK</u>*** Make a list of your dog's top 10 reinforcers. These could be anything. They could be a walk, a specific treat, being on the couch, attention, a certain toy, a certain game etc. The only ones to avoid writing down are the ones you do not want to use such as biting the mail man. List them in rank order, number one being the highest valued and number ten being the tenth favorite thing. Write your list and put it into your file.

Suzanne Clothier, in her book Finding a Balance Issues of Power in the Human/Dog Relationship suggests an exercise in which you make two columns on a piece of paper. On the left side write "I do" and on the right side write "dog does". Under I do write a list of all the things you do for your dog that he cannot do for himself. Be creative. Don't limit yourself to letting the dog outside, offering dinner etc. Anything that is taken positively by your dog should be included. Make your list at least 25 items. Think like a dog. Clothier describes how her dogs seem to find it enjoyable to watch her go to the bathroom. This would be on her list of things the dog enjoys and she provides. Think like that. Now on the right hand side write next to each item exactly what your dog does presently for that item. What is he required to do in payment for that thing. Now if you get to the end and find that getting all those good things is not contingent on any deference or consistent payment of any kind, then that indicates that you may have a problem with the leadership you provide in your relationship. It also gives you a good place to start with your NILIF program. From now on, all good things in life are contingent upon some relevant deference. For example: the dog way have to sit and wait until released in order to be allowed outside or get food. He may have to drop the ball and sit, then down, then sit again every so often during a session of fetch. He may have to sit before being allowed to wear his collar. He may have to walk close to you on a loose leash to be allowed to continue a walk. This is all about leadership skills. The control freak and the fearful dog alike need for you to be an effective leader. Being a leader does not mean teaching him who's boss all the time and dominating him. It means you will not spoil or coddle him. It means you will not be permissive and give things away for free. It means you will not make excuses for or rationalize about his behavior. The root of many aggression problems is a messed up relationship between the dog and the owner. The owner of such a dog is usually permissive and coddling. This must stop. You must become a benevolent leader now. Spoiled children have lots of temper tantrums and so do dogs. We know we have to be careful not to spoil our children, but then some people are even proud of how they spoil their dog. If you really want to do your dog a favor, then raise him like a child; provide clear and consistent boundaries.

Yielding

Many dogs have a problem with being displaced (Directed to move from one location to another). If your dog does not, then this is a preventative measure since aggression generalizes quickly. The goal of this exercise is to frequently direct the dog to move, and then displace the dog and to reinforce it heavily. Do not bribe the dog. The reward should be a surprise. Use a combination of sometimes using a placement command and other time physically displacing the dog. Targeting also works well for teaching a dog to move to another location. By physically displacing the dog, I do not mean to correct or otherwise act harshly with the dog; simply take him by the collar and move him gently. If your dog has problems with you touching his collar, do some desensitization work to make this a more enjoyable experience. This is supposed to become a pleasant and rewarding experience. The dog should start to look forward to being displaced. Immediately upon displacing the dog, reward him with very special treats or a game of tug perhaps. Try to use life rewards. Start with displacements from places that do not actively provoke defensiveness. If the dog is a place guarder then do not force those trigger stimuli. This is meant to turn a mildly irritating event into an event that is enjoyed. You can also occasionally call your dog to you from where he is.

Another way to go about this is to clicker train your dog to yield. Get your clicker and treats ready. Walk toward your dog. When he moves out of your way click and treat. Repeat. When this is reliable, you can put a cue of it by giving the cue, then walking toward him; and when he moves, you click and treat. Once this is reliable, you can perform the exercises when the dog is sitting and then laying down, and finally in more contentious situations like when he is on the couch etc. Work up gradually.

Time-Out & Time-In

A time-out is based on the notion that a behavior can be negatively punished by using social isolation. Time-outs may be used for excessive attention seeking, controlling behaviors or anger related aggressive acts. They are not to be used for more fear-related forms of aggression. Time outs can be frustrating for many dogs so it is important to try to focus, if you can, on other methods and only to use the time out selectively, and discontinue it's use if it does not start to work fairly quickly. An *exclusionary time-out* involves removing the dog to a place that removes him from social contact and continued reinforcement. Usually a bathroom is a good choice. It may be wise to avoid using the dog's crate, as this can be detrimental to crate training if the dog starts to associate the crate with punishment. To perform a time-out, the dog is verbally directed to the time out area, be it a bathroom or the dog's crate. This will require you to train the dog to go to the time out place before you start using the time outs. Use a cue specific to the time out such as, for example, "time-out", rather than using a cue you might use when you simply would like your dog to go to his crate for some other reason. *Nonexclusionary time-outs* involve withdrawal of reinforcement or social contact without removing the dog from the training environment. This can be as simple as folding your arms and looking away for a few seconds to tying the dog's leash to a door knob or tree and walking a way for a few minutes. Proper time outs should act as a negative punishment and not as a positive punishment. Exclusionary time-outs tend to work better than nonexclusionary time-outs.

There are important guidelines that make the difference between effective time-outs and abusive isolation. Observe the following guidelines.

Bridging Stimulus

Dogs are not very good at connecting events and their consequences, when they are separated by more than a few seconds. Just as a clicker becomes a conditioned positive reinforcer and informs the dog that what he did at the moment he heard the click won him the reward, so can a sound indicate to the dog that when he heard it he lost social contact and has earned a time out. The word you choose can be anything but you should avoid words you will use on a daily basis. "time out" is a good choice.

Timing

Timing is vitally important so that the dog knows or comes to know exactly what lost him social contact and continued reinforcement. You must deliver the conditioned negative punisher CNP (the bridging stimulus, the "time out", for example) exactly when the dog performs the behavior. Ideally the word should be delivered as soon as the behavior begins also. The CNP acts as the cue to direct the dog to the time out area (the crate or bathroom or a matt in the corner for example).

Repetition

You should follow every single unwanted event with a time-out. *Consistency* and *contrast* are the keys to making this process clear.

Duration

For aggressive behavior, it has been found that 2 - 3 minutes is appropriate duration for time-outs. [Nobbe and colleagues, Use of time-out as punishment for aggressive behavior, Canine Behavior,1980] More may, depending on the dog, be too aversive or the dog may simply settle in and habituate to the isolation. Less time may not be adequate. I know that is *feels* like more time would be better but this is not the case with dogs so stick to the 3 minute maximum.

Time-in

There must be *contrast* between the time-out and non-time-out so that the dog can appreciate the meaning of the time-out. To do this there should be time-in opportunities. The time-out causes all of the "good things" to stop happening, and hence the dog will avoid it more, if, when he is not in a time-out, he is experiencing good things. Once the dog has been removed from a time-out he should be allowed to offer an alternative coping strategy or behavior in the same or a similar context that got him the time-out. If he commits the illegal act again; he is timed-out again but if you can achieve an alternative behavior that you can positively reinforce you will contrast the time-out with the time-in. This is *not* to suggest that you expose the dog to a situation in which he will respond aggressively; that *must* be avoided. If you get more than 2 time-outs in a row then you are moving too quickly. Back up and instate some prevention measures, such as ensuring that the dog understands what you want, through remedial training.

Target Behavior

Dogs do not learn well when they are expected to learn multiple behaviors at the same time. For appropriate results you will have to choose target behaviors. Work on one specific behavior at a time.

Emotional Content

It is VITALLY IMPORTANT that the time-out process possess NO emotional content. No yelling. No harshness. No yanking the dog by the collar. If you express anger, this will overshadow the effect of the time-out and will distract the bridging effect; your exercise as negative punishment will instead become positive punishment. Harshness will be more likely to be perceived as a positive punishment, and the aversive nature of this may make the time-out a negative reinforcement, or, a removal of bad things. That means the target behavior may INcrease in frequency. This is a very important point. The inclusion of emotional content will be likely to not just disrupt the process but actually make the problem worse. If you cannot manage to divorce emotion from your CNP or bridging stimulus, then either say nothing, or use a marker such as a whistle to mark the time-out. Get the dog and calmly place him in a time-out. No words, no yanking, no hitting. If you cannot manage that without emotional content then do not perform time-outs at all.

Teaching Bite Inhibition to Aggressive Adult Dogs

Bite inhibition is, simply, the amount of pressure that a dog puts behind his teeth when they come into contact with flesh. In a perfect world, dogs will learn this skill during their formative months as young puppies... but many don't have this opportunity, for lots of reasons. Our goals in teaching bite inhibition are many: not only does this training help the dog to understand the pressure he exerts with his jaws, but it also teaches the dog a much higher degree of self-control under circumstances where he'll become excited and stimulated. In addition, these games are used to help vent some of the frustration and physical energy that may be exacerbating the problem in the first place. [Rushman, Brenda, personal communication]

Developing bite inhibition in level 1 through 3 biters can be established through setting up situations in which you can provide the dog with feedback. Games like Tug-of-war and Frisbee, in which your hands come into close contact with the dog's teeth, and hand-feeding small pieces of food can be done. If the dog is snatchy or touches skin when using food, set the dog up for success by only doing the exercises after a meal... he'll have a softer bite, if he's not hungry. [Rushman, Brenda, personal communication] Conversely, a dog that isn't as food-motivated as the grabby dog will work better before a meal. Always remain calm in the beginning stages of these exercises; building excitement in the dog will cause him to lose control of his bite, and will set him up for failure. [Rushman, Brenda, personal communication] Start by using the trick that horse trainers use: hold the treat in the folds of your palm, rather than between your fingers. This forces the dog to use his lips and tongue more than his teeth. [Rushman, Brenda, personal communication] Only after the dog has learned to do this, should you begin to offer the treat between your fingers; accidents cause you to screech in pain and storm out of the room immediately with the toy or piece of food if possible but without it if necessary. Continue these exercises until the dog is noticeably gentler with his jaws, and then continue to spot-check throughout his life by purposely introducing your fingers into his mouth when offering treats or toys. When the dog is proficient in not applying pressure, add obedience commands into the game. Starting at very low levels of excitability, have the dog sit and down before continuing; as his proficiency progresses, you can do this at higher levels of excitability. This builds self-control. [Rushman, Brenda, personal communication] If you think a bite was accidental, keep in mind that these are the same animals who can catch a fly buzzing past their head. If it was an accident, then they can learn to be more cautious and careful. Keep these exercises up as reminders. This will help develop a sense of carefulness in the dog, but it effects the real life bite less than in the context of the inhibition exercises. If a dog's flight / fight or predatory mechanism is triggered, the bite inhibition you developed will have varying degrees of effect on the outcome of that bite. It is still a part of the total package of treatment, though, as this training also helps the dog to develop self-control. Remember that we will throw everything we can at the problem.

Developing bite inhibition in level 4 through 6 biters is a whole different matter. You must use your judgement with these exercises, as the risk is high and the risk may outweigh the benefits. I include this for sake of completeness and so that dog behavior counselors reading this can make their own judgement, but I should say that I rarely suggest this myself in my own practice, because with these hard biters the risk is too high and I am convinced there are factors involved in producing a hard biter that are not modifiable to any reasonable degree. I usually just attack the problem on other fronts. I'll leave the decision to your judgement. The exercises will be the same ones for less risky dogs but you will have to use more safety precautions. If your dog has a problem with food then the hand feeding may not be the way to go. If your dog guards toys, then tug of war may not be the way to go. If your dog has a problem with having his head or mouth touched, then tooth brushing must be avoided for now. If at any point you feel uncomfortable with this exercise then stop immediately and do not do them. Softening a mouth is good if you can do it safely, but in some cases a hard mouth may be beyond conditioning, and if the risk is high then it is not worth it. Here is something else to consider: we are taking special precautions, but I think Patricia McConnell put it best when she explained in her book The Cautious Canine that all the bites she has received always appeared to be in the past tense, not the present or future. She was describing how fast an attack can happen. There will be little if any time for you to react. I would not suggest these exercises for level 5 or 6 biters! I hesitate to include them for level 4 biters.

Notes to consider: in playing games, your dog will not be muzzled. This means that you (and any helpers present) will be more at-risk for these exercises. Don't do them if you're not comfortable with this. Obedience commands are used throughout any game that you play with your dog (whether aggressive or not), so it's important that your dog be proficient at the very basic commands before starting to play the games. The use of obedience commands is important... it helps the dog to maintain focus, and builds self-control in situations where he's likely to become excited and aroused. In addition to the obedience commands, it will be necessary for your dog to have a working knowledge of commands like "drop it", which will allow you to re-gain control of the toy. These commands should be taught in advance of actually playing the game. Do NOT allow children to engage the dog in these games until the dog is VERY good on all counts... and NEVER allow it if the dog has ever aggressed toward children! [Rushman, Brenda, personal communication]

Step #1. Keep the dog's arousal level at a nonproblematic level. Be careful. Be safe.

Step #2. Avoid "hot" items or behaviors, concentrating on exercises that do not set the dog off. Be careful.

Step #3. Have a helper hold the leash which you will have attached to a Gentle Leader that the dog will be wearing. If you are alone you can have the leash tied to something so that you can escape if needed.

Step #4. Keep the fun and games interactions with the dog to a minimum when not performing the exercises so that the continued fun with you has more value. Preferably this should follow a reversal of social polarity program. Refer to section on treating control complex aggression for details.

Step #5. Start playing tug of war (if this is a viable choice for the exercises for you and your dog). You must remain in control of the game. Tug-of-war should only be played with one specific toy, which is reserved for this purpose, and this toy should be put away when you're not playing. He must drop it when told. He must not take the toy until he is told to, and above all else he cannot touch human skin or clothing. Keep it fun and continuous. Keep arousal levels manageable and use lots of obedience breaks. The second he touches skin or clothing say "OUCH" as if it hurt very much, even if it was light, immediately get up and walk away with the toy if you have it, but without it if it will slow you down to get it. After a few minutes, reenter, request a sit and perhaps a few other obedience exercises, and resume play as reinforcement for obedience. Repeat through many sessions, being consistent with the feedback. If any part of this provokes real aggression or it is not diminishing the strength and frequency of the bite, discontinue the process and seek the advice of a professional.

Step #6. The same process and concerns apply to hand feeding. In the beginning stages, again, use small pieces of food in your palm, held in the folds of your palm. As the exercises progress, put a small (pea sized or smaller) piece of treat between your index finger and thumb with little sticking out. Present the treat. If he is gentle, let go of the food and perhaps tell him how good he is, and drop a couple of pieces at his feet. If he is snatchy or bites skin without much concern for you, say "OUCH", do not let go of the treat if you can manage that, stand up and walk out on him. Try to perform all of these exercises in a room without his bed, crate or toys so it is a boring room except for your presence. Use a baby gate that you can step over when you leave or just close the door behind you. Give him a few minutes to appreciate the contrast between your fun presence and your boring absence, then return, request some obedience and try again. Repeat through several sessions.

Step #7. Continue these exercises on an ongoing basis.

Remember with these hard biters that if you do not feel comfortable doing these exercises do not do them. It has been argued [Lindsay] that hard biters may be that way for physiological or anatomical reasons at least in part. It can be difficult to soften a hard mouth, so if you cannot do it safely then do not attempt it.

Nonconfrontational Compliance Training

Verbal control will be vitally important for any dog with aggressive tendencies. Verbal control will not just give you a way to prevent or stop a tragic event, but also the opportunity to more easily desensitize the dog to trigger stimuli and teach the dog proper replacement behaviors.

I strongly suggest clicker training. If you are not using a clicker then you are simply not communicating as effectively with your dog as you could be. The clicker is more clear, concise and unique than words or tossing of treats. A clicker is a small device that makes a click-click sound when squeezed. Initially the click sound has no meaning to the dog. It is a neutral stimulus. Via classical conditioning we pair the two stimuli (click and reinforcement) until the click sound stimulates a response that is very similar to the response the dog would experience when receiving the actual reinforcer. The treat for example, would be the unconditioned reinforcer, and once the association is made, the click would be the conditioned reinforcer. So once they are associated in the dog's mind, he will hear the click and immediately feel reinforced even though he has not received the treat yet. The click communicates to the dog "that right there, what you just did when you heard the click, is exactly what I like, want more of, what just won you a treat and will win you more treats in the future!!". Many behaviors happen so fast or beyond your reach the clicker gives you a way of marking these behaviors in a very concise way! You could simply say "yes", but you will ruin the word in every day language (it will be de-valued, because you'll often say it without any meaning for the dog), so the association fails, it will be different depending on who says the word and you cannot possibly be as concise with a word as you can with the split second click. So, get yourself a clicker and a clicker book. A nice one is The Clicker Workbook A Beginner's Guide by Deborah Jones, Ph.D.. It's a nice concise book and not very expensive. You can purchase these at www.dog-wise.com. www.SitStay.com sells clickers. You will not have to have a clicker with you for the rest of your life. The clicker is used to build new behaviors, or "brush up" on existing behaviors, and is not required forever. Once a behavior is well conditioned you will be able to reward on a schedule without the clicker. There are now even electronic clickers so that if you are in a group class each clicker will be on a different frequency so that their is no confusion. The only problem, is that by buying this product, you support the manufacturer who makes shock collars.

Charging the Clicker

To get your clicker 'charged' or 'loaded', meaning to create the conditioned response to the clicker, you will simply pair the two repeatedly. The simplest way to charge the clicker is just to click and treat (c/t) and repeat several times in a row. The treat must follow the click within 3 seconds. Try to make sure the dog is not doing anything you do not like when you click and treat. Remember that the treat must always follow the click. Never click and then fail to deliver a treat. If your timing is off on one or two trials that is okay. You will simply shape the behavior away from that but do not degrade the charge on the clicker by failing to follow up with the treat. You will know it is charged when you click and the dog shows any behaviors or facial expressions that show he is excited about getting his treat. At first especially, use treats that the dog really loves. Little bits of fried liver is often a good one. One of my dog's favorites is chicken hot dogs chopped up and microwaved so they are not slimy. My dog will also work for Cheerios which is better for him. Please remember that the value of the reward lies with the dog, and is relative; each reward will hold different values in different contexts. The treats should be pea sized or smaller. If he is spending time chewing it will ruin the flow of training and he will get full fast. Later you can have a little bag with both Cheerios and the really yummy treats. You will use the Cheerios for the not bad ones and the super yummiest for the exceptional ones. And, combining (for example) Cheerios with hot dog in the same bag will give you hot-dog-flavored Cheerios; another favorite! This will help you "shape" better responses.

The Behaviors

The three most important behaviors that you will need when dealing with an aggressive dog are "sit", "look" and "leave it". Each will be explained briefly below. A private lesson with a clicker trainer would help get you started.

Look

Start with a set time frame for training. 10 - 15 minutes is a good time frame. Once you get behaviors solid you can start using them in retraining your aggressive dog. Also start training in a very low distraction room.

Look means to make eye contact and not break it until you are released with either the click or with a release cue such as saying okay and throwing your hands into the air. Eye contact will help you in a few very important ways. First it will open the lines of communication. You cannot communicate with your dog if he is not paying attention to you, or if he's afraid to look at you. You need your dog's attention. Next, it allows you to redirect his attention from something else. If he stares focused intensely on another dog, for example, he will develop tunnel vision and his arousal level will rise until it climaxes into an explosion. Eye contact will allow you to keep the dog's attention on you. You may put a verbal cue on this, but we want this as a default behavior primarily. That means that you do not have to actively request it, that the dog will choose voluntarily to make eye contact with you all the time. You get this to happen by making it really worth his while. Here is how.

First smile. Always smile when working your dog. Take a treat and hold it out to the side as far as you can. The dog will look at the treat. Your job is to be patient and wait. Do nothing with your face or voice to get the dog to look at you. I know it's tempting but resist that urge. He will eventually look at you, even if just very briefly while he wonders what is going on. The split second he looks at you c/t. Timing is vital here. Think of clicking the clicker like the shutter on a camera. The thing he is doing at the exact split second you click is what is reinforced. Not what he was about to do or what he did before the click, but what he was doing just then. It is not easy to click at the exact right moment when he glances at you but get it as close as humanly possible. Repeat several times.

If you are having a hard time getting this glance you can try the intermediate level. First start clicking for him looking away from the treat. Repeat that several times. Once he is looking away from the treat more frequently or quicker move onto the next level. Expect him to look at you. It should go smoothly from there with that intermediate step.

The next level once the dog is making eye contact even very briefly is to expect just a little more. Now wait for the committed look. That means he is now willing to make eye contact but he will have to make eye contact for an extended duration now. He will look at you and then wonder why he was not clicked so he will look back at the treat. Wait for him to make eye contact and maintain it for three seconds. In a committed look he will probably briefly hold his breath and close his mouth. When you get your first committed eye contact, click and jackpot that. A *jackpot!* is when he makes a major breakthrough and you dump seven treats at his feet so they spread out a bit (or hand him several treats individually in a row rapidly), rather than handing him one treat. Now repeat the exercises several times through several sessions.

Start varying the direction you hold the treat in so that he does not develop any funny ideas that you must have your right arm out to the right in order for this to work.

Next start gradually introducing distractions. To do this have another person in the room or another dog (Do not use anything that has proven as a trigger in the past; it's entirely too soon for that!). Try to make it gradual so you set him up for success. When he makes eye contact, c/t. Continue to increase the duration and distraction levels gradually. Introduce distraction and duration separately, and relax one of those while starting the other. More on this below.

Try to start recognizing when your dog offers eye contact voluntarily, and reinforce that. You may also start finding that it is so reinforced and calming that he will start making eye contact when he becomes concerned or stressed. If he makes eye contact, and is also acting calm and relaxed, then jackpot those moments. That is exactly what you want. You want the behaviors offered voluntarily as a coping strategy or replacement behavior for various unacceptable behaviors.

Sit

Sit means when cued, immediately put your rear end on the ground while your front end remains upright, and stay right there until you are released. It's important to have a full definition, so that you know what your goal is. Here is how you do it.

Have a treat in your hand between your thumb and fingers. Present the treat for your dog to sniff and target. Keep your hand palm side up. Once the dog is targeting the treat move your hand up and out, between his eyes and toward his tail, while he continues to target the treat. As he looks up and back his rear end should hit the ground. The second it does, c/t. If he jumps up it is probably because you raised the treat too high. Keep the treat very close to his nose for the entire process, to avoid this. If he continues to simply shuffle backwards, try doing the exercises in a corner or against a wall so he cannot, as long as being cornered will not attack his sensitivities (make him feel uncomfortable). Repeat 3 times. This time show the dog that you have nothing in your hand. Keep the food in your clicker hand behind your back or in a treat pouch. Now lure the dog into the sit, using the hand that previously held the treat. When he sits, click and jackpot. Drop several treats at his feet. When you get a breakthrough such as this, reward it more heavily. Repeat a few more times with treats in hand and then one or two with no treats in your hands. Start 'fading' the lure now. By "fading the lure", I mean making the motion less and less like the original motion, and more like what will ultimately be the hand signal. The hand signal will look like this: hand out, elbow bent 45 degrees, palm up. Motion hand up toward shoulder. Gradually make the lure look more like the hand signal. Once things are going smoothly and consistently, put the delivery of the treats on a variable schedule. Don't give a treat every time. Keep him hoping for the treats and also keep him guessing. You do not want to give so few that he gives up trying but you want to avoid giving too many treats also. Try to c/t the excellent ones; the ones that are quick and enthusiastic. If you are choosy about which ones you reinforce and which ones you fail to reinforce, you will shape a better response. Ping-pong the reinforcements to keep him guessing. Avoid reinforcing say every third or fourth one. Reinforce a few in a row sometimes and then others expect several sits before he gets a treat. Dogs are capable of detecting a pattern even if you do not realize you have one, so be clever. Keep the hope alive.

I suggest that you keep the hand signal. The problem with verbal cues is that many owners tend to repeat the command if it is not responded to, which is not a good idea (refer to section Learned Irrelevance) and many owners become more demanding and threatening each time they have to repeat the cue. This is attacking a social or noise sensitivity, and many people do not recognize this. This can be avoided by simply using the hand signal only. This will also encourage your dog to keep an eye on you. Remember though, up until this point there has not been any verbal cue. Don't use a cue until you're sure that the behavior is the way you want it; attaching a cue to a behavior means that "this word will ALWAYS mean this behavior". So, make sure that what you're seeing is REALLY what you want! If you want the behavior quicker or more accurate continue to shape the behavior before you put the verbal cue on it. You don't start with a verbal cue; you end with it. If you want to put a verbal cue on it here is what you do next: once the behavior is smooth and consistent on hand signal give the cue then deliver the hand signal and c/t the dog when he sits. Repeat this several times through several sessions. Then test it. Say "sit" and wait. If the dog sits, jackpot him. If not go back and do the initial sequence several more times before you try again. Do no repeat the cue, or you will simply train the dog to either ignore the cue altogether or to wait for x number of cue deliveries to respond. In other words, the cue will no longer be "sit", but "sit, sit, Sit SIT!!". You don't want to get into that trap. If he does not perform the behavior just perform a No Change Response© discussed below. Do not overlap the cues either. You deliver the verbal cue, and then you initiate the hand signal. If you do them at the same time, or if they overlap at all, the hand signal will simply overshadow the verbal cue because dogs are more visual, and this will make it difficult if possible at all to get the verbal cue established.

Once the behavior is smooth and reliable and you are sure he knows the cue well you can start proofing it. That means increasing *distraction* levels. You can do this by very gradually taking the sit into other rooms which are more distracting and eventually 'taking it on the road' as Jean Donaldson puts it.

When you train a new element of the behavior, drop back your expectations for other elements. For example, you can start working on *duration* now. That means bring distraction back to very low levels. To work on increasing duration, simply wait for a very short period of time after he sits before you c/t. Build it up gradually but don't forget to ping pong it. Throw in easy ones frequently. Request the sit and count to three silently. If he is still sitting c/t. Next time expect 4 seconds. Next time throw in a 1 second. Then wait for 7 seconds. It must be variable. Keep building the duration up gradually. Try to use DRE (differential reinforcement of excellent behaviors) also and really encourage the great ones. The occasional jackpot for exceptional service helps keep the dog motivated.

The next element is *distance*. To do this, relax distraction and duration temporarily. Request the sit, and when the dog sits, take one step back and then forward again. If the dog is still sitting, c/t. Repeat several times. Next, take two steps back and then forward. Then try one step to the side. Then one step to the other side. Work your way up gradually to further distances. Some goals could be to be able to walk around the dog once or to walk briefly out of sight. Once this is going smoothly, add in duration and stay out of view for increasing duration before returning. Then start adding distraction also. Do all of this gradually; keep them guessing and set them up for success. If they are failing a lot then you are going too quickly. Back up and go more slowly.

When you are at a level where the dog should understand what you are requesting but fails to perform the behavior, perform a No Change Response NCR© [Chuck Tomkins, Behavior International, Using the No Change

Response©]. You have been animated, fun and reinforcing generally, so when he fails to comply you will not be providing the fun stuff. When he fails to comply, do not make eye contact and do not say anything. Stand still and offer nothing to the event; no punishment and no reinforcement; nothing. Count to four in your head, and then re-request the behavior. The NCR© will take on meaning to the dog after a while. It will come to mean that he did the wrong thing, and will get nothing from you for it. This will be more effective than corrections or punishment, and just about anything else you do will be taken as reinforcement, so do nothing. If you get more than two NCRs© in a row, this indicates that you are moving too quickly or that the session is degrading for some other reason. In this case, request a few behaviors that you know he knows and will comply with, and then end the session on a positive note.

Leave it

Leave it means to ignore and walk away from whatever you are presently focused on.

Start walking on leash with the dog. Toss a treat or toy out to the side so you have to walk past it, or make sure something was placed there ahead of time. The dog will probably strain on leash to get at the treat or toy. Continue walking as if it is not happening. The second the dog gives up on trying to get it, c/t. This will no doubt be at the point at which you are so far from it he can barely see it. That is okay. As you repeat this process over and over, you will find that he gives up on the object at less and less distance. Continue to c/t for leaving it. At some point you will find that the dog gives up on the object immediately upon being given a choice. That is excellent. The dog is really getting it. He is learning that he will not get everything he wants directly, but that if he looks to you or gives up on it, it will probably be worth his while. Initially the dog struggles on leash to get the treats. You will probably find that a slight tug (not a correction by any stretch of the imagination) becomes a cue for him to leave it. This will come in handy also as you will inevitably want him to leave something and you do not want to add anything to the event. So, when you simply keep walking, the action of the leash tightening will act as a cue to leave it alone and look to you for reinforcement, which you will give. This is exactly the kind of choice you want him to make. I'd like to thank Chris Bach and Angelica Steinker M.Ed, Dip.C.B. (who both independently discovered it) for that little tidbit.

Once this is smooth and reliable, start increasing distractions. That means instead of the treats use a favorite toy or another person or another dog. Once this is smooth and reliable, take it on the road and gradually increase distractions. As with the other foundational training behaviors, work this to a very high level of distraction. As with "sit", put the reinforcement on a schedule and heavily reinforce for the really good ones, especially.

To put a verbal cue on this, deliver the verbal cue, present the choice, and when they choose to leave it, c/t. Repeat several times through several sessions, and you should be able to make "leave it" mean "walk away from it". This would come in handy for when the dog is off leash. But, of course, if you have an aggressive dog, there will not be many times he will be, except in his own securely-fenced yard. However, it will give you a cue to help redirect his focus when he becomes aroused.

Teaching Impulse Control

Teaching a dog impulse control comes with many of the exercises in the foundational program, but there are some exercises you can do to specifically teach impulse control.

For dogs that are easily aroused, speak slowly and calmly while moving in a relaxed and slow manner. These dogs are unlikely to be in a frame of mind to think clearly and relax, if you speak in an animated and excited manner. They are highly aroused or arousable, so you do not want to amplify that with tightening leashes or yelling commands.

Use the sit command to teach impulse control. Start with low levels of distraction, and teach the dog to sit. Increase the duration of the sit randomly but gradually longer and longer. Then, take a step back in duration, and start adding a bit of distraction gradually, always setting the dog up for success. Request the sit before he becomes aggressive or highly aroused, rather than after, so that you have a fighting chance of showing him that he can indeed sit and calm himself down. Use eye contact with the sit. The sit position is perfect because it is a non-reactive position, but he is less likely to feel vulnerable than if he were required to maintain a down position. Once you have achieved success with this to the point where you are using it to help calm your dog down in potentially volatile situations, you will have to observe your dog carefully. You want to request the sit before he becomes too aroused. This means you have to watch his ears, his tail, his breathing, his glare, his hackles and everything else about how he expresses his growing arousal level. Request him to control his impulses with a sit before he reaches a sensitized state of mind. Start the whole process in a very unchallenging environment, and work your way up.

Train, don't restrain. This is why clicker training is so great. You can free-shape behaviors, and avoid any physical contact by successively reinforcing closer and closer approximations to the (terminal) behavior you want to see.

Train behaviors that promote impulse control. Commands like "wait" and "stay" teach a dog to control himself. Training with an emphasis on duration and distraction will promote a sense of performing even when he would rather do something else at that time. Start in low-distraction environments and work your way up at a pace that will ensure the dog's success.

Play

Play provokes incompatible emotional responses to aggression. Play is a major source of affiliative bonding for dogs. Through play, dogs learn how to relate to others with other options. Play can also build appropriate confidence. Play promotes joy, and emotional / behavioral flexibility. Make play constructive and structured. Use play breaks as reinforcement for compliance training. If your dog loves his throw toy or a tug toy, then use a brief toss or tug as reward following a click for an excellent behavior.

If you are dealing with a possessiveness problem, please avoid playing with toys that might provoke a problem. If predatory issues seem to be at work, avoid having the dog chase you. If arousal is a big issue with your dog, keep things calm but still fun.

If your dog is difficult to predict and seems to be experiencing control-related frustrative arousal, play can be very dangerous. "Initiating play with dominant-aggressive [read control complex aggressive] dog with a history of serious attacks is potentially very dangerous. Such activities are only slowly and carefully introduced after significant behavior modification has taken place to reduce the risk. Dominant-aggressive [read control complex aggressive] dogs often exhibit a striking lack of interest in play and may resent playful initiatives and respond aggressively if prompted to play." [Lindsay,vol2,253] Play should only be initiated gradually (and sometimes not at all) following a change in social polarity in control related dogs. Refer to control complex treatment exercises below.

Hand Feeding

Hand-feeding is a good idea even if your dog does not have specific issues surrounding his food or food bowl. Hand-feeding is meant to teach your dog that hands are good things, not bad, and that you, the hand-feeder, are a source of good things, which strengthens the bond between you and the dog. Start hand-feeding without a bowl. Simply request a sit as part of the NILIF program and when he does allow him to eat a handful of food from your hand. If he has issues with his food bowl, you will need to gradually desensitize him to your presence near the bowl. Refer to treatment for possessive aggression, below.

Smile

If you train your dog to see a human smile as a high level predictor of good things, you can use it, particularly when faced with a scary stranger. In that case, you can smile and suggest that your stranger (be it a set up with a friend or an actual stranger) smile also. This can get you over the initial leeriness hump. To train this, simply smile before delivering good things repeatedly, until the dog is visibly pleased to see a smile. You should help the dog to generalize the lesson by having others perform this training also. Then when faced with training exercises, you can use the smile to offer the dog a competing emotional response.

Nutritional Intervention

Nutrition can have significant effects on the behavior of your dog. If you are feeding a low quality food to your dog, chances are good that he is getting inadequate nutrition. By-products and cereal fillers are bad enough, but some chemical preservatives, colorings and chemicals that are used to keep food moist may be potential problems. Many dogs react negatively to these ingredients and this can manifest in behavior problems. The lower quality food also make use of a lot of corn, in many cases, which decreases the level of serotonin in the brain. "A common protein source in dog food is corn. Corn, however, is unusually low in tryptophan and may represent some risk to animals sensitive to serotonergic underactivity." [Lindsay,vol1,100] The follow diets are suggested by this author:

Canidae www.canidae.com

Innova www.naturapet.com/display.asp?ch=2&pg=0

California Natural www.naturapet.com/display.asp?ch=3&pg=0

Nutrience www.rchagen.com/canada/english/dogs/nutrience.html

The benefit of feeding a better quality food is that they are usually more energy dense, and hence you feed less of it, but that the dog gets the same number of calories. For example, Innova Dog Food contains 557 calories per cup. That is compared to the usual 350 to 400 in most lower quality diets. The dog on the lower-quality diet requires nearly 1 1/2 times more food than the dog who eats Innova. The dog will also produce less feces since more of the food is being digested. On top of that, the dog eating the higher-quality food will be healthier, which means that you'll visit the vet's office less often, and purchase fewer over-the-counter remedies..

"Dietary intake of the amino acids tryptophan and tyrosine, and other large neutral amino acids, significantly influences the biosynthesis and concentration of a group of neurotransmitters - serotonin, noradrenalin [otherwise known as norepinephrine (NE)] and dopamine - which are collectively known as the Monoamines." [Strong, The Dog's Dinner, 19] Noradrenalin is responsible for inducing high arousal which leads to aggression, dopamine is responsible for attention and reactivity and serotonin is responsible for controlling mood, arousal levels, sensitivity to pain and is thought to be one of the key elements, when deficient in the brain, responsible for impulsivity, aggression, anti-social behavior, attention disorder, hyperactive disorder, anxiety and conditioning problems. [Strong,The Dog's Dinner,19] Dogs that are found to be deficient in serotonin in the brain are extra sensitive to pain, overly reactive, emotional and aggressive.

Individual amino acids which form the precursors for these monoamines compete for reuptake from the blood into the brain. If the balance is off, or if a deficiency occurs, the effect will be an imbalance in brain chemistry. "The brain's production of serotonin depends on nutritionally derived tryptophan. Tryptophan, like other precursor amino acids used in the manufacture of neurotransmitters, reaches the brain by passing through the blood-brain barrier." [Lindsay,vol1,99] It is at the blood-brain barrier that these precursors compete to enter the brain. This is because there are limited pathways for this transport. Dietary tryptophan is the precursor for serotonin while tyrosine is the precursor for norepinephrine and dopamine. Dietary tyrosine acts as a sort of anti-tryptophan, and hence an anti-serotonin. It is therefore very important to insure that excess tyrosine is avoided and sufficient tryptophan is provided. Protein sources generally have a higher ratio of tryptophan to tyrosine than do carbohydrate sources. In many cases a switch to a lower protein diet has resulted in dramatic behavioral changes for the better. "... diets rich in protein tend to deplete brain tryptophan levels." [Lindsay,vol1,99] "... diets high in carbohydrates actually increase available tryptophan for serotonin synthesis, even if the food itself contains only modest amounts of tryptophan." [Lindsay] The question remains as to why a carbohydrate rich diet affects serotonin levels in the brain so significantly given that there is not more tryptophan in carbohydrates than protein. In The Handbook of Applied Dog Behavior and Training, Steven Lindsay explains that insulin production when carbohydrates are present affect other amino acid precursors such that tryptophan wins a competitive advantage in transport through the blood-brain barrier. "(1) Naturally occurring tryptophan represents only a small proportion of various amino acids making up protein (approximately 1% to 1.6%). The other larger and more prevalent amino acids all compete with tryptophan for a limited number of transport channels passing through the blood-brain barrier. The result of the foregoing biochemical scenario is that tryptophan is blocked out and the brain may be quickly depleted of available stores of the amino acid needed for the steady production of serotonin. (2) A more complicated metabolic process is needed to explain how a high-carbohydrate diet raises brain levels of tryptophan. Diets containing a proportionately higher level of carbohydrates than protein (at least 1 part protein to 5 to 6 parts carbohydrate) stimulates the secretion of insulin. An important effect of insulin production is it's diversion of large neutral amino acids (other than tryptophan) into muscle tissue. Because of it's unique molecular structure differentiating it from other amino acids, tryptophan is not similarly affected by the secretion of insulin. The outcome is that the proportion of plasma tryptophan is greatly increased, thus obtaining an advantage over other amino acids competing for transport through the blood-brain barrier. As a result, the brain's production of serotonin is significantly increased." [Lindsay,vol1,99]

In case you come across results from a study by Dodman and coworkers (1996) [http://www.sonic.net/~cdlcruz/gpcc/library/protein.htm], as I did in researching this topic, their results may not discredit the theory presented above as much as it purports to. In that study the only form of aggression affected positively by a reduced protein diet was territorial aggression with strong fearful component. The study is criticized (Lindsay,vol1,100) for not maintaining sufficiently low levels of protein in the study diet, Carbohydrate levels may not have been maintained at a high enough level and the dogs may not have been exposed to the diet long enough to affect positive change. A more recent study published in the JAVMA, Vol 217, No 4, on August 15, 200 titled "Effect of Dietary Protein Content and Tryptophan Supplementation on Dominance Aggression, Territorial Aggression, and Hyperactivity" by DeNapoli, Dodman, Shuster, Rand and Gross showed that reduced protein does indeed tend to significantly reduce aggression, but only insignificantly reduced hyperactivity. Reduced protein with tryptophan supplementation more significantly reduced aggression.

Here is the rub, though, which may suggest a more efficient intervention. "However, brain tryptophan can only be significantly raised by carbohydrate intake if the carbohydrate meal is given within two to three hours of protein ingestion. Insulin is secreted in response to carbohydrate ingestion, to regulate plasma glucose levels. Insulin also diverts other large neutral amino acids to peripheral skeletal tissues where they are involved in energetic and immune system pathways." [Strong,The Dog's Dinner,20] Also, Vitamin B6 is a co-factor for tryptophan synthesis into serotonin so this should be manipulated in a nutritional intervention.

This all boils down to the following intervention procedure for aggressive dogs:

Step #1. Take 10 days to switch to a high quality diet if the dog is not on one presently. Look for independent information on this. Do not ask the pet shop employee; they all have house brands to push and they generally know very little about nutrition. Try to focus on rice, oats, potato or barley as a carbohydrate source rather than corn which may have high levels of tyrosine. Start with 90% of the old diet and 10% of the new. Increase the percentage of the new diet by 10% each day until the dog is on 100% of the new diet. This will prevent stomach upset and diarrhea.

Step #2. Reduce the kibble meal to make room for a smaller pure carbohydrate meal.

Step #3. Within 2 hours after the kibble diet offer a smaller pure carbohydrate meal. You may have to experiment to see what will be accepted. Examples of sources can include potatoes, sweet potatoes, barley, brown rice, carrots. Include a B complex vitamin or specifically a vitamin B6 at 1 mg./kg body weight/day in the carbohydrate meal.

Signs of improvement may appear within 1 - 10 days. [Strong,The Dog's Dinner,19] Continue this regime until significant improvement in behavior through all forms of behavior modification interventions. At that point you may experiment with offering a lower protein kibble, rather than offering the separate meal. If you switch to a "light" diet for this purpose do not switch to one with a fiber content higher than 6% at the max, but preferably 5%. If your dog will not accept the carbohydrate meal you may try simply adding the carbohydrates mixed with the kibble, or if that is not working try to find a diet with as low a protein source as possible.

Mental Enrichment

By engaging your dog's mind in active focused enjoyment of something, you promote activation of the cerebral cortex, which as was discussed, inhibits the limbic system from activating problematic emotions. "A dog or person who is focused on a task is not easily overwhelmed by powerful emotions. In fact, they may tune out stimuli not relevant to the task. This is why even dogs that loathe each other are often able to work peacefully side by side - their focus is not on their emotional responses to each other but on their task. (of course, in their leisure hours...)" [Clothier,27]

What follows are some ideas for how to increase mental stimulation in your dog.

#1. Feed meals in a Buster Cube or similar puzzle ball. This will allow the dog to work at getting his food.

#2. Put some portion of meals hidden around the house in small piles. This will encourage him to forage.

#3. Training. This can be toward obedience or a canine sport such as agility, flyball, freestyle etc. As long as the dog enjoys the training it will help him exercise his mental power. Make it challenging but still lots of fun. I highly recommend clicker training, in all training venues.

#4. Road trips. Visiting new places for a hike or some other activity can be stimulating for most dogs. This is a very good source of mental stimulation.

#5. Free Shaping and clicker training. Refer to a good book on clicker training. Games such as 101 things to do with a box and other free shaping training engages your dog's mind and actively encourage thinking. Dogs who are free shaped think more and are less impulsive. Free shaping is so great because there are no coercive or aversive stimuli. The dog thinks to get the rewards. Clicker training "keeps your dog on his toes", mentally. This method teaches your dog to THINK, and a by-product of this training is that it allows you to gradually increase the amounts of stress that the dog can handle, emotionally. Each time that you withhold the click for a behavior (in free-shaping), you're adding very small amounts of stress to the situation. Small amounts of stress are quite beneficial to learning, and help your dog to learn valuable coping skills.

Exercise

A tired dog is a good dog. You have no doubt heard this quite a bit. It turns out that there is a sound physiological basis for this statement. Research indicates that physical stimulation exerts a significant, therapeutic influence on the physiology of the dog. [Lindsay,vol1,112] Exercise stimulates the production of serotonin, NE and certain endorphins which account for the positive mood-altering effect of physical stimulation. "In addition to the release of various HPA [hypothalamic-pituitary-adrenocortical] system hormones (beta-endorphins, ACTH [adrenocorticotropic hormone], and cortisol), exercise also increases the production of NE." [Lindsay.vol1,113] Physical stimulation that is short and explosive in nature may have a distressing influence on the body, whereas more moderate and longer duration physical stimulation is what they call eustressing, and produces the noted beneficial effects. "Although acute and forced treadmill exercise appears to deplete NE stores in the brain (as observed in learned helplessness), and is physiologically stressful for animals, chronic exercise appears to enhance noradrenergic activity and increases the amount of NE stored in several parts of the brain. Besides enhancing noradrenergic activity, exercise was also found to increase serotonin levels in the central amygdala." [Lindsay,vol1,113] It would seem that there is a physiological basis for the suggested use of chronic physical stimulation is cases involving any form of stress, anxiety, reactivity or aggression. Lindsay describes it's use this way: "The finding that exercise enhances serotonergic activity is of considerable importance with respect to the use of exercise for the management of stress-related behavior problems. Within the brain's neuroeconomy, serotonin plays an important modulatory role over stress and the control of undesirable impulsive behavior. Promising evidence in support of a functional link between serotonin production and exercise has been reported by Dey and his associates (1992), who demonstrated a significant alteration of central serotonergic activity in rats exposed to chronic exercise. Daily exercise was found to generate pronounced and sustained enhancement of serotonin metabolism in various areas of the brain, including the cerebral cortex. The authors suggest that the cortex is the most likely neural site mediating the beneficial effects of exercise over depression. ... The aforementioned studies support the hypothesis that exercise, especially daily and long-term exercise, has potentially beneficial effects on the neuroeconomy of the dog." [Lindsay,vol1,113] "In general, the response of serotonin receptor subtypes to exercise was very similar to the effects produced by tricyclic antidepressants." [Lindsay,vol1,113]

Dogs are much like humans. Some are in good physical shape and others are not. If your dog has not been leading a physically active life, you will have to gradually increase physical stimulation over a period of weeks. Avoid starting a heavy physical exercise program all at once. This will likely stress your dog out and potentially lead to injury or illness. Carefully assess the amount of exercise that your dog has been getting. Having access to 20 acres of property for 9 hours per day does not necessarily mean your dog has been getting any exercise at all. If he lays at the back door or in a dog house for the whole time, then he is getting no exercise. If on the other hand he runs around the yard for a total of a couple hours each day then he may be getting an adequate amount of exercise. You cannot answer the question of what is adequate without assessing the exercise requirements of the breed and the age of the dog. Dogs under 1 year of age require lots of exercise but should avoid any form of exercise that is jarring on the joints, especially large breed dogs. Certain breeds such as Siberian Huskies and Border Collies were bred to require extreme amounts of physical stimulation. Generally speaking, sled dogs, herding dogs and sporting dogs require hours of physical stimulation each day. Certain sight hounds such as the grey hound are not very active generally but they have spurts of energy when they will run around a yard as fast as they can with sod flying in the air as they whiz past you. This is natural for them. Other breeds such as the English Bulldog are difficult to motivate, and if given the chance, would choose to lay on the couch all day. This is natural for them. Speaking of the Bulldog it is important to note that brachycephalic (short muzzled) dogs can have difficulty breathing when exerting themselves. It is especially important to be extra careful with the introduction of physical stimulation in these breeds. Don't forget to do warm ups and cool downs with your dog before an exercise session. The bottom line is this: do research on your breed regarding any special circumstances regarding physical stimulation. Then visit your veterinarian for a full examination. Get the veterinarian's okay before you start an exercise program. Then gradually, physically condition the dog for a breed and context-specific amount of daily exercise. Expect to have to maintain exercise for several weeks before sustained behavioral effects can be expected.

Regarding choices of exercise programs, you should choose one that closely relates to what the breed was designed to do. It would be ideal if water dogs could swim, herding dogs could herd etc., but this may not be viable. Swimming for most breeds and especially the water dogs is probably the safest and most beneficial exercise that a dog can perform. It saves the joints the jarring impact that other forms of exercise can cause. Be careful with heavy fronted dogs such as Boxers; they do not swim well as their front end tends to sink. They also have less fat than most breeds so they have to work harder to stay afloat. If you have purchased a dog who requires more physical stimulation than you are able to keep up with, then retrieve games are a solution. You can remain motionless and throw a Frizbee, Cool Kong, tennis ball or what ever else is safe for the dog. Not all dogs take to fetch games immediately. You may have to hide the toy when not playing to make it more valuable. You may have to use two balls to get one back, and then throw the other. You may have to refer to a good training book or consult a trainer to train the dog to fetch. A good article can be found at http://www.dogscouts.com/retrieve.shtml on this topic. By the way, even long walks are not adequate for almost all dogs. Dogs need to at least trot to get proper exercise. Walking even for long distances is not usually sufficient except for some breeds or for when you are just starting to condition the dog for exercise. Jogging and cycling are other choices. You must be careful that your dog does not trip you or run under bicycle wheels. Another option is canine sports. Agility is probably the most valuable canine sport as you work closely with the dog at something physically and mentally stimulating. Flyball is another choice, as is musical freestyle. These are all options. The bottom line is to meet your dog's physical stimulation requirements in a safe manner.

Designing a Treatment Plan

Applying Learning Theory to Trigger Stimuli

Various learning principles can be used in the design of a treatment protocol. Generally speaking, classical conditioning techniques are used to affect the reflexive elements of emotional responses, while operant conditioning techniques are used to affect voluntary behaviors. Since most behavior is a complex amalgam of emotional responses and voluntary behavior, it seems reasonable that both forms of learning will take place simultaneously and hence both kinds of techniques should be taken advantage of. Generally, the more fear is involved the more classical conditioning is required, and the more frustration or anger is involved the more operant conditioning is required. But, of course the usual course of action will involve an interplay between both sets of techniques. As discussed previously, if you focus on operant conditioning you will promote active thinking in the dog, and classical conditioning will occur as a by-product of positive reinforcement based operant conditioning.

How to Put Operant and Classical Conditioning to Work

We have reviewed both operant conditioning processes and classical conditioning. Now it is time to decide how to put it all together and design both a general plan and specific treatment protocols. This section will help you do that.

All aggressive behavior is a complex amalgam of emotional responses and operant behaviors. Some forms of aggression are primarily based in fear, while others are primarily based in frustration, anger and impulsiveness. Think of it as a spectrum with fear on the one side, and frustration, anger and impulsiveness on the other. This is not to say some dogs do not have serious problems with both, but usually it can be determined to be on one side or the other.

As mentioned above the general rule is that the more fear based the problem is, the more classical conditioning will have to play a role in treatment, and the more impulsiveness, frustration or anger based the problem is, the more operant conditioning will have to play a role in treatment. The primary techniques of classical conditioning are systematic desensitization and counter conditioning. The primary techniques of operant conditioning are proofing and differential reinforcement. We discussed how operant conditioning should be focused on, since we want dogs to think and make wise choices, but we also need the fearful dog to have a modified emotional response. If your dog's problem is primarily fear based, you would be wise to start with systematic desensitization and counter conditioning. Once you have made a little progress with that, you should change your focus to operant conditioning. For anger based aggression you should start with operant conditioning right off the bat. Refer to the appropriate descriptions above for more details on how to design a program based in either paradigm. Basically the difference between proofing - differential reinforcement protocols and systematic desensitization - counter conditioning protocols is that with operant conditioning, you will train alternative behaviors prior to performing exercises, and then apply them to the trigger stimuli with gradually increasing intensity so that the dog does not actually trigger. With classical conditioning, you do not necessarily use an alternative behavior. Rather you gradually increase intensity so that the dog does not trigger, and pair the stimulus with good things. They look very much alike in practice except for the alternative behaviors, and in reality both forms of learning take place.

One of the most important guiding principles to setting up exercises is volunteerism. You must never force a dog into a fear eliciting stimulus. If you do, the dog will go "limbic" on you and will sensitize. He will learn nothing except that he cannot trust you, and that he will have to defend himself. Keep the dog cerebral (operant).

One of the first things you will have to do, is find a way to present either the stimulus or something that resembles the stimulus at the appropriate distance such that the dog is aware of it, but still operant. It helps to train before a meal or if you are using toys as reward, for you to deny the dog access to that toy for at least a few hours (if not days) before. You want the food or toys to be very valuable (salient), and if you allow free access to them you devalue them.

When performing operant conditioning techniques either sit with eye contact or heel with eye contact are the most commonly used alternative behaviors. I prefer to use toys for toy-motivated dogs; a tug-rope is an excellent choice for this, because it will allow you to keep the dog securely-leashed during the exercises (of course, if you do this, you'll need to forego the muzzle -- if your dog has done harm, it's NOT a safe alternative!) Don't forget to smile and act upbeat. Be happy. Breath normally. You must not convey anxiety to the dog. By using the Gentle Leader or other pieces of equipment you should be in a position to feel confident. Remember to reward heavily for the performance of the alternative behavior. I suggest that you use your clicker for this. Some people have too much to think about and cannot manage to use a clicker under this kind of stress. If you cannot maintain the attention of your dog and you are not sure you are using the clicker correctly, right then perhaps you should not use it, or better yet contact a clicker trainer and have them go through the basics with you. If on the other hand, you can manage it, then the clicker will help you communicate with your dog more effectively and it will give you something to focus on also. Apply the responses you have trained in your dog to the proofing procedure described previously.

When working a classical conditioning technique, follow the guidelines previously discussed, but be prepared to switch to operant conditioning on a moment's notice. It is your job to prevent full sensitized responses, but if you cannot, then you should try to avoid reinforcing the behavior. Immediately disengage from any aggressive responses. Get the dog out of there. The second that you choose when to present the good stuff and when not to present it, you are now performing differential reinforcement. In a way you are really always using operant conditioning, but just setting it up so that you never have the opportunity to fail to present good stuff. Whichever way you look at it do not allow a dog to remain in a sensitizing situation, and do not actively reward with treats or games aggressive behavior.

If the dog cannot manage to focus on you, then the distraction (or stress) level is too high. You need to slow down and take a few steps back. Work up more gradually. If he does respond, reinforce that immediately and heavily. Repeat through a few trials and then withdraw from the fear eliciting stimulus on a good note but end the fun there. Make contrast between the fun and games when he responds appropriately when the stimulus is presented, and the boringness of when the stimulus goes away. Do not fall into the common trap of reinforcing the dog AFTER he has met the stimulus and it has gone away. This may reinforce the removal of the stimulus. For example, if you have arranged for a stranger (the stimulus, let's say) to walk in the opposite direction as you on opposite sides of the street while you work with the dog, avoid reinforcing after the stranger has passed. Reinforce as the stranger approaches and then stop when the stranger is going away. This is particularly important if your dog has territorial issues, which are rewarded when people move away. Always reinforce the dog for appropriate behavior when the scary thing is approaching.

Repeat the process at increasing levels of intensity. As you progress, you should also attempt to achieve these exercises in various places and under various situations. Proofing involves reducing the discriminative stimuli. That means doing the exercises in many different contexts so that the dog does not get any funny ideas, like everything is okay as long as we are in the house, but out of the house is a whole other matter. The same can be true of being in the presence of various people. Try to allow the dog to generalize.

Once you are achieving success with this process, keep up the socialization and differential reinforcement program. Think of your efforts as a muscle. If you fail to exercise it, it will atrophy, but if you do exercise it, it will become stronger. Keep up the good work.

Common Behavior Modification Protocols by Classification

Fear Related Aggression

Step #1. Instate a prevention and management program that will allow you to avoid all sensitized responses. It is vital that you establish a safety history with this suspicious and scared dog. Establishing a safety history involves WORK -- train twice daily, using a clicker, and manage the HELL out of any situation that may prove to be stressful for your dog. Always provide for his safety and comfort, so that he looks to YOU for these things. Don't allow ANYTHING bad to happen, and make sure that he sees you providing for these things. If a stranger approaches, and your dog is afraid of strangers, TELL the stranger not to approach. Move between your dog and the scary thing, supplying a safety buffer. It's your responsibility to protect the public, but you also have a responsibility to provide for the physical and emotional well-being of your dog -- take it seriously, and you'll see immense improvements in your relationship. You will have to be creative and think ahead. Use the Gentle Leader for control just in case you make a mistake or things go wrong. Most fear related aggressive dogs give plenty of warning but if warning, has been punished and suppressed you may not get any. If the dog is an experienced one, he may not offer many warnings except avoidance-motivated preemptive attack. Know the trigger stimuli well and avoid them. Keep the safety buffer intact.

Step #2. Start nonconfrontational compliance training and the NILIF program. Really focus on confidence building, by providing the dog's life with structure. Recognize positive default behaviors and reward them. This way the dog may start using them as coping mechanisms, which help him regulate his own stress levels and perform alternative behaviors to active defensiveness. Recognize and reinforce these. Set aside 15 minute training sessions twice or three times daily if possible. Be upbeat and have fun. If the dog is generally risk-averse rather than fearful toward a specific stimulus, instate play which is not intimidating. It might take a bit of gentle coaxing. You may also instate other noncontrontational parts of the foundational program such as nutritional intervention, exercise and mental enrichment.

Step #3. Mouth softening. Unless in your case the risk seems too high, start softening the mouth and working on bite inhibition.

Step #4. Remedial socialization. Many fear-related aggression problems are the result of inadequate or improper socialization. Remedial socialization will involve getting the dog out into the world frequently. You may have to focus on nonbusy times and places at first, but build up gradually to more stimulating walks or hikes. Keep adequate distance from feared things, but avoid making it seem to the dog like you are responding fearfully toward it. You could use this opportunity to pop a treat into the dog's mouth every time he notices something that he might be scared of as he gets nearer to the object, and is remaining relaxed and calm. Repeated and positive exposure to many stimuli will go a long way.

Step #5. Once you are well on your way to improving the dog's confidence and establishing a safety history, you are ready to start instating more specific behavior modification techniques. Start by either proofing or systematically desensitizing and counter conditioning. Once you have made a bit of progress in changing the emotional response, which should not take more than a couple weeks in most cases (and I have seen some major progress in DAYS), you should start using the sit-eye contact or heel-eye contact behaviors as a replacement habitual response.

On-leash aggression is a common fear-related problem. Here are some ideas on how to handle it:

Most dogs do not, in fact, explode into aggression. Most go through a few levels of heightening states of arousal before they start lunging. Observe and take note of your dog's behavior. You must look closely. If you see the initial signs use this information and intervene early in the sequence rather than trying to fight with a lunging maniac. Once a dog triggers, there is nothing you can do, except remove him from the situation.

Either change directions and move away from the dog or person or cue a behavior such as sit, in an upbeat and happy manner. No tension in your voice. Be delighted, and smile. Breath and do not tense your muscles. The way to decide is if by having the dog sit the dog or person will approach so closely that you cannot prevent the aggressive behavior then redirect with a change in direction. Do it happily. Avoid acting urgent and tense.

If your dog becomes aroused and stands, walk away. The arousal makes it difficult for him to focus on you and indicates that you are pushing it. Offer mild praise, a smile and perhaps a petting for a good attitude.

ıat the leash stays loose. The best way to do that is to have the dog el.

: dog in question has not had stellar socialization with what he is lunging . big part of treatment will also include remedial socialization on top of proofing and habituation. Increase significantly the amount of sensitive and pleasurable contact the dog has with the target. This does NOT mean that you should allow your dog close contact with strangers and other dogs when he's fearful. It means that you should set up exercises involving feared objects (often stranger people and dogs) at a distance, so that your dog can build up a safety history around them. When I say increase I mean as much as possible. If the problem is strangers in general then perhaps spending a few hours every day in a mall parking lot at the far edge of the action would help. Get closer to the center of action every day. Tons of remedial socialization! Take it slow; this is not a flooding exercise but a habituation and learned irrelevance exercise.

Alternatively...

Identify your dog's trigger and comfort distance (safety buffer). Find a volunteer and run passes. You may have to start in a field, or on opposite sides of a street. If you have the room, each person will walk large circles in a clockwise direction such that you meet and pass at a certain point. Start by passing at a distance that you can still maintain your dog's attention and eye contact. You and your volunteer will perform these passes over and over, getting closer only as dictated by the tolerance of the dog. Each time you pass, try to encourage the attention of your dog to heel with eye contact. Use the obedience training you have worked so hard to instill in your dog. Praise good passes, and ignore tense ones. Try to achieve only good ones, though, by the distance you use. Be upbeat and happy. Alternatively, passes can be done by walking on opposite sides of the street, and getting closer with each pass and rewarding tolerance and ignoring intolerance. Over time you should be able to develop impulse control and habituation as well as a trained alternative behavior. Keep in mind that a large volume of training must occur to achieve success with this program. It may be necessary to re-a assess your commitment and ability to carry out the program.

An ingenious trick for retraining an on leash aggression problem was taught to me by Angelica Steinker, M.Ed., Dip.C.B. (www.courteouscanine.com). The rationale for this training exercise is that it can be very difficult to not tighten the leash. The trick is to train the dog that a tug on the leash is a cue to play a quick game of tug, or something else the dog enjoys. You could also train the dog to make eye contact when cued by a tightened leash. This is also the basis of "leave it" as discussed above. In either case train this by setting up several trials of tightening the leash under low distraction circumstances at first, and then following it immediately with either a quick game of tug or the cueing of eye contact. Then you can start proofing it in more distracting and potentially volatile situations. This is a very clever trick, especially if you are having a hard time not tightening the leash which most people, including trainers, do.

Control Complex

Step #1. Instate a prevention and management program that will allow you to avoid any reactive conflicts. Get a Gentle Leader on the dog. He will wear it at all times while he is supervised for at least a month, even if he is just laying around the living room chewing on a bone while you watch TV. It will have a leash attached to it which will allow you to control him, just in case you need it. He is not to be let off leash in public, possibly for the rest of his life. Do not become complacent. This problem usually targets the family, rather than strangers, and but you must remain safe.

Step #2. Start nonconfrontational compliance training, preferably three training sessions per day of 15 minutes each. Do not proceed with active behavior modification techniques until training is coming along; at least 2 weeks, probably more likely a month. At the same time initiate the NILIF program. You may also initiate other parts of the foundational program that are nonconfrontational, such as nutritional intervention, exercise, mental enrichment etc.

Step #3. Mouth softening. Be very careful with softening the dog's mouth, and if you sense that it is dangerous in your case discontinue it. The risk outweighs the potential benefit, if you are unsure.

Step #4. Social Polarity is a term coined by Lindsay (2001). This technique may help in cases in which the dog accepts or demands affection, but rarely offers affection. In this case the sequence is simple:

(a) Ignore the dog completely for several days, until they begin to initiate affectionate behavior toward you. It may be that they realize they have taken you for granted, or it could simply be that they are adapting to less affection. In any case this can be a turning point. You need to act aloof. And, if you are the type of person to think of it in that way, (I'm not) that is how the leader of the pack acts; aloof.

(b) Once the dog begins showing affection, you may start showing affection in return but only contingent on deferential behavior. Be aware of the sociopathic faked affection which is actually a challenge. If you are facing this, the risk is too high to perform this technique at least without a muzzle. A default sit is good, or a requested sit or down is also good. In some cases you can do doggie push-ups and request a sit - down - sit before returning a small amount of affection. Keep it brief and leave him wanting more.

(c) From now on, your affection will not be devalued by over use. It will be contingent on deferential behavior, and you will leave him wanting more. I know this is hard; you got a dog so that you could have a source of affection, but if you want to control this problem, you need to turn the tables in this way. Right now, he expects your relationship to work one way -- his way -- and we will help him expect it to go your way in a caring and nonconfrontational way. Remember, we are not out to get him, we are out to help him.

Step #5. Once social polarity has changed, and deferential behaviors are being offered on a default basis (or at least reliably on command), you may begin working on specific behavior modification techniques. Below are some examples of common ones. Apply your knowledge of learning and behavior modification techniques to adapt them to your circumstances.

Many control complex dogs have a problem with being stepped-over. If this is the case, start by designing a differential reinforcement and proofing program. Use differential reinforcement for any pro-social behaviors. The program may go something like this.

A. Start in a place that does not really provoke that much response. You can move onto hotter areas such as the favored hallway or whatever later, when you have achieved some success in the not-so-hot area.

B. Walk past the dog at such a distance that the dog is not reactive. As you pass, surprise him by dropping a favorite treat toward him. Make sure he does not know that you have them before-hand. Just keep walking.

C. Repeat until the dog is either bored silly with your pass or preferably happy to see you coming.

D. Walk a little closer in the next approximation. Not so close that he becomes tense and suspicious, but make some progress toward him. Repeat the basic pattern of step B.

E. Gradually decrease the distance through repeating the basic pattern and not progressing until the dog is enthusiastically happy to see you coming. Progress until you are able to step over him. The incremental steps once you get that close must be very very small. Remember, you MUST NOT progress to the next level of intensity until the dog is pleased with your behavior. This is the classical conditioning by-product of DRO that we have been talking about.

F. Once you have achieved success in the 'cold' areas, you can start performing these exercises in 'hotter' areas (ALWAYS start at Square 1!!), and then progress to waiting until the dog has chosen a place to rest, as opposed to having you request him to down for the exercises.

G. Once one person has graduated to hotter areas, another person in the family should perform the program, starting in the not-so-hot area and moving up as dictated by the progress of the dog.

Many control complex dogs are triggered by leash corrections. This practice can be discontinued. Problem solved. If you have a choke chain or prong collar on the dog, then get rid of them. This may be a big part of the frustration and fear. I'd lash out, too, if you tried to strangle me! We are lucky dogs are so forgiving. I am probably more appropriately aggressive than most dogs. I'm not so quick to forgive someone who harms me and I'm probably even quicker to defend myself, than most dogs are.

Many dogs are triggered by reprimands and they "talk back". In this case focus on positive reinforcement rather than reprimanding. As much as is humanly possible, avoid provocation. If need be, walk away. While that can be reinforcing, it also reinforces less than a full-on confrontation will reinforce. If it is easy to do, in a particular situation (such as when he wants something that you have) do not give it. Just walk away with it.

Many control complex dogs are triggered by staring at them. The best way to handle this is to set up a differential reinforcement and proofing exercise in which counter conditioning will tag along.

A. Start by having the dog sit.

B. Now glance at the dog so quickly it was more like he was in the line of fire as you moved your head past him. Click and treat as you glance.

C. If he could handle the split second without responding, he will probably be able to handle a slit second longer. If he can handle that, then he can probably handle a glance of about one second. Each time you glance, click and treat, unless he becomes tense or defensive in any way. Make him look forward to your looking at him. Go at his pace, and do not push it. As before, start each new session by reviewing previous levels, before carrying on.

D. Once one person is progressing quite far in these exercises, another person can start the program at the beginning. We want him to positively anticipate being stared at, and to use any other behaviors than aggressive ones. Work your way up to several seconds of being stared at. Then you can start training eye contact.

Be very careful with 'eye contact' with these dogs. In this case you will have to build up. In using eye contact with a dog that doesn't display control complex aggression, you would be looking at the dog, waiting for him to look at you. In the case of a dog that does display this problematic behavior, though, he may be looking at you; but his problem is that you are looking at him. Eye contact can be perceived as a threat to these dogs, so you must help him learn that it means good things -- not bad things.

Many control complex dogs are triggered by handling, usually of the muzzle, hips or head / neck. If this is the case with your dog, design a systematic desensitization and counterconditioning program, making use of differential reinforcement. If you can come up with an alternative behavior, concentrate on operant principles. Remember the basic principles of starting at an intensity of exposure that the dog will tolerate, even if that level does not even resemble the final product yet. Do the exercises in a non-'hot' area, and go at the dog's pace. Start with the dog wearing a muzzle, if need be. At the very least he should be wearing his Gentle Leader and leash. When you have gotten through the exercises totally, with the muzzle, you can go back and start over without one. In this case, you may want to do a run-through with a Gentle Leader and leash. Once one person has gone through the exercises in a non-hot area, and then a hotter area (if one exists), then another family member can go through, starting at the beginning.

Territorial Aggression

Step #1. Instate a strict prevention and management program. This may mean window treatments that do not allow the dog to look outside. It may mean music as white noise when you are away to prevent frustrative stimulation by outside sources. It may mean baby gating the hallway at the entrance. It may mean installing a mail box at the road so the postal carrier does not come to the door. It may mean having to pick up mail at the post office. It may mean bringing the dog outside on-leash rather than letting him out. It will definitely mean NEVER tying the dog out. The dog should never be allowed out in the yard unattended, and in many cases, never off-leash, either. I know that this will require a lot work. That is what it will take. The dog should be fitted for a Gentle Leader and it should be on the dog at all times when he is supervised.

Step #2. Start nonconfrontational compliance training, preferably 3 training sessions per day of 15 minutes each. Do not continue with active behavior modification techniques until training is coming along; at least 2 weeks, probably more likely a month. At the same time initiate a NILIF program. You may also initiate other parts of the foundational program that are nonconfrontational such as nutritional intervention, exercise, mental enrichment etc.

Step #3. Mouth softening. Be very careful with softening the dog's mouth, and if you sense that it is dangerous in your case, discontinue it, and consult a professional trainer who uses clicker training. The risk outweighs the potential benefit.

Step #4. Remedial Socialization. If you can get the dog out into the world more, perhaps he will not find it to be such a threatening thing when it approaches his environment. Many of these dogs are just so set in their ways, and have such a narrow sphere of safety, that they are triggered by the slightest nudge to their comfort zone. Try to make every experience out there a good experience. Meet lots of people as long as it is safe to do so. Broaden the dog's horizons, and widen the dog's comfort zone.

Step #5. Once other steps are well underway, you can start designing treatment exercises. What follows are some common protocols. Remember the basic principles, though, and adapt the concepts to your own situation.

The first series of steps in primarily operant. You will work on verbal control, and reinforce alternative behaviors. The second set of steps will help to make the stranger intruder a welcomed guest.

Stage 1 Verbal Control and DRI

If the dog is set off by seeing people come on or by the property, the first order of business is to block that visual. Put up curtains or blinds that cannot be moved, and cannot be seen through. You can also purchase an adhesive "frosting" from home improvement stores, that you can use on the window glass to inhibit the dog's view. You may be able to move furniture that the dog stands on to see outside. Do whatever you have to do to prevent him from seeing what is going on. If it is noise that sets him off from outside, then leave a TV and the radio on to add white noise that will break this cycle of responding to every little stimulus.

If the problem is knocking at the door or the door bell, you can do a couple things. First, put up a sign for a while asking for no knocking or bell-ringing. Wanted guests can be asked to call ahead, so that you'll know that they're coming. You can take this down after you get the dog to not respond badly to every sound at the door. You can ring the bell or knock every time you or other family members enter. That will help break the predictability of the bell or knock representing an intruder; learned irrelevance. VERY IMPORTANT: Ask all family members to vary their knocking and bell-ringing habits. If one of my client's family members knocks to enter the house, every one of their dogs knows immediately who it is, by the knock. They have to slide the dogs out of the way, in order to open the door. This is a very different response than the one seen if a stranger knocks. In entering the house yourself, you can ring the bell immediately before entering so that if he does react, he sees very quickly that it is only you. Do this several times daily until the dog is quite sure that it is not an intruder when the bell is rung or there comes a knock at the door.

If anyone has ever run to the door when the bell rings or someone knocks on the door, then this may be the reason the dog is reactive with it. The dog will perceive you as responding reactively, and he will get involved. If this might be the case, change that right away. No one runs to the door. Wait for 3 seconds after a bell or knock comes, and then walk very slowly to the door with a smile on your face.

Here is one training program. An alternative program will follow.

A. Temporarily subdue attention levels and other reinforcers except for obedience shown when visitors arrive and for other prosocial behavior. You can actually invite people to your home, and build exercises around this. It's best if the visitors are people that the dog has met previously (and liked) at first, to build a history around what's expected when greeting visitors. I recommend at least one visitor per day -- if you can arrange for 10 every day, though, your program will progress much more rapidly and smoothly. Don't neglect this all week, though, and then have 10 visitors on Sunday afternoon; it is important to try to even things out through the week, so that the dog has lots of practice.

B. Have your dog sit at least 10 feet from the door. Let him see you walk toward the door a few steps, then return. If he is calm, in place and quiet through the exercise, reinforce it with a game, the presentation of a toy or a treat. If he barks you can say "Oops" and walk away from him. The general lack of reinforcers otherwise will motivate him to avoid hearing "Oops" (conditioned negative punisher). Repeat until he does not respond with concern or tension.

Note: if you have misinterpreted your dog's enthusiasm for aggression, your dog will be completely uninterested in any food or games that you may be using as reinforcement, when there is a guest on the other side of the door. It's best to be safe, of course, and these exercises will help to build overall manners, so that your dog isn't relegated to the back room when company arrives. I just want you to be aware that this is a common occurrence, and that the exercises will still help you to solve the problem of over-exuberance. In these cases, though, the opportunity to greet the guest is far more reinforcing than any food or toy; you will need to build exercises around that eventuality, with safety of everyone involved in mind.

C. Do the same thing as above but walk closer to the door, returning and rewarding tolerance.

D. The same as above but walk to the door, touch the handle and return, rewarding tolerance.

E. Same as above but turn the knob and return, rewarding tolerance.

F. Same as above but open the door, close the door and return, rewarding tolerance.

G. Same as above but open the door, step out, step back in, close the door and return to the dog rewarding tolerance.

H. Same as above, but do not close the door. Ring the bell while the dog can see you, and return to the dog to reward tolerance. You can take a little side-step here if you want and spend some time in position in the doorway ringing, and then tossing a treat. Repeat the bell - treat sequence several times, just to make it extra clear in a classical conditioning context that the bell equals a treat.

I. Same as above, but close the door so that he cannot see you ring the bell. Return and reward tolerance.

J. Once the dog is remaining in place and tolerating this, have a family member run through the same process, as you remain by the dog to give the sit command.

K. Once this is working, have the bell ring before you request the sit. Have the family member exit by a different door if you can, so that you get to perform several exercises per session without the dog seeing who is coming to the door. If the dog is reactive, then just enter after the bell, ignoring the dog completely as in the previous step of ringing before entering each time.

L. Same as above, but you will go to the door to greet the "visitor" (not a stranger at first). You can practice with the visitor leaving again or coming in. Return to the dog and reward tolerance and staying put. The visitor must be instructed to completely ignore the dog.

M. Run through the same process with a non-familial acquaintance of the dog.

N. Run through the process, but now with actual strangers.

As things are going smoothly you should request that the visitor at least ignore him for the first few seconds, only greeting the dog after that and only if the dog is calm and quiet. You may have to use a muzzle through many of these exercises. If that is the case, you can try the exercise without the muzzle ONLY after you have run through the program with one and everything has gone smoothly. In this case, you should attach a leash and Gentle Leader so that you can regain control of the dog, should anything happen to cause concern. Greetings of the dog should be low key and not threatening. That means letting the dog sniff the visitor and perhaps take a treat. Quick movements or pats on the top of the head should be avoided at least at first.

I would encourage you to use your clicker for this training. At first, keep the click and treats coming in rapid succession.

Stage 2 Visitors Are a Good Thing

To convince a dog that, not only is it worth their while to be obedient when visitors arrive, but that they are actually something to welcome (rather than chase off), you will have to employ a little more counterconditioning.

A. Run through the program described above for verbal control before starting this series of steps.

B. Restrict the dog's access to his list of valued things or reinforcers, except when visitors are over. So, when no visitors are present, life is boring; but when they show up and he is obedient with a sit to greet, then out come the fun and games. You want to pay close attention to arousal level. If all of the fun and games are promoting a high arousal level that is causing problems, then you will have to tone it down, focusing on things that create a pleasant experience, but does not promote a state of aggressiveness.

C. You may have to start with having the visitor ignore the dog, and generally not do much at all while you or other family members reinforce for behavior other than aggressiveness or tension, and thereby start the association between visitor = fun. Start with visitors that are unlikely to cause any reactivity (perhaps friends and family members that the dog already likes), and work up to unknown guests. When the visitor arrives all the fun and games start. Then a few minutes later the visitor leaves and so does all the fun and games. Repeat. Manage arousal levels by taking breaks when necessary, and always end on a positive note. These visits should be set up as exercises, lasting only 10 to 15 minutes each.

D. After C is going smoothly, you should be able to get the visitors involved, having them participate in the fun and games. They may have to start by tossing a treat gently to the dog, but eventually they should be in a position to hand the treats or play fetch down the hallway with a favored toy. The visitors should avoid directly facing the dog, leaning over the dog and staring at the dog. Have visitors face slightly away from the dog. If the visitor does approach the dog, have him do so in an arc, rather than walking in a straight line toward the dog. Approaching a dog in an arc has a calming effect, and is one of the rituals that strange dogs use with one another. Averted eyes, lip-licking, and yawning may also be helpful in defusing a tense situation. The treat can be handed or tossed from the side.

Visitors = fun. No visitors = not so much fun. The consistent presentation of this lesson should, over time, create a classically-conditioned positive response to strangers which will replace the negative emotional response. The dog will come to anticipate games and treats when visitors show up. This will make visitors a good thing. This takes a significant amount of time and effort.

Alternative Program

The idea for this method came to me from Brenda Rushman of PAWsitive Solutions Canine Behavior Counseling Ltd. (www.PAWsitiveSolutions.net) The goal is to train the dog to deliver his alarm bark perhaps, but then the dog will immediately run to his crate, where it becomes safe for the visitor to enter and be greeted.

This is basically a placement command, with the cue being the door bell (or knock), rather than a verbal cue. If the dog knows a verbal cue for going to and remaining in his crate until released, then you can use that. In that case, as with any time that you may want to change or add a different cue for a behavior, you simply present the new cue followed immediately by the old cue and then get the response. So you would have the door bell rung, cue the dog to his crate (encouraging him along if you have to at first), go and close the crate, click and reward him heavily for doing so and repeat. Perform as many repetitions as remains fun for the dog (10 to 15 minutes at one time is recommended). After you have done several sessions of several trials per session, you might already notice that the doorbell itself cues the response. You may just see it click with the dog (no pun intended). If you think he may have it, try having the bell ring and then wait a few seconds before giving the verbal cue. This will tell you if the new cue (the door bell) is installed yet or not. If he does not do it, then you need more sessions to connect the cues. If he does do it, jackpot that -- as it is a major breakthrough. Once things are going smoothly you can put the reward on a differential schedule. My advice is to maintain a fairly high percentage of reinforced responses, and always at least offer verbal praise. Because this is an either / or behavior, meaning he either enters the crate and remains, or he does not, you will not have a lot to shape except perhaps for speed, so I would keep the rewards potent and really make it worth his while. Once you have it smooth and reliable you can start proofing it by gradually covering the many bases of distraction. That might mean having the bell rung a few times in a row or perhaps having someone knock and ring the bell. It is a good idea to also cover knocking at the door; many people prefer to knock, and you want the dog to understand that either of these contingencies will require his going to his crate. Cover the bell or knock occurring when you are not in sight. You can ring it when you get home and spy to make sure he went in the crate then you can click, enter and reinforce. You should also gradually introduce actually answering the door, so as to desensitize the dog to a stranger's presence. This will help reduce the anxiety felt when in the crate.

If the dog does not yet have a placement command for entering the crate then you will simply perform the above exercises, but this time the sequence will go a little more like this: Encourage the dog to go in the crate with inviting noises and patting the ground in front of it or what ever else works. Tossing a treat into the crate (especially if it's really good), usually works. Don't close the door; let him come back out, then play the game again. Start feeding him in his crate, and give him really cool stuff (like stuffed Kongs) that he's only allowed to have while crated. Reward him heavily when he goes in. Once this is smooth and reliable, add on the cue such as "crate". You give the cue, encourage the dog and reward successes. After a while, you will be able to drop the encouragement part as with the above procedure. From there, it will just be a matter of switching the cue as described in the above paragraph.

This method can be a very practical method, especially if you are having a hard time with the first method described. You can also combine the techniques in order to not only have the dog go to his crate, but also to come to like it when strangers come to the door.

Possessive Aggression

Step #1. Instate a prevention and management program. That will involve removing any toys or beds or whatever items are guarded. If that is not practical, then you will have to resolve not to make a conflict out of his possession of it. I teach clients that if they leave an object where the dog can get it, that item is sacrificed. It's NEVER advisable to try to remove an object from a dog with this problem unless the item will do him great harm. Do not accept any challenges and do not try to remove the item. If he plays the keep away game, then simply do not play along. If he gets something that you absolutely cannot allow him to have for his own safety, toss a piece of steak or chicken away from him, so that you can retrieve the item. Note: This step is designed to prevent confrontation, but removing something increases it's value, which in turn can cause possessive problems with the item later on when you reintroduce it. Your options are to allow access to the items on a permanent basis, but never make a confrontation out of it, or, remove it forever, or try the basic version of this step and be careful when reintroducing the items not to make a confrontation out of it until he gets a bit more bored with it again.

Step #2. Instate the rest of the foundational program. Begin nonconfrontational compliance training.

Step #3. You have many options. Here are some of them:

A. Get rid of the offending item altogether. If he guards a bed get rid of it. If it is rawhides, then he is never to get rawhides again. If it is a food dish, then for this option you could feed him by simply spilling dry food onto the kitchen floor, or he could eat it out of a Kong or Buster Cube. My dog guarded his food bowl, and when I started putting his meals in his Buster Cube, he actually began to bring it to me, because I was better at getting out more pieces. If he brought it to me I would give it a good shake and dislodge several pieces and then put it right back down. No bowl, no problem.

B. If dogs are fighting over their food or water bowls, you could try setting down several bowls, in several different locales. If the dog guards it's food, you could do one of 2 things: either offer food around the clock, rather than at scheduled times. If he eats too much provide light food. This has the added benefit of being less tasty and less valuable hence less worth guarding. Or, you can feed the guardy dog in his crate. If dogs are fighting over an object, then you could manage the use of the toy, making sure that the possessive dog is alone when they have access to that toy.

C. You can perform active behavior modification techniques to counter the possessiveness.

Food Bowl Guarding

Guarding of a food bowl is a common resource-guarding scenario. The following program is called the delinquent waiter routine and was originated by Dr. Ian Dunbar. This exercise will condition the dog to associate your presence at the bowl as better than your absence from the bowl.

A. Put the dog's dinner ration in a bowl (not the dog's food bowl) on the counter. Instruct the dog to sit, put down his usual bowl, empty, and give the command to eat. He will most likely sniff around the bowl and look to you for evidence as to what is going on. The dog will anticipate food and when he does not receive it right away, he will be in a better frame of mind to have you approach the food bowl because he wants the food. Now the dog WANTS you to approach the food bowl, not remove yourself from the area. On top of that, since there is nothing to protect, he will be less likely to act protective. By doing this you set the dog up for success.

B. Approach the food bowl, have him sit if he is not already seated, drop in 1 kibble and walk away to the counter again. Now he will gulp that piece down and quickly look to you again. Again you have the food bowl reactive dog "asking" you to approach a bowl he usually "asks" you to go away from. That is habit-forming.

C. Continue to feed the dog his dinner in this manner, letting only a small portion go at a time and eliciting an eager anticipation of your approaching the bowl. It is the attitude that is what is at the heart of the problem, and this motivates him to adjust that attitude.

D. Hold the dog's bowl in your hand with a handful of food in it. Now, with the other hand feed him a special treat. Feed several in a row allowing him to eat his relatively boring kibble in between offers of the special treats. Perhaps liver cooked in butter and garlic. If at any time he stiffens and then growls or raises a lip, immediately walk away with the food bowl in tow. Remember you were hanging onto it still. If this provokes reactivity, then you were going too quickly. If the dog reacts to your leaving with the bowl, then do not do so in future exercises, but then take a good look at the sequence and figure out a way to prevent the reactivity by going more gradually.

E. Once you are convinced that he is okay with that stage, in that he looks to you eagerly and happily for your presence around his food bowl, you can move onto relinquishing possession of the bowl. Until now you have not removed a bowl that you have not already had continued contact with. When you maintain contact with an item, it is considered by dogs to be in your possession; but as soon as you let go of it, it is then in their possession. So, this will be a big step. Prepare your best treats. Hang onto the bowl that he eats his boring kibble from. Let go of the bowl for a very brief moment and simultaneously offer a very special treat with the other hand, then immediately take hold of the bowl again. Timing may have to be pretty good depending on the dog. Continue to feed small allotments at a time in the bowl, so that if you get a bad response from the dog and you say "Oops" and walk away the bowl is never more than a gulp or two from being empty. DO NOT attempt to take the bowl, if you get a poor response!!

F. Repeat the process, letting go of the bowl for increasing durations, then placing your hand back on the bowl.

An easier and relatively simple alternative is the walk-by method.

A. Determine the distance at which you can approach the bowl without an aggressive display.

B. Have some extra special treats that the dog loves, ready.

C. Request a sit and when he sits place his food bowl down. Then release him to eat.

D. Walk by him while he eats just on the edge of his comfort zone, and toss a treat in or near his bowl. Perform this as many times as you can, until he is finished eating.

E. Once he has come to anticipate your approach with treats, and appears pleased with your approach at that distance, push it a little bit again; walk a bit closer in your approach. Continue to toss treats.

F. Continue this process until you are able to place a treat into his bowl as he eats. When you get close to the bowl you should be prepared to move very gradually as this will be tougher for the dog than previous distances.

G. Take a few steps back in the distance and do the same exercises but put the treats on a schedule. Start by tossing treats 95% of the time and gradually get it down to around 5%. You may want to keep the 5% permanently to help maintain the conditioning.

Switch to a food that the dog does not like as much, and it will be less worth defending. You can switch back once you are achieving some success with training. Or, you could offer the less tasty food when he eats on his own, but the really good stuff always comes from you, and by hand.

Toy and Object Guarding

If the object guarded is not essential, you may want to simply get rid of it. If it is something that cannot be disposed-of easily, or something that he will most likely come in contact with outside of your control, then it may be worth intervening. Also, if you get rid of the object and he simply chooses a new item to guard, then again you may want to intervene. ***HOMEWORK*** First, if you have not already done so specifically, rank the items he guards from hottest to coldest. Make an actual list and add it to your file. Start with the coldest item and get your best treats ready. Keep the treats out of sight, e.g. on top of the refrigerator. Please note: if, at any time, the item is dropped on the floor, toss a treat away from the dog (away from the item), before attempting to retrieve it. NEVER attempt to pick the item up off of the floor.

A. Offer the dog a "cold" item.

B. IMPORTANT: your hand never leaves the item, in these beginning exercises. To take your hand away automatically gives over possession of the item, and it will not be safe to try to re-gain possession. Instead, allow the item to simply "catch" behind the dog's canine teeth, then immediately remove it and reward. Do this several times, in preparation for the following steps. This step helps to "prime" the dog for the steps that are to come.

C. Repeat step B, but allow the object to remain in his mouth for a second (with your hand still on it), say "drop it", and remove it. Repeat this particular step for 3 days, 3 times per day, for 5 minutes each time. Do it more often, if you can.

D. Repeat step C, but allow the object to remain for 3 seconds.

E. Repeat step C, but allow the object to remain for 5 seconds.

F. Repeat step C, but allow the object to remain for 7 seconds.

G. Insert the object, remove your hand for ONE second, then replace it and allow the object to remain in his mouth for an additional 6 seconds (with your hand still on it), say "drop it", and remove it. Repeat this particular step for 3 days, 3 times per day, for 5 minutes each time. Do it more often, if you can.

H. Repeat step G, but remove your hand for TWO seconds, then replace your hand on the object and allow it to remain in his mouth for an addition 8 seconds.

I. Repeat step G, but remove your hand for FIVE seconds, then replace your hand on the object and allow it to remain in his mouth for an additional 5 seconds.

J. Repeat step G, but remove your hand for SEVEN seconds, then replace your hand on the object and allow it to remain in his mouth for an additional 3 seconds.

K. Insert the object behind the dog's canine teeth, remove your hand for TEN seconds, then replace your hand on the object, give the "drop it" command, remove it from his mouth (he should do so quite readily at this point), and reward.

L. Proofing: repeat this last step WITH THE SAME ITEM, but change positions: if you were sitting, stand. If you were in the kitchen, move to another locale. Walk away for the 10 seconds, then come back and ask him to "drop it". If all of these go well, then you're ready to move on:

M. Use other COLD items, starting at the beginning. This will go much faster, this time around.

N. Have other family members go through all of the exercises with him, WHILE HEAVILY SUPERVISED.

O. Change to a variable system of reward.

P. Once he is eagerly giving up the cold objects on command and getting treats on a variable schedule, move to the next hottest item. When you move to the next hottest item go back to Step A, rewarding every single time.

Q. Work your way through the items up to the hottest item. Once one person has gone through the process, the next family member should run through it. It may go a little quicker with each successive person, but do not rush it. Reward; don't bribe unless you have to for safety's sake. The reward should be hoped for, but not offered up front. In going through this process, the dog will learn that if he gives up his prized toy on-command, he can not only get a treat for it, but he will also get the toy back. Yes, he will expect these things, but he will also learn to trust in the system, and when you need for him to have these skills, they will be there for you. Continue to reward your dog for tolerating sharing. [Much of the above sequence was described by Brenda Rushman, personal communication]

Teaching a dog to fetch can not only improve the physical and mental condition of the dog (and owner), it also encourages the dog to bring things to you and give them up. Having an object thrown for a dog can be a potent reward for giving it up.

Bed, Crate, Couch, Under a Table or Other Place Guarding

The first and most obvious solution to location guarders, is to deny access to or get rid of, if possible, the location. This works fine if the location is your bed or his bed since you can close doors or throw away his bed, but is difficult with couches or hallways. The key in these situations is two-fold: verbal control and, specifically, placement commands. Really work on yielding as described in the foundational plan. If you can request your dog to occupy and move away from a location on command, there is likely to be less conflict over it. I'll use a couch as an example.

A. Say "Couch" and coax the dog up on the couch by patting the cushions and making inviting noises. When he gets up on the couch tell him how smart he is. Save the really good rewards for getting off. Do this when he is not showing interest in getting onto the couch on his own.

B. You may want to request that he lie down, to properly simulate his enjoyment of the couch.

C. Say "Floor" and pat the floor, making inviting noises. If he moves to the floor, immediately give him a great treat, or pull out a favorite toy or whatever is highly reinforcing for him. If he does not get off, say "Oops", and walk away. In that case, find a less "hot" location to work on placement commands for a while.

You can have him go up and down several times, and end with a good game and on a positive note.

D. Repeat several times in several sessions, so that he comes to understand the command and trust in the reward system.

E. Once things are going smoothly try a cold trial. Use the command when he is already on the couch and comfortable. Make the rewards variable after the first several sessions. Sometimes when he gets down, you pull out the leash and ask him if he wants to go for a walk; while other times you play tug or fetch, and yet other times you give a liver treat. Try to keep it variable and fun. Keep the dog in the game and winning.

F. Once this is going smoothly and cold trials are working well put the rewards on a variable schedule. You want him to continue trusting in the system, but you do not have to give a heavy reward every time. Continue to praise the dog for being displaced.

Idiopathic Aggression Treatment Plan

Unfortunately there is no treatment protocol for dogs with idiopathic aggression. Given the high risk level and lack of treatment options, euthanasia is recommended in any case severe enough to be diagnosed idiopathic aggression. Remember that this diagnosis should only be made if the attacks are particularly violent and after seizure disorders have been ruled out. For the sake of confirmation and prevention of some amount of guilt on your part, it would be a good idea to have a professional behavior counsellor back up your diagnosis. In some cases, heavy duty medication such as Paxil or Prosac may help, but they take time to fully load, the dog will be heavily medicated, perhaps on a permanent basis, and the risk is still very high with no certain chance of improvement at all, even with the medication. The bigger the dog the more dangerous this is. You may elect to try the medication route first. In this case be very careful and use equipment to reduce the risk.

Pathophysiologic Aggression

Treatment for health-related aggression starts with medical treatment and moves onto other measures for the learned component, if one has developed. The basic program is instated if aggression is not completely diminished by medical care. The specific issues are then addressed as needed for any remaining learned component.

Maternal Aggression

There are not many formal treatment plan options for maternal aggression. Management is central to dealing with this issue, unless surgical intervention can be considered. If maternal aggression presents with false or phantom pregnancies during each cycle, rather than with actual puppies, the dog may choose toys, slippers etc., and this may be confused with possessive aggression. In either case, spaying the female at the appropriate time in her cycle can often produce positive results, but it must be done at least 6 weeks after estrus. There may be a learned component, and in this case a plan for possessive aggression can be designed.

Predatory Aggression

Treatment for predatory aggression will involve the basic program and will focus heavily on management and solid verbal control. Time outs will be used for early stages of the predatory sequence of behaviors. Differential reinforcement will be used for appropriate behavior. Impulse control will be very important.

Step #1. Initiate a prevention and management program such that the dog is never able to harm anyone. If triggering stimuli live within the house, then either the triggering stimuli must be rehomed or the dog must be rehomed. The dog must not be left unattended outside. The dog must never be off leash in public and preferably should be wearing a Gentle Leader. Management will be key.

Step #2. Even though this is largely a drive related behavior, I would still suggest working through the foundational program and verbal control. Catch the dog early before he triggers. That is how the prey drive of competing herding border collies is controlled. The handler orders alternative behaviors prior to the dog triggering into the next stage of the predatory sequence. By knowing what triggers the dog and when, the handler can toggle the predatory sequence on and off.

Step #3. Continue to train the dog and develop solid verbal control.

Step #4. Formulate a treatment plan in which you teach the dog to maintain an alternative and mutually exclusive behavior in the face of the triggering stimuli. Focus on operant conditioning techniques. The dog is not fearful of the trigger.

Play Aggression

Step #1. Ban all rough play. Develop a prevention program. This will likely involve using a Gentle Leader and ground line.

Step #2. Proceed through the foundational program with an emphasis on verbal control and consistency. Really increase exercise significantly!

Step #3. Notice and reward proper behavior and contrast that with preventing aggressive, uninvited play as much as possible. When the dog chooses to initiate rough or aggressive play, you should ignore him or he should be placed in a time out until his arousal level is waned. Don't accept the challenge, and if you find his behavior amusing, stop laughing or smiling at it.

Redirected / Displaced Aggression

The basis of treating this form of aggression will be to manage arousal levels and prevent where possible the stimulation. On top of that the owner should learn to predict the triggering stimuli, and have management tools such as a Gentle Leader and leash in place to help control the highly aroused dog. Treatment for any forms of aggression that are the underlying cause for redirected aggression should be treated on their own terms.

Resident Directed Dog - Dog Aggression

There may be many reasons for resident directed aggression. Aside from the usual competitive problems and learned impatience, one dog may have simply become very fearful of other dogs or another particular dog in the household. If the fear is intense enough, it might be termed social phobia. If the aggressor is much larger than the aggressee then consider predatory drift. This occurs when a big dog's predatory instincts are triggered by another, smaller dog. Medical causes might be the problem. One dog might have become a bully through the constant reinforcement of being competitively successful. Clashes of personality are common among dogs who live together. These dogs do not choose each other, after all. If both dogs are driven in the same way, or if one dog's drives conflict with another dog's sensitivities, then there is going to be trouble. In any case, prevention of rehearsal and solid training in impulse control will stop fights and head in the right direction toward controlling the chaos and conflict inside your house.

Handling aggression among housemates is a dynamic process which requires micro and macromanagement. Given the dynamic quality of the problem and complexity of treatment and management, you must understand the basic principles. These principles will guide you in how you handle the dogs. Aggression toward house mates must be prevented, and if and when it cannot be prevented it must result in as little reinforcement as possible. Instate the foundational program with a heavy emphasis on training. Make sure each dog gets enough exercise and general consistency. Instate the NILIF program for each dog.

Management

Management will be vital. You can use baby gates, crates, doors etc. to keep dogs apart if necessary. If two dogs have a history of fighting, then do not allow them access to one another when you cannot be there. If a serious fight breaks out throw a bucket of water on them or yank them away by their tail or hind legs. If you break up a fight, be prepared to get bitten. It is not safe to break up a dog fight. With small dogs and some medium sized dogs you can get a suitable sized piece of plywood and insert it between fighting dogs. If you have help, each person can grab the rear legs of the 2 main fighting dogs, and lift up. This works even with giant breeds, and keeps the dogs from redirecting their aggression to you; they can't reach you. At any rate, if there is a fight, the reinforcement has already occurred, so minimize continued reinforcement with a time out for the offending dog or dogs. Many conflicts are over objects so you will have to manage objects, carefully. If it's over water dishes, then put down seven water dishes throughout the house. You will have to get very clever and be an expert observer and diplomat. Don't forget to reinforce them for tolerance. If one dog is tolerant of the other let them know it. Make it really worth their while to be patient and tolerant.

Train Each Dog Individually

The first order of business will be individual training. You will make arrangements to have time alone with each dog in which you will train them. This should be a pleasant time, and can incorporate walks and play sessions or exercise sessions. The training must get done, but get some bonding time in also, so that the dog respects you and becomes used to paying close attention to what you want. When there are a bunch of dogs running around all the time, it is easy for the dog to get used to not paying attention to you. You must train the dog to a high level of reliability individually, in basic control cues that will allow you to verbally control each dog, but the training will possess a component that will teach the dog to be patient and show impulse control. It is easy to train a dog to come when called or sit when asked, but will he come away from playing with another dog? If not, then you need to go beyond the level of training that gets you the response only in low distraction levels. I can't tell you how many people tell me their dog is well-trained in something, and then we see that the dog only does it if there is a treat in sight, or if the owner has to offer both the verbal cue and hand signal, or if the owner is standing or whatever. The dog is not trained beyond the elementary school level. It might be a nice elementary level sit but we are going to need more. If I ask the person to face away from the dog and say "sit", the dog does not do it; or if they say it from a distance, or if they say it from out of sight, or when there is something distracting going on. If the dog does not respond reliably under all these conditions, then no, the dog is not well-trained in that response. You need to take that nice elementary sit to a P.hD. level (solid under many distracting contexts). Continue to proof the basic responses of "off", "here", "sit" and "down" until he will perform them under high levels of distraction. Refer to the section on training for more details on training processes. The more individual training sessions you put in, and the more proofed the responses are, the better off your treatment plan will be. You might want to attend clicker training classes with the most problematic dog or dogs, but only one dog goes to any one class.

Train in Pairs

Once you are at a nice reliable point in individual training, you will start training in pairs. Even if you have several dogs, you will start with one pair. Start performing the training with each dog in a way that rewards each for tolerating the attention payed to the other dog. Have one dog sit and then have the other dog sit. You will want to use the name of the dog you are addressing prior to the cue, so that they know it is for them. Release and reward one, and then release and reward the other. Start when they are in a receptive mood, and start with them far enough away from one another that they are not triggering. Start with easy ones and work your way back up to more difficult ones. Once you have worked with one pair, work with another pair if you have more than two dogs. If it is only one dog that is the main problem you can focus on that one, but you should still perform the training with each pair combination that exists.

You can also make group commands. To do this, come up with a group name such as "everyone" and then deliver the cue. Reward only those who perform it, and repeat, encouraging the other dog to do so. This group command will come in handy when you want all the dogs to all respond to a cue. "Sit" delivered to all dogs at once, for instance, can be valuable.

Training in Groups

Once you have worked your way through training each pair combination to a reliable level of distraction, you can start combinations of three. The training will go pretty much the same way as with pairs. Have them separated and work each dog in turn. Once you have made significant progress in these small groups in each possible combination of three, you can start adding in any other dogs within the household, until you have your whole pack working together. Maintain the training by continuing to work with them individually and as a group. Apply the training to everyday life when you can.

When the Dog Triggers

If a dog loses his cool and snaps at another dog, immediately perform a time out on that dog. Impatience, frustration, displays of anger or frustration will not result in continued reinforcement. But as with any time out application, you must make sure that you make clear what the appropriate alternative is. Reinforce for signs of tolerance and impulse control. Refer below for some ideas on specific training exercises.

Specific Exercise

What follows is an actual step by step training exercise that you can perform. It not only allows you verbal control, but it teaches the dog to be patient and control his impulses.

Training Tolerance

I learned this technique from Brenda Rushman of Pawsitive Solutions Canine Behavior Counseling Ltd. (www.pawsitivesolutions.net). It can be useful for dogs who guard food or other resources, or for those who do not tolerate it when the other dog is favored in some way.

Start by setting up the environment. You should have a muzzle on the temperamental dog. Next set up an area in which you can sit comfortably with a dog on either side of you and a barricade between you. If you are dealing with large dogs then a kitchen table should do. If you are dealing with medium sized dogs then another chair in front of you would be good. For smaller dogs use a foot stool or other similar object. Work in ten minute sessions as many times daily as you can find time for. Act just up-beat enough to make it fun for the dogs, but not so much that they are more highly aroused.

Step #1. Both dogs get treats simultaneously. Feed each dog a treat at the same time repeatedly so that they start to realize that just because the other dog gets treats does not mean they will lose out. Repeat through several sessions beyond the point at which you think the aggressor is okay with the proceedings.

Step #2. When step one is established, the next step is to offer the treats at the same time, but this time continue to hold onto the aggressor's treat as he licks or nibbles at it. Let the other dog have his treat and then let go of the aggressor's treat. There should be a split second between the time you let go of the one dog's treat and the aggressor's treat.

Step #3. Very gradually start increasing the duration between offering the treats. You can also very gradually start feeding the one dog his treat and *then* offering the aggressor his treat *after* the first dog gets his treat. This process must go very gradually.

You may have to also not even look at the other dog so that your aggressor does not become intolerant. You can add the variable of looking at the other dog later. Remember the basic process whereby you work on one variable at a time until it is solid and then you relax that one while you add in another. You may also experiment with verbally encouraging the aggressor. As long as he remains tolerant and does not tense up, you can offer verbal praise and the treats of course. One more trick of the trade is to use crummy treats for the one dog and great treats for the aggressor. You can work on increasing the difficulty level later, once you are getting a solid success with the easy ones. Another factor of difficulty you will work on when you can, is decreasing the distance between the dogs until they are shoulder to shoulder, standing side by side.

Step #4. Generalize further by using other dogs if there are any and other treats and toys.

A variant on this method with toys might involve performing object exchanges with each dog in the presence of the other dog. Reinforce heavily for tolerance and obedience.

Rehoming

If the dogs are fighting all the time and you cannot seem to diminish it, then you might want to consider rehoming a dog. If one dog is terrorizing another, intentionally or not, you may want to rehome one of the dogs. If one dog is doing serious harm to the other dog or attacks the feet then you must either rehome the dog or consider euthanizing him. You cannot ask a dog to live in a relationship that is traumatizing, abusive or dangerous; it is unfair. Look at your dog's quality of life.

Non-Resident Directed Dog - Dog Aggression

Non resident directed aggression usually has a lot to do with either bullying or inappropriately establishing socially competitive event expectations and social boundaries or fear and undersocialization.

If your dog has mild arguments with other dogs in which no one gets hurt, either physically or emotionally, then there may not be a problem. If, on the other hand, the arguments are not brief and appropriate, and followed by appropriate apologies and acceptance, or if one dog harasses or physically / emotionally harms another dog, then you do have a problem. These kinds of events can cause fear of other dogs and future aggression problems too easily, and it is not fair to expose this dog to a bully. If your dog is the bully, do not fool yourself into thinking that they are just "getting to know one another" or that they will "work it out themselves". That does not matter. The fact is that a single bad experience like that can ruin a dog for other dogs forever. If your dog is the bully, do not allow your dog to rehearse this behavior under any circumstances. Yes, this may mean not allowing your dog off-leash, and it may mean he does not get the kind of socialization that would be good for him. That does not matter. You cannot harm others for the sake of allowing your dog to socialize, and let's face it: he is not socializing; he is rehearsing how to be a better bully. Management and solid verbal control will be very important. From within that framework, you can set up proofing and DRI exercises in which you do passes, reinforcing for tolerance.

If your dog is the one being bullied, then you can talk to the other owner about their responsibilities, but they are most likely going to be defensive and in denial; or you can walk your dog elsewhere. If your dog is fearful of all other dogs then you can design a systematic desensitization and counter conditioning program, or a proofing and DRI program. In some cases remedial socialization off leash is possible. In that case find a dog that is well socialized and a canine diplomat. If your dog's problem is primarily with intact males, then start with a well socialized female. You can start adding other dogs to the play group over time. You may not ever be able to add intact males, but you might be able to make your dog a little more socially-savvy. Concentrate on general confidence building also.

Growl Classes

A recent development in the dog to dog aggression treatment arsenal is the "growl class". Growl classes involve group training classes in which all of the participating dogs have aggression problems. Often the dogs are initially muzzled and retraining techniques are taught to the owner by the instructors. Growl classes have been praised in books by some of the most well know trainers in the industry but I am not familiar with any real research to suggest that they benefit dogs at all. Any time a situation is set up so that dogs are allowed to rehearse unwanted behaviors, it is bad. It does not matter if they are muzzled and that there are trainers around or if they try to match up the combatants. If two dogs are allowed to become sensitized and just go at each other, then they are being flooded. Remember that flooding involves exposing the dog to the sensitizing stimulus at full strength and is a very tricky procedure and likely to backfire. It is made worse by some growl classes in which the dogs are not even allowed to continue interacting until they become exhausted and then finally start to actually habituate. The dogs are separated before they even start to habituate. I am not suggesting letting dogs fight until they are exhausted, because I am not suggesting growl classes. This form of growl class operation is a failed flooding, technique. You get the fallout of flooding but none of the benefit (if indeed there is any). I attended a growl class seminar in 2000 given by a quite well-known trainer who I will not name, in which this exact process was demonstrated. It was very clear to me that many of these dogs left there worse off than when they went in, and I could not identify a single dog that left better off. There was one little Viszla who I'm sure is ruined for other dogs now, for good. Please keep this in mind if you are considering entering a growl class or designing and running a growl class. Do not allow a 'professional' to allow your dog to become sensitized and flooded. If you are a professional, do not allow someone's dog to become sensitized; they will learn nothing good. Beware of growl classes. I do not suggest them.

Take Home Message

Treatment for aggression problems is highly variable, and is guided by the particulars of the case. You must get a decent understanding of the principles of learning theory and behavior modification techniques in order to deal with this problem on your own. If you cannot get a good solid grip on the principles, or if you are having a hard time applying them to reality, then you need to reassess the situation; and if the risk is significant then you should either euthanize the dog or call in a professional dog behavior counselor with experience with aggression problems and who is dedicated to positive reinforcement methods. You cannot hope to tackle this alone, unless you are firm on what needs to be done. Remember also, that it is you who has to live with this dog and the risk so one way or another you need to learn what to actually do. Don't send a dog off to be trained; you need to do the training.

Instate the foundational program first. Along with all the other elements start training the dog. Avoid dealing with the actual problem situations until you have worked extensively with the dog, he loves training, and you have begun proofing the behaviors under higher levels of distraction.

The goal of treatment is not to cure the dog; that is not possible. There are books on aggression out there that will suggest to you that if you follow their one true way you will be able to cure your dog. That is not accurate. You are indeed very likely, if you work really hard, to gain control of the problem and increase the dog's trustworthiness, but he will never be *cured.*

Aggression is rewarding for the dog and it is habit forming. That means that when he is stressed, he will fall back on behavior that is automatic (habitual). Your goal for treatment is basically two-fold: you want to set up the right circumstances so that he may get used to the 'thing' that sets him off, and, you want to instate replacement behaviors and make them habitual. I strongly suggest clicker training, as communication is very important and this device will allow you to more accurately communicate to your dog what you like and want.

Chapter 5

Children and Dog Aggression

Prevention

Children, as a group, are the most frequent target of dog aggression, and when a dog bites a child, substantially more damage is done. Bites to children represent more than 50% of the total number of cases and 26% of dog bites to children (compared to 12% in adults) require medical attention. [www.bogbite-law.com] Most deaths occurring as a result of dog bites are children. [www.bog-bitelaw.com] The chances that a victim of a fatal dog attack will be a child is 7 out of 10. [www.bogbitelaw.com] Children between the ages of 5 and 9 are at particular risk. [www.bogbitelaw.com] Given the significant over-representation of children in dog bite statistics, the topic deserves special attention.

Children do all the wrong things. They imitate wounded prey animals. They are jerky and spastic. They squeal and squeak. They hug dogs (who may not have been prepared for this behavior, through training and socialization). They pull fur, ears and tails. They hit dogs. They tease dogs. They run away from or toward dogs. On top of all of this, most dogs who come into contact with children were not properly socialized toward them when they were in their sensitive period as a puppy. This lack of socialization makes the dog leery of children, at best. It is a disaster waiting to happen. There is yet another factor; parents. Many parents forget that these are animals, and not little furry people. Many parents are paranoid of strangers, but then allow very high risk confrontations between their children and dogs.

Treatment?

The decision to treat a dog who is aggressive toward children will include several factors. Answer the following questions and ponder the conclusions.

Has your dog bitten so hard he has broken the skin? If you answered "yes" you have a very risky situation that could potentially result in the maiming or death of a child. I'm being blunt, because the statistics suggest that someone NEEDS to get blunt, and quick. These dog owners are always so sure that their dog would never harm a child. It could happen to you.

Is your dog aggressive toward children who live in the same household? If you answered "yes", the children are at great risk.

If your dog is aggressive toward children, and there is a possibility that he will come in contact with children in a less than fully-controlled manner then there is risk; and the risk is greatly increased if you cannot guarantee that you can control the child, as well as the dog. It blows me away when I see parents allowing their toddlers to run around in dog park fields. If you think the risk is at an unacceptable level, you must consider your options. Trying to find a home for such a dog such that he will never come in contact with children is pretty unlikely. Eventually the dog will come in contact with children in one way or another. It is risky to rehome such a dog. If you decide to go ahead with this option, you must be very honest with the potential new owners and make them sign a liability waiver (Even with the waiver, if the dog bites a neighbor's child, you can be held liable!). This can be a very difficult option to realize. You must very carefully consider the option of euthanasia. Try not to feel guilty about this option. Aggression is a life-long tendency and the risk is just too high. If you want to save a life, after you have gotten over the grief, visit a Humane Society and adopt a dog who is not aggressive and who desperately needs a home. There are many homeless dogs who are not aggressive at all, and would make great pets that do not put the community at risk. You could save one of these dogs by your decision. Think long and hard about keeping a child-aggressive dog in your house, even if you do not have children in your house. There is no call more scary to a dog behavior counselor than the child-aggressive dog call.

The following suggestions will help you to prepare a non-aggressive dog for a child, but I've purposely left out detailed instructions on teaching a child-aggressive dog to cope with children. The risk is simply too great. For the budding dog behavior counselors out there you should seek an apprenticeship in which you can work closely with a professional before handling this kind of case. It's just something that requires supervision and experience; not a book.

Preparing a Dog For a Child

If you have a dog and plan to have children follow some of these guidelines. Many of these guidelines are from Child-Proofing Your Dog by Brian Kilcommons and Sarah Wilson. I strongly urge the reader who will be bringing children into contact with dogs to get and read this book.

Start scheduling your dog's time now, so that when the child comes the dog will not have to adjust to a new schedule.

Stop games in the house that promote the dog getting highly aroused. Better to make these games outside-dependent so the dog is not jumping all over you and onto furniture, without regard to where the child is.

For several weeks prior to the child arriving start paying less attention to the dog. You want him to get more attention when the child arrives, not less.

Play tapes of children crying, screaming and squealing. When the tape is on be upbeat and happy. Give a treat. Make the crying represent good things. Systematically desensitize the sounds.

Allow your dog to become familiar with things like diapers, children's toys etc.

Provide the dog with toys that do not resemble what the childs toys are going to resemble. Buy the childs toys now and teach the dog to leave them alone. To do this allow him to choose which to grab. If he grabs his own praise and reward him by playing with him with it. If he chooses incorrectly, use the leave it command and encourage him to choose correctly. You may also make the distinction more clear by applying a minuscule amount of Listerine to the child's toys. A better choice is to train yourself to always ensure that the dog doesn't have access to the child's toys.

Socialize the dog now to as many children as possible. Try to keep the leash loose. Cover as many ages as possible. Never allow the children to harm the dog and always allow the dog to leave if he wants to, but watch the circumstances surrounding his leaving; if he's just tired, that's fine. If he's leaving because he's uncomfortable, desensitize to the situation that made him feel that way. Make this a fun event, with praise and treats. Laugh and be fun (from the dog's perspective) when around children.

Avoid allowing your dog to play with a doll in hopes that it will get him used to children. The dog is likely to see this as a toy and then see a child as a toy.

Desensitize the dog to child-like handling now. Stroke the dog on the head and give a treat. Stroke a little harder and give two treats. Pat on the head and give a treat. Pat more forcefully and give a few treats. Pat vigorously and drop several treats in front of the dog. Touch and ear and give a treat, Gently tug the ear and give a couple treats. Tug a little harder and offer a few treats. Do the same for the tail and paws. Try to get him to love being touched in ways that he will likely be touched by children. Do not forget to included hugs and dressing up. Of course you will try your hardest to prevent children from doing these things but you prepare for the inevitable errors.

Dos and Don'ts

- Do teach children to always ask permission before approaching a dog.
- Do instruct the child to tickle the dog on the chin or chest, not the top of the head.
- Do instruct the child to not bother the dog when he is sleeping.
- Do instruct the child to not go near the dog's bed or crate.
- Do instruct the child to not follow the dog if he walks away.
- Do instruct the child to not stare at a dog.
- Do instruct the child to avoid running toward or away from a dog.
- Do instruct the child to avoid jerky motions around dogs.
- Do instruct the child to respect the dog's toys and food.
- Do not leave a child with any dog unsupervised, ever!
- Do not force a dog to meet a child.
- Do not allow a child to pick a dog up.
- Do not ever tie a dog out unattended where he can be teased or get frustrated.
- Do not ever allow a child to tease or bother a dog. It is not cute. It is a disaster waiting to happen.

Above all else simply keep in mind that dogs are animals with their own motivations and feelings. They are not stuffed animals. Be extremely careful when dogs and children are in contact and do not rationalize it or think it will not happen to you. Do not think that YOUR dog would NEVER harm a child. The statistics show that a lot of people are SURE of that, and wrong!

Take Home Message

Children and dogs can be a disaster. If a dog is not ready to deal with a child well, or if a child is not ready to deal with a dog well, then they should not be in contact until they can both learn how to do so. If a child is young and does not understand or follow the rules, then they should not be living in the same house with a dog. The risk is too high.

If you are expecting a child, and have a dog, follow the guidelines in the text to prepare the dog for the change in life-style. If you have a child under the age of 9, then wait and get a dog after the child is old enough to deal with a dog safely.

Never leave a child and a dog unattended no matter what you think the risk is, ever!

Resourses

Below are links to articles on the internet. I urge the reader to explore each of them. I do not necessarily agree with everything expressed in them, but they will offer you different perspectives from what is contained in this book.

A special note should be made for www.DoggieDoor.com. Members have access to message boards where knowledgeable dog owners and professionals offer advice. If you will not be seeking the services of an in person behaviorist, you can discuss your options and get advice here. Doggie Door has helped many owners over the years and has become a well respected resource for dog owners.

Article on medicating behavior: http://www.allbreed.net/chows/factors.htm

Behavioral genetics and animal behavior: http://www.grandin.com/references/genetics.html

Aggression article: http://www.vetshow.com/friskies/cani.htm

Aggression article: http://www.gooddog-training.com/aggression.htm

Aggression aricle: http://www.labradornet.com/daggression.html

Canadian Statistics: http://www.hc-sc.gc.ca/hpb/lcdc/brch/injury/dogbit_e.html

Aggression article: http://www.homepagez.com/tailsawaggin/aggression.html

Flying Dog Press articles on aggression:

http://www.flyingdogpress.com/onldagg.html

http://www.flyingdogpress.com/selfpg.html

http://www.flyingdogpress.com/sayhi.html

http://www.flyingdogpress.com/attitude.html

Aggression article: http://www.doggiedoor.com/aggressi.shtml

Aggression article: http://www.k9shrink.co.uk/page86.html

Bite prevention: http://www.dogscouts.com/biteprevention.shtml

Finding a Trainer:

Certfied Canine Behavior Counselors & Certified Canine Trainers http://www.acbt.ca

Canadian Association of Professional Pet Dog Trainers: http://www.cappdt.com

Association of Pet Dog Trainers: http://www.apdt.com

Bibliography / References

Beaver, Bonnie, DVM, MS, Dipl ACVB. 1999. Canine Behavior: A Guide for Veterinarians, W. B. Saunders Company

Burns, Steven, M.D. The Medical Basis of Stress, Depression, Anxiety, Sleep Problems, and Drug Use, http://www.teachhealth.com/index.html

Burch, M. Ph.D. & Bailey, J. Ph.D., 1999. How Dogs Learn. Howell Book House.

Cacioppo, John. 1999. Annual Review of Psychology

Clothier, Suzanne. 1996. Body Posture & Emotions Shifting Shapes, Shifting Minds. www.FlyingDogPress.com

Clothier, Suzanne. 1996. Finding A Balance Issues of Power in the Human/Dog Relationship. www.FlyingDogPress.com

Clothier, Suzanne. 1996. The Seven C's A Guide to Training & Relationships. www.FlyingDogPress.com

Clothier, Suzanne. 1996. Understanding & Teaching Self Control. www.Flying-DogPress.com

Coppinger, Raymond. Coppinger, Lorna. 2001. Dogs A Startling New UNder-standing of Canine Origin, Behavior & Evolution. Scribner

Cornell University College of Veterinary Medicine. 1999. Dealing with your Dog's Aggressive Behavior A special Report from the Editors of Dog-Watch.Torstar Publications, Inc.

DeNapoli, Jean S., Nicholas H. Dodman, Lousis Shuster, William M. Rand and Kathy L. Gross Effect of dietary protein content and tryptophan supplementation on dominance aggression, territorial aggression, and hyperactivity, JAVMA, Vol 217, No 4, on August 15, 2000.

Dodman, Nicholas. Dr. 1999. Dogs Behaving Badly. Bantam Books

Donaldson, Jean. 1998. Dogs Are From Neptune. Lasar Multimedia Productions.

Donaldson, Jean. 1996. The Culture Clash. James & Kenneth Publishers

Dunbar, Ian, D.V.M., Ph.D., MRCVS. Dog Aggression Biting (video of seminar). James & Kenneth Publishers.

Dunbar, Ian, D.V.M., Ph.D., MRCVS. 1999. Dog Behavior. Howell Book House.

Houpt A. Katherine, VMD, Ph.D., Watanabe E. Myrna, Ph.D.., 1999, Dealing with your Dog's Aggressive Behavior A special report from DogWatch, Cornell University College of Veterinary Medicine

Jones, Deborah Ph.D. 1999, The Clicker Workbook A Beginner's Guide. Howln Moon Press.

Kilcommons B. & Wilson, S. 1994. Child Proofing Your Dog. Warner Books

Lindsay, Steven M.A. 2000 Handbook of Applied Dog Behavior and Training Volume One. Iowa State University Press.

Lindsay, Steven M.A. 2001 Handbook of Applied Dog Behavior and Training Volume Two. Iowa State University Press.

London, Karen, Ph.D. & McConnell, Pactritia, Ph.D. 2001. Feeling Outnumbered? How to Manage and Enjoy Your Multi-Dog Household. Dog's Best Friend, Ltd.

McConnell, Patricia, Ph.D. 1998. The Cautious Canine How to Help Dogs Conquer Their Fears. Dog's Best Friend, Ltd.

McLennan, Bradi.1993. Dogs & Kids Parenting Tips. Howell Book House

Meisterfeld, C.W. 1889. Jelly Bean Versus Dr. Jekyll & Mr. Hyde. MRK Publishing

O'Farrel, V. 1996. Manual of canine behavior. British Small Animal Veterinary Association.

Overall, Karen L., M.A., V.M.D., Ph.D., 1997. Clinical Behavioral Medicine For Small Animals. Mosby.

Overall, Karen L., M.A., V.M.D., Ph.D., 1996. DVM News magazine

Page, George.1999. Inside the Animal Mind A Ground-breaking Exploration of Animal Intelligence. Doubleday

Pryor, Karen. 1999. Don't Shoot The Dog! Bantam Books.

Reid, Pamela. Ph.D. 1996. Excel-erated Learning. James & Kenneth Publishers

Reid Pamela, Ph.D.. Getting Dogs Off Death Row [video] June 1997.

Serpell, James. 1995. The Domestic Dog its evolution, behaviour and interactions with people. Cambridge University Press

Strong, Val. 1999. The Dog's Dinner. 1999, Alpha Publishing, Tel: 01753 89004, isbn: 0-9532814-5-0

Strong, Val. 1999. The Dog's Brain - a simple guide. 1999, Alpha Publishing, Tel: 01753 89004, isbn: 0-9532814-6-9

Unruh, La Vonn. 1996. Canine Aggression. The Middle Atlantic States Komondor Club, Inc.

Further Study (Must Have)

Reisner, R. Llana, DVM, Ph.D., DACVB. Canine Aggression: Neurobiology, Behavior and Management [Article on the internet at http://www.vetshow.com/friskies/cani.htm

Dunbar, Ian, D.V.M., Ph.D., MRCVS. Dog Aggression Biting (video of seminar). James & Kenneth Publishers.

Donaldson, Jean. 1998. Dogs Are From Neptune. Lasar Multimedia Productions.

London, Karen, Ph.D. & McConnell, Pactritia, Ph.D. 2001. Feeling Outnumbered? How to Manage and Enjoy Your Multi-Dog Household. Dog's Best Friend, Ltd.

Reid Pamela, Ph.D.. Getting Dogs Off Death Row [video] June 1997.